netzwerk recherche

D1984780

nr-Werkstatt:
Fact-Checking:
Fakten finden, Fehler vermeiden

Dokumentation zur nr-Fachkonferenz im SPIEGEL-Redaktionsgebäude in Hamburg am 27. und 28. März 2010.

mit freundlicher Unterstützung von:

DER SPIEGEL

G+J

message

Initiative Wissenschaftsjournalismus

Fact-Checking: Beispiele aus der Praxis

Herausforderungen für das Fact-Checking

message-Werkstatt: Fact-Checking

„Wer immer die Wahrheit sagt,
kann sich ein schlechtes Gedächnis leisten."
Bundespräsident Theodor Heuss, 1949-1959

Thomas Leif

„Qualität kommt von Qual" – Warum Fact-Checking das Leistungsversprechen des Qualitätsjournalismus ist?

Als jüngst ein altgedienter Berliner Politiker seine Aktivitäten am Ende seiner Karriere reflektierte, überraschte er mit einer ungewöhnlichen Bilanz. Es gebe heute „keine Bereitschaft mehr, sich zu quälen," diktierte er dem Lokalreporter in den Block, der nach Lösungen für einen Problembezirk fragte. Dieser altmodische Leitgedanke gilt offenbar nicht nur für die modernen Ghettos. Die Bereitschaft zur wiederholten Nachfrage, zur Fakten-Überprüfung und zum Quellen-Zweifel sinkt. Die Neigung zur Übernahme der Mehrheitsmeinung, der bequemen Agentur-Veredelung und der Verarbeitung von interessengebundenen Textbausteinen nimmt zu. Zeitmangel und Tempospirale, Kostendruck und Verlegerpolitik werden gerne zur Entschuldigung für den zunehmenden just-in-time-Journalismus angeführt. Aber wohin führt der langsame Wandel des Journalismus vom Beruf zur Tätigkeit?

Wer auf diese Zukunftsfrage eine Antwort möchte, bekam in der ersten Juniwoche 2010 reichlich Anschauungsmaterial. Nach dem überraschenden Rücktritt von Bundespräsident Horst Köhler interessierte sich kaum ein Medium für die tatsächlichen Gründe für dessen Rücktritt. Niemand fragte danach, o b der interne politische Druck der Regierungskoalition über mehrere Jahre möglicherweise ausschlaggebend gewesen ist? Köhlers kristallklare Positionen zur Verantwortung der Banken in der Finanzmarktkrise, seine Forderung nach erhöhten Energiepreisen, die skeptischen Bemerkungen zum tabuisierten Afghanistan-Einsatz und die Dauerkritik an einer überforderten politischen Klasse irritierten Liberale und Konservative. Sie hatten einen Bundespräsidenten ins Amt gehievt, von dem sie eine neo-liberale Begleitung ihrer Politik erwarteten. Stattdessen mutierte Köhler immer stärker zu einem harten Mahner und skeptischen Beobachter, der halbgare Gesetze kassierte und vehement die Regulierung der Finanzmärkte forderte. Dieser Gedanke wurde in den meisten Medien nicht einmal aufgegriffen.

Stattdessen wurde selbst in den Hauptnachrichtensendungen Ursula von der Leyen bereits als Nachfolgerin des Bundespräsidenten ausgerufen. Journalisten wollten – just in time – Ergebnisse und gingen „ihren" Informanten aus Kanzleramt und Regierungsfraktionen erneut auf den Leim. Auch dieser Zusammenhang wurde von der Medienkritik nicht bilanziert.
Hätten die gefürchteten Fact-Checker in den Verlagen diese Pannen vermeiden können?
Wohl nicht. Denn noch werden sie nicht für vorsichtiges Nachdenken, gründliches Ausleuchten des Terrains und den skeptischen Umgang mit interessengeleiteten Informanten eingesetzt. „Fakten-Checker" betreiben n o c h eine Orchideendisziplin, sind für viele Journalisten eher „lästige Besserwisser" und „nervende Nachfrager."

Damit sich dieses angstbesetzte Zerrbild langsam auflöst, hat netzwerk recherche auf einer Fachkonferenz Spezialisten und Insider in Hamburg versammelt. Der hier diskutierte gesammelte Sachverstand kann nun ‚nachgearbeitet' werden. Die in dieser nr-werkstatt dokumentierten Texte, Analysen und Praxistipps spiegeln das Chancenpotential einer unterschätzten Disziplin. Denn der besondere Charme des Fact-Checkings liegt in den zahlreichen indirekten Wirkungen, die von der Überprüfung der Fakten und dem Klären der Sachverhalte ausgehen. Factchecking ist Gift für die grassierende copy and paste-Kultur und Treibstoff für den oft geforderten Qualitätsjournalismus. Dass es dabei nicht nur um Qual geht, zeigen die Autorinnen und Autoren, die den Horizont öffnen und für eine ganz selbstverständliche Kultur der Verifikation im Journalismus werben.

Bertram Weiß

Fact-Checking und redaktionelles Qualitätsmanagement

Bertram Weiß studierte Journalistik und Biologie (Schwerpunkt Wissenschaftsjournalismus) und arbeitet seit 2006 als Autor und freier Redakteur vornehmlich für die Zeitschriften der GEO-Gruppe. Im Auftrag des netzwerk recherche und des Spiegels konzipierte er gemeinsam mit Günter Bartsch, nr-Geschäftsführer, die Fachkonferenz zum Thema „Fact-Checking".

„Qualitätsmanagement“ gehört zu jenen Begriffen aus der Wirtschaft, die in der deutschen Presse am häufigsten genannt werden.[1] Denn die Frage, wie sich Qualität erzielen und sichern lässt, wird in unterschiedlichsten Bereichen diskutiert. Als sie auch in der deutschsprachigen Erforschung des Journalismus Anfang der 1980er Jahre zögerlich Fuß zu fassen begann und sich im Laufe der 1990er Jahre zum Teil des wissenschaftlichen Kanons entwickelte, wurde vielfach betont, dieses aufkeimende Interesse setze sehr spät ein – viel später als in vielen anderen Wirtschaftsbranchen und Forschungsdisziplinen. Seitdem hat „Qualität“ auch in der Journalistik geradezu eine Konjunktur erlebt.
Dabei lassen sich eine Vielzahl der Merkmale erkennen, die der Sprachwissenschaftler Uwe Pörksen in den 1980er-Jahren für Begriffe (z. B. Kommunikation, Energie, Prozess) fand, welchen er die Bezeichnung „Plastikwörter“ zuwies: „Sie sind griffig und sie sind der Schlüssel zu vielem, sie öffnen riesige Räume“.[2] Entsprechend ist Qualität auch im Journalismus kaum zu greifen, ja eine klare und unstrittige Definition scheint unmöglich: „Qualität im Journalismus definieren zu wollen, gleicht dem Versuch, einen Pudding an die Wand zu nageln“.[3] Dieser Ausspruch des Kommunikationswissenschaftler Stephan Ruß-Mohl ist zu einem „Mantra“ in Debatten um journalistische Qualität geworden. Allerdings wird dabei vielfach vergessen, dass Ruß-Mohl in dieser Beobachtung keineswegs einen Anlass zur Resignation sah: „Es heißt nur, daß man sich über Qualitäts-Ziele und über deren Gewichtung verständigen sollte“.[4] Ebenso wird oftmals vergessen, dass Ruß-Mohl seinen Ausspruch später maßgeblich modifizierte: „Es gehört zu den amüsantesten, aber auch schmerzlichen Erfahrungen wissenschaftlichen Arbeitens, daß gerade dieses Zitat noch immer munter zirkuliert, während sein Urheber sich längst eines Besseren belehren ließ und inzwischen mit empirisch ausgerichteten Kommunikationswissenschaftlern der Auffassung ist, daß sich journalistische Qualitätskriterien im Gegensatz zu Wackelpeter eben doch ‚festpinnen‘ lassen“.[5]

Faktentreue als Qualitätsmerkmal

Denn Qualität bezeichnet jenes Maß, in dem Ziele erfüllt werden. Demnach prägen immer jene die Definition der Qualität, welche über die Erfüllung von Ansprüchen ein Urteil fällen können.[6] Diese Subjektivität der Qualität führt dazu, dass sie nur mittels definierter Kriterien oder Indizien zu erkennen ist. Ein Indiz für journalistische Qualität ist etwa die Faktentreue: Der Begriff „Fakt“ ist lateinischen Ursprungs und von der englischen in die deutsche Sprache eingeflossen.[7] Er bezeichnet im allgemeinen Verständnis „etwas, das tatsächlich, nachweisbar vorhanden oder geschehen ist“[8] oder, in den Worten des Kommunikationswissenschaftlers Denis McQuail: „Facts can be considered as self-contained units of information in any account which claims to report on actual events or situations. A fact should, in principle, be verifiable by reference to reliable sources or to other independent accounts".[9]

„Faktisch" ist demnach, was als „verbürgt", als „real" oder gar „wahr" gilt.[10] In umgangssprachlichen und wissenschaftlichen Kontexten sind Fakten Merkmale der Wahrheit,[11] obwohl der lateinische Wortursprung „facere" so viel wie „machen" bedeutet, und somit vielmehr auf das „Gemachte"[12] verweist: „Verum ipsum factum", heißt es bei dem Renaissance-Philosophen Giambattista Vico – „Das Wahre ist dasselbe wie das Gemachte".[13] Aus dieser Perspektive weist der Begriff Fakt auf das Gemachte im Sinne einer Konstruktion hin; folglich eben nicht auf das eindeutig Wahre, das eindeutig Reale oder Gegebene.

Fakten gelten aber als konstitutives Element des Journalismus. Unbesehen aller wissenschaftlichen Dispute um Definition und Abgrenzung von Begriffen erhalten Fakten in der Medienpraxis und journalistischen Selbstreflexion zumeist eine zentrale Rolle. Denn Journalismus lässt sich als sozialverbindlich verstehen, so dass er faktisch wird. Der Journalist muss natürlich „insbesondere auf unbestrittene Mitteilungspartikel zurückgreifen, will er die Subjektivität der Erkenntnis möglichst weitgehend ausschließen. Diese Bedingungen erfüllen annäherungsweise am ehesten Kommunikationspartikel", stellte etwa der Kommunikationswissenschaftler Detlef Schröter fest. Kommunikationspartikel, „welche im allgemeinen Sprachgebrauch als Fakten" betrachtet werden.[14]

Allein ein flüchtiger Blick in die Markenstrategien einiger Massenmedien zeigt, wie wichtig der Begriff für deren Selbstverständnis war oder heute noch ist: Beispielsweise setzen das ARD-Fernsehmagazin Fakt, die Werbeslogans „Fakten, Fakten, Fakten" des Nachrichtenmagazins Focus oder „Alles Fakt" des Sportmagazins Kicker die Fakten in das Zentrum ihres Angebotes. In einer Werbekampagne in den 1960er-Jahren fand das Nachrichtenmagazin Newsweek ein besonders eindrückliches Bild: Auf Werbeplakaten wies Walter Lippmann, der den Begriff des „Stereotyps" in die Auseinandersetzung mit Kommunikation einführte, auf den damaligen Nachrichtenchef mit den Worten: „The facts he gets are often ‚firsts' – are always facts".[15]

Qualität als Managementaufgabe

Je höher die Ansprüche an Qualitätskriterien wie die Faktentreue sind, über die sich Journalisten, Medienunternehmer und Publikum verständigen, desto eher gilt es, die Qualität durch gezielte Maßnahmen zu erlangen und zu sichern – sie zu managen. Der Begriff „Qualitätsmanagement" bezeichnet im Journalismus daher die qualitätsbezogene Arbeit innerhalb der Medieninstitutionen und gewinnt als strategische Aufgabe des Medienmanagements an Bedeutung.[16] Maßnahmen des Qualitätsmanagements betreffen insbesondere die konkrete Organisation der redaktionellen Arbeit.

Dazu gehören etwa Gegenlesen (bzw. Beitragsabnahme im Rundfunk), Redigieren und Blattkritik. Dies hat Vinzenz Wyss (2002)[17] für den Journalismus in der Schweiz, Sandra Hermes (2006)[18] für den Journalismus in Deutschland, in einer Studie gezeigt, in der u. a. regelmäßig angewandte Maßnahmen zur Qualitätssicherung erhoben werden sollten. Der Vergleich der repräsentativen Hamburger Studien „Journalismus in Deutschland I & II"[19] belegt sogar, dass die Praxis des Gegenlesens zwischen 1993 und 2005 in deutschen Redaktionen deutlich zugenommen hat. 66 Prozent der Befragten der jüngeren Untersuchung gaben an, dass ihre Beiträge „immer oder fast immer" gegengelesen oder abgenommen würden. Eine Befragung deutscher Nachrichtenredakteure ergab sogar, dass 76 Prozent der Beiträge regelmäßig gegengelesen werden. [20]

Jedoch gibt die bloße Quantität noch keine Auskunft darüber, wie reflektiert, systematisch, routiniert und aufwendig dieses Handeln in den Arbeitsprozess eingebunden wird. Gegenlesen, Redigieren und Kritik mögen nach der Selbstauskunft von Journalisten einen besonders hohen Stellenwert haben. Tatsächlich wenden sie aber durchschnittlich nur knapp eine Stunde der täglichen Arbeitszeit dafür auf.[21] Und wie genau diese Arbeiten ausgeführt werden, ist kaum erforscht und in Lehr- sowie Handbüchern nur vereinzelt zu finden. Ebenso verhält es sich mit dem „Fact-Checking" im Sinne eines institutionalisierten Verifikationsprozesses, der in die redaktionellen Arbeitsabläufe eingebunden ist – so wie etwa die Inspektion bei der Fertigung von Maschinenteilen.

Zu gering ist (bislang) die Bereitschaft, durch „Total Quality-Management" (TQM) ein ganzheitliches Leitungskonzept und eine damit einhergehende Organisation der Qualität zu etablieren. Das TQM orientiert sich vornehmlich an betriebswirtschaftlichen Ansätzen und zielt in erster Linie darauf ab, Arbeitsprozesse zu optimieren.[22] Aus Angst vor einem Verlust der professionellen Autonomie, so vermutet Wyss, werden Bemühungen um eine derart systematische Qualitätssicherung im Journalismus selten unternommen oder gar heftig abgewehrt.[23] In der Wissenschaft haben sich Forscher jedoch verstärkt diesem Thema gewidmet und sowohl fundierte Pro- als auch Contra-Positionen eingenommen.[24] Insgesamt zeigt sich, dass eine qualitätsorientierte Strategie und Unternehmenskultur vor allem durch das übergeordnete Management und die gesamte Firmenorganisation forciert werden müssen. Gerade diese Perspektive, die TQM in der Auseinandersetzung mit journalistischer Qualität betont, rückt redaktionelle Strukturen und Prozesse in den Vordergrund.

Die Organisation deutscher (Zeitungs-)Redaktionen begann sich in der zweiten Hälfte des 19. Jahrhunderts zu differenzieren. Einerseits orientierte sich der Aufbau der Redaktion an gesellschaftlichen Teilbereichen, etwa Politik, Wirtschaft oder Kultur, andererseits an Interessen einzelner Zielgruppen[25] – insgesamt also an inhaltlichen Kriterien. Die Arbeitsteilung in deutschen Redaktionen erfolgt daher bis heute vornehmlich nach thematischer Zuständigkeit.[26]
Eine Differenzierung entlang funktionaler Tätigkeiten ist im deutschsprachigen Raum dagegen nur schwach ausgeprägt. Nach einer solchen Logik haben sich vor allem Textproduktion (mitunter mit eigener Archiv- und Rechercheabteilung), grafische Produktion und Schlussredaktion bzw. technische Redaktion als eigenständige Arbeitsprofile etabliert. Im Gegensatz dazu entwickelte sich im angloamerikanischen Raum auch eine verbreitete Ausdifferenzierung auf der Ebene der Textproduktion in (mehrere) „Editor" und „Reporter",[27] zu der etwa Text- und Bildarchiv bzw. -recherche, Ombudsmann und Schreibcoach als weitere funktionale Aufgabenbereiche hinzutreten können.[28] Insgesamt weisen angloamerikanische Printredaktionen eine so hohe funktionale Differenzierung auf, dass die Bezeichnungen der einzelnen Aufgabenprofile vielfach nicht einmal treffend ins Deutsche übersetzt werden können. Tatsächlich folgt die organisatorische Logik angloamerikanischer Redaktionen nach Wyss dem „Muster der Werkstattfertigung".[29] So wird der Schwerpunkt auf den Verarbeitungsprozess der Medienaussagen gelegt, nicht auf das Recherche- oder Quellenmaterial. Auf dieses legt im Zweifel ein eigener Produktionsschritt das Augenmerk – das Fact-Checking.

Ausdifferenzierung des Fact-Checking

Vermutlich etablierte sich Fact-Checking als eigenständiger Arbeitsschritt, als sich die „factstory" als Artikeltypus aus dem „objective reporting" formte. Diese Maxime der Berichterstattung bildete sich etwa in der Mitte des 19. Jahrhunderts zuerst in den USA und wurde im Verlauf des Ersten Weltkrieges zur beherrschenden Idee der journalistischen Massenmedien.[30] Michael Schudson ist 1978 ausführlich der Frage nachgegangen, wie und warum so genannte objektive Fakten zu Paradigmen des Journalismus wurden: Er stellte fest, dass diese Werte vor 1830 keine besondere Rolle in den Medien spielten und erst mit dem Begriff „Nachricht" an Bedeutung gewannen.
Bis in die ersten Jahrzehnte des 20. Jahrhunderts unterschieden Journalisten nicht grundsätzlich zwischen Fakten und Wertungen, jenen individuellen Sichtweisen und Einschätzungen von Erlebtem und Erzähltem. Im Vordergrund des „objective reporting" stehen dagegen umfassend und selbst recherchierte,

unparteilich dargebotene Informationen, welche als wahrer Kern der durch Partikularinteressen verfälschten Informationen verstanden werden. Fakten gelten dabei als unabhängig nachvollziehbare Aussagen über die Welt, die sich von Wertungen trennen lassen. Dass das Ergebnis dennoch ein Amalgam aus Faktizität und Meinung bleibt, ist oft Gegenstand der Medienkritik.[31]

Zum Inbegriff der factstory wurden die Beiträge der „Time", welche 1923 gegründet wurde: Diesem Nachrichtenmagazin wird auch die erstmalige Einführung eines professionalisierten Fact-Checking in die redaktionelle Organisation zugeschrieben.[32] Wenig später folgte das Magazin „The New Yorker". Als herausragender Vorreiter dieser Idee gilt außerdem die „New York Times", welche seit 1886 erscheint und nachhaltig den Informations- und Faktenbegriff in den Vordergrund des Journalismus stellte. Als erste US-Zeitung beschäftigte sie Mitarbeiter allein für die Recherche von Informationen. Heute fahnden bei der Zeitungsbeilage „New York Times Magazine" Fact-Checker vor der Veröffentlichung nach Fehlern in allen Beiträgen.

Diese Entwicklung hin zur arbeitsteiligen Suche nach Informationen und Fehlern ist eng verknüpft mit gesellschafts- und geistesgeschichtlichen Innovationen. Walter Lippmann konstatierte dazu treffend: „The study of error is not only in the highest degree prophylactic, but it serves as a stimulating introduction to the study of truth. As our minds become more deeply aware of their own subjectivism, we find a zest in objective method that is not otherwise there. We see vividly, as normally we should not, the enormous mischief and causal cruelty of our prejudices".[33] Was dies für das journalistische Handeln bedeuten kann, bringt Maury auf den Punkt: „Without good fact-checking it's hard for truth to win out over stereotype".[34]

Fact-Checking beobachten und verstehen

Das Streben nach objektiver Berichterstattung förderte also in angloamerikanischen Redaktionen eine personelle Trennung von Erkennen, Prüfen und Bewerten der Realität. Während diese Merkmale journalistischen Handelns bei deutschen Tageszeitungen meist in einer Person, dem Redakteur als „Allrounder", vereinigt werden, können sie bei Zeitschriften mit geringerem Aktualitätsdruck mehr Bedeutung erhalten. In Deutschland führte wohl erstmals „Der Spiegel" die inhaltliche Prüfung, das Fact-Checking, in die redaktionelle Organisation ein. Es ist ein langwieriges, mühsames und teures Procedere, das nur wenige Medienunternehmen bereit sind zu etablieren. Nicht zuletzt, weil vieles eher ungewiss ist: Wie wirkt es sich auf journalistische Inhalte aus, wenn Fact-Checking wegfällt? Wie reagiert das Publikum darauf? Welche Fehler durchdringen das

Sicherheitsnetz? Oder welche werden gar erst darin produziert? Was bedeutet es für Autoren, mit Fact-Checkern zusammen zu arbeiten? Was bedeutet Fact-Checking für den Schreibprozess? Wie werden Konflikte zwischen Fact-Checking und schreibenden Journalisten ausgehandelt? Ist es möglich, dass Journalisten durch Fact-Checking in einen „moral hazard" geraten – also in die Versuchung, nachlässig zu werden, weil sie sich in der Sicherheit einer Prüfinstanz wiegen? All diese Fragen erscheinen besonders sinnvoll angesichts der seit der Jahrtausendwende wachsenden Einsparungsmaßnahmen, mit denen Archiv- und Dokumentationsabteilungen von Verlagshäusern (und somit mitunter auch das Fact-Checking) konfrontiert sind. Und all dies sind Fragen, deren Antworten wichtige Anregungen für das Qualitätsmanagement in Redaktionen geben könnten.
Die finanziellen Belastungen, die mit der Einführung eines institutionalisierten Fact-Checking einher gehen, lassen es unwahrscheinlich erscheinen, dass Medienunternehmen dies künftig in stärkerem Ausmaß bei der redaktionellen Organisation berücksichtigen – zumal die Frage, wie Fehlerzahl und Medienwahl der Rezipienten zueinander stehen, empirisch bisher nicht befriedigend beantwortet ist. Eine stärkere Integration von Fact-Checking-Prinzipien und Erfahrungen aus der Fact-Checking-Praxis (auch in der Journalistenausbildung) oder eine zumindest punktuelle Einführung von Fact-Checking erscheinen dagegen eher realistisch.[35]
Angesichts der zu erwartenden Steigerung der Qualität und Glaubwürdigkeit von Medienaussagen durch Fact-Checking erscheinen diese Maßnahmen im wachsenden Verdrängungswettbewerb des Mediensektors sogar geboten. Vielleicht werden am Zeitschriftkiosk oder im Internet ja einmal Publikationen angeboten, auf deren Frontseiten steht: „Diese Ausgabe wurde aufwendig von unseren Fact-Checkern geprüft".

Die Referenzen in Fußnoten stehen auf www.factchecking.de zum Download bereit.

Scott Maier

News Accuracy: Transatlantic Perspectives

Prof. Scott Maier, Ph.D., lehrt Journalistik an der School of Journalism and Communication der University of Oregon. Bevor er sich als Wissenschaftler der Qualität journalistischer Berichterstattung widmete, schrieb er als Zeitungs- und Agenturjournalist vor allem über politische Themen, Lateinamerika und investigative Rechercheergebnisse. Im Jahr 2009 war Maier am Journalism Observatory der Università della Svizzera italiana als Forscher zu Gast. Für seine Forschungen zur Richtigkeit der Medienberichterstattung erhielt er (zusammen mit Philip Meyer) den „National Award for Research About Journalism" der „Society of Professional Journalist's".

We all probably agree that accuracy is the foundation of media credibility – after all, how can audiences believe what they read in the newspaper or hear on the television news if the facts aren't right? In the United States, the code of ethics of the Society of Professional Journalists states: "Test the accuracy of information from all sources and exercise care to avoid inadvertent error. Deliberate distortion is never permissible." The International Federation of Journalists has a similar mandate: "Respect for truth and for the right of the public to truth is the first duty of the journalist."

Yet clearly journalists fall short in meeting these high-held principles. The public in the United States is increasingly convinced that the media commonly makes mistakes. The latest public opinion survey indicated that only 29 percent of the people believe the news media get their facts straight.

But the question remains: How often do errors really occur? Is the public correct in its perception that mistakes are frequent? And when mistakes are made, does it matter? In answer to these questions, I seek to provide baseline data.

U.S. Study of News Accuracy

For more than 70 years, U.S. communication researchers have asked people in news stories whether the information reported was correct. As early as 1936, a news accuracy study of three U.S., newspapers found that nearly half of the stories had one or more errors. Factual errors identified by news sources included incorrect information regarding names, ages, numbers, titles, addresses, locations, time, and dates. Researchers also have tracked "errors of meaning" with a separate listing of subjective categories such as overemphasis, underemphasis, omissions, and misleading quotes. Following this model, researchers through the years have documented that accuracy persistently eludes the press.

In the largest and most recent accuracy study, Prof. Philip Meyer of the University of North Carolina and I examined news accuracy of 22 U.S. newspapers (Maier 2005). It was an enormous undertaking. Researchers clipped every bylined news story appearing in the front, metro, business and lifestyle sections of each newspaper examined until a sample of 200 to 400 stories had been compiled for each newspaper studied. Over a two-year period, 7600 news stories were copied and mailed to the primary news sources cited in the articles. We provided a four-page questionnaire that asked the news source to evaluate the accuracy of the news article and to assess the newspaper's credibility. The response rate was 68 percent, relatively high these days for survey research.

A limitation of this study is self-evident: Perceived error lies exclusively in the eye of the news source. Indeed, research shows that news sources and reporters frequently disagree about what constitutes error, especially when issues of interpretation are involved. For that reason, I will focus today's presentation on matters of factual accuracy – such as whether a name or location is correctly reported – for which there tends to be little debate.

Findings:
Nearly 50 percent of the news stories had at least one factual error – such as incorrect name or title, the numbers were wrong or location in error.
Multiple errors were common: On average, three errors were identified for each story perceived as inaccurate.
The error rates were the highest in 70 years of accuracy research.

What kind of errors were made? The most common factual error was misquotation, accounting for 20 percent of objective errors reported. Errant headlines and incorrect numbers also were among the leading factual errors (see Table 1 for listing of error frequencies and severity ratings). I know how difficult spelling in English can be for foreign speakers. But take heart, U.S. journalists also have difficulty getting their words letter-perfect. Typographical and spelling errors (not including misspelling names) accounted for nearly 10 percent of factual errors. Despite automated spell-checkers, this is an error rate nearly as high as the rate reported in 1936!

	N	*Error Severity*
Misquotation	690	3.01
Inaccurate headline	482	3.09
Numbers Wrong	423	2.83
Misspeling	330	1.94
Job Title Wrong	279	2.57
Name Wrong	113	3.11
Location Wrong	90	2.93
Time Wrong	71	2.75
Date Wrong	71	3.07
Address Wrong	56	3.30
Age Wrong	46	2.57

Table 1: Factual Errors I – Sources were asked to rate the severity of errors identified. On a scale in which 1 is a minor error and 7 a major error, the average rating was 2.8.

What about subjective errors -- information considered technically correct but misleading? These kinds of errors — for example, a quote taken out of context -- are by definition matters of opinion, but we believe that these perceptions are still important. Here's what we found: Subjective errors were identified in 47 percent of the news stories examined. The most common subjective error involved not what was reported in the newspaper but what was left out: 30 percent of subjective errors comprise what news sources considered "essential information missing." As shown in Table 2, news sources also frequently complained that their quotes were distorted or out of context (accounting for 23 percent of subjective errors). Not surprisingly, survey results provided further evidence of the tendency of journalists to hype news stories. Nearly twice as many stories were considered "sensationalized" (20 percent of subjective errors) by news sources than stories considered "understated" (11 percent of subjective errors). Moreover, news sources often considered these kinds of subjective errors to be more serious than the fact errors they identified. These results suggest that how the story is conveyed is as important as getting the facts straight.

	N	Severity
Essential Information Missing	918	3.03
Quotes Distorted	699	2.90
Story Sensationalized	603	3.22
Numbers misleading	419	3.12
Story Understated	348	2.95

Table 2: Subjective Errors

Just as you would suspect, errors are frequently found. Why were they made? As shown in Table 3, the top response was that the reporter didn't understand what he or she was writing about, a complaint given by about one in four news sources reporting errors. Deadline pressure and lack of research also were leading reasons given for inaccuracies, providing further evidence that reporters blunder when they don't take the time needed to comprehend and interpret the information they seek to convey. Relatively few news sources attributed errors to laziness or the pressure to scoop other media. Even fewer news sources blamed themselves: About one in a hundred acknowledged providing incorrect information.

	N	%*
Lack of understanding	520	25.9
Deadline pressure	379	18.9
Insufficient research	346	17.3
Didn't ask enough questions	254	12.7
Events were confusing	252	12.6
Didn't ask right questions	243	12.1
Laziness	198	9.9
Pressure to scoop others	135	6.7
Source provided misinformation	18	0.9

*Percent of stories with errors

Table 3: Causes of error

This study indicates that newspapers – whether small or large – suffer from unacceptably high rates of errors. So clearly, accuracy remains a challenge among the U.S. press. But does it matter? Indeed it does. By every measure, we found that inaccuracy had a toll on credibility. When asked to assess the story's overall credibility, news sources finding one or more errors rated the article nearly a full point lower on a 7-point scale than sources finding no error. The errors in a single story also measurably had a negative effect on news source perceptions of the entire newspaper. Even mistakes judged "small" diminished respect for the news media. In fact, statistical analysis showed that error explains a third of perceived story credibility. That might not sound impressive, but it is significant when you consider all that goes into judging a news story – its authorship, placement, style, as well as the newspaper's prestige, political orientation and other attributes.

In spite of the abundance of errors identified, news sources generally remained trusting of newspapers in which they were named. On a scale in which 1 is the least trusting response and 7 indicates the most credibility, news sources gave the newspapers studied a 5.1 rating. Sources also reported that they were quite willing to serve as news sources again, with sources characterizing themselves as "eager" to cooperate with the newspaper outnumbering by 12 to 1 sources who characterized themselves as "reluctant".

Nonetheless, we found that newspaper errors tarnished the media's working relationship with the sources they relied on for information. Even though news sources were remarkably forgiving of errors, recognizing that journalists have a difficult job, their willingness to be a news source again diminished with every error found.

European Journalism Observatory Study

The evidence is compelling that the U.S. media have a problem with news accuracy. Do the media in Europe share this malady? To explore this supposition, the European Journalism Observatory, a research institute based at Università della Svizzera italiana, tested the news accuracy of Swiss and Italian newspapers. Replicating the U.S studies, principal investigators Colin Porlezza and Marta Zanichelli sent surveys to 1000 news sources quoted in five Swiss (German-language) daily newspapers[1] and 1000 news sources quoted in five Italian newspapers[2]. The response rate from the Swiss newspaper sample was 50 percent; only 15 percent for Italian newspaper sample (Hence, the Italian results lack statistical significance and should be viewed as exploratory at best).

Before I share their results here, let me ask: Would you expect errors to be more or less frequent in the Swiss press than in the U.S press? In the Italian press? In your own newspaper or news media?

Here are the preliminary results recently reported by the European Journalism Observatory: Sources identified factual errors in 60 percent of news stories in Swiss newspapers, in 52 percent of Italian newspapers, compared to 48 percent of U.S. newspapers. In fact, more factual errors were identified in Swiss and Italian newspapers than in U.S. newspapers in every category except "wrong numbers" (see Table 4). Sources also reported subjective errors at a rate higher in Swiss news stories and in Italian new stories than in U.S. newspapers. But errors – both factual and subjective -- were considered somewhat less severe in Swiss and Italian newspapers than in U.S. newspapers.

	US (%)	Swiss (%)	Italian (%)
Misquoted	21.0	26.5	22.1
Headline wrong	14.7	26.6	26.6
Numbers wrong	12.9	12.4	14.9
Misspelling	10.0	12.9	13.6
Job title wrong	8.5	11.6	13.6
Name wrong	3.4	8.0	7.8
Address wrong	1.7	2.7	52.6
Age wrong	1.4	2.6	1.5
Location wrong	2.7	3.1	3.9
Time wrong	2.2	4.3	3.9
Date wrong	2.2	3.1	2.6

Table 4: Factual Errors II

The reasons attributed to errors (factual and subjective) were similar across nationalities, though Swiss and Italian sources considered deadline pressure to be a larger issue than US sources. Despite the abundance of errors, these news sources remained remarkably trusting of the newspapers and willing to serve as news sources again. This was especially true among Swiss sources: the majority of Swiss sources characterized themselves as "eager" – the highest rating – to cooperate with the newspaper again, compared to slightly more than a third of U.S. or Italian sources who characterized themselves as "eager".

From these results, I do not believe its fair to conclude that media accuracy is better or worse in Switzerland or in Italy than in the United States. After all, only five newspapers were studied in each European country and, as I stated earlier, the response rate was not adequate to draw solid conclusions from the limited Italian sample. Accuracy rates also might reflect differences in expectations of news sources and their willingness to attribute error. In other words, European sources may be harder on the media than their U.S. counterparts. Another possible explanation: The results reflect differences in editing procedures in Europe and the United States. As academics are fond of saying, I submit, "further study is needed".

So what can be concluded from all this? These studies show that news inaccuracy is an issue across nations and journalism cultures, with remarkably similar errors reported in each nation studied here. Furthermore, accuracy really matters: Across nations, errors had a measurable effect on news credibility. News sources clearly have high expectations that the media should get the story right. Especially in Switzerland, there appears to be a high level of trust that shouldn't be squandered.

I hope these results pique your curiosity and inspire some to consider conducting an accuracy study of their own newspaper or magazine. With that wish, I will end by providing a brief outline how you or your news organization can conduct such a study. Here are some guidelines:

Guidelines for studying news accuracy

Sample: Collect 200 to 400 news stories for each news organization studied.
Sources: Identify and locate at least one primary news source for each article. Consider partnerships: Research shows that the return rate is higher and respones are more honest when surveys are administered by independent academic researchers than by editors of the media studied.
Survey: Provide a personally addressed letter and the news article with each questionnaire.

Promise confidentiality: Sources fear their complaints will be used against them.
Consider rewards: A small gift or promised donation to charity can increase participation.
Delivery: Send questionnaires by postal mail AND email for maximum response.
Follow-up: Repeat the mailing process two to three times for every source who does not initially respond.

Fußnoten

1 Tages-Anzeiger, Aargauer Zeitung, Berner Zeitung, Südostschweiz, and the Basler Zeitung.

2 L'Eco di Bergamo, Il Resto del Carlino, Il Giornale di Sicilia, Il Giornale di Brescia and Il Secolo XIX.

Literatur

MAIER, Scott (2005): Accuracy Matters: A Cross-Market Assessment of Newspaper Errors and Credibility. In: Journalism and Mass Communication Quarterly 82/3.

Sarah Smith

Lessons Learned: Fact-Checking Disasters of the Past

Sarah Smith ist seit 2005 Managing Editor des New York Times Magazine, der wöchentliche Beilage der New York Times. Zuvor leitete sie dort die Recherche-Abteilung und erarbeitete einen neuen Fact-Checking-Prozess. Smith studierte englische Sprache und Literatur an der Columbia University und der Oxford University, arbeitete als Fact-Checkerin für das Magazin The New Yorker und verfasste das Lehrbuch „The Fact Checker's Bible".

I wrote a book about fact-checking a few years ago that was geared toward people who fact checked for a living at a major magazine with a checking department. When the book proposal sold to a publishing house, I was totally floored, because the total number of professional fact checkers in the United States has got to be under a thousand, and outside of the states, fact-checking is largely a cultural joke. So who exactly was going to buy this book I certainly couldn't imagine. But the fact is, of course, that many publications don't have checking departments and are just as concerned about, and responsible for, the accuracy of their content as a larger magazine would be. I've seen some very scary errors go into print despite good fact-checking and like all checkers, I've used unchecked sources – newspapers and books, for example, as a successful part of the fact-checking process. There isn't a firm line of accuracy dividing checked and unchecked stories in different media, and that's because in a normal editing process, several different people are reading content before it is published, each bringing to it a degree of skepticism and their own stores of knowledge, plus, as time allows, their own "non-professional" fact-checking skills.

The Editorial Trinity

That sounds pretty good – a smart editor, a smart writer, a good copyeditor to check the names a dates – you might be very successful with this editorial trinity. But depending upon how ambitious your writers are, dangers lurk. Working at The New Yorker and at the New York Times Magazine, where, I would argue, we publish some of the most seasoned, reliable writers on a weekly basis and have experienced fact checkers, copyeditors and assigning editors, we've gone to press with some absolute horrors and had our editorial methods scrutinized from both without – on blogs, and online magazines like The New York Press – and, at The Times, from within, by our own public editor, who as an ombudsman for the newspaper investigates reader complaints from a privileged and feared position. From each horror we've honed our institutional methods a tiny bit more, learned to be that much less credulous – though of course the next horror is usually one we hadn't anticipated.

If one could generalize about the horrors and their origins, I would say that they could be classified as having at their roots at least one of the following four factors: First: an unreliable editorial process, second, an unreliable source, third, an unreliable author, and fourth, incomplete reporting. Horrors of the magnitude I'm going to describe – in the sedate world of magazine, these qualify as spectacular horrors – could happen anywhere, at any ambitious publication, and I'm hoping they will expand your sense of what lurking dangers are out there.

I don't think you have to be a fact checker to catch one of these horrors before it goes into print, because in every case, these horrors WEREN'T caught by the fact checkers working on them. Which is not to say, forget about hiring fact checkers, but rather, be aware of how hard it is to get everything right, even with the smartest, well-trained, polyglot checkers at your disposal.

Horrors of Fact-Checking

The first fact-checking horror I want to describe – the one that changed fact-checking history as we know it happened at The New Yorker magazine a few years before I joined the checking department there. The New Yorker was famous for its fact-checking department, though it was actually Britten Hadden at Time Magazine who seems to have invented the job when he began that magazine in the 1920s. His all female fact-checking crew verified names, dates and facts and marked news items for writers to use when compiling their stories. Edward Kennedy, an editor at Time, can also be credited for writing the first fact-checking manual, in which he advised, "Checking is sometimes regarded as a dull and tedious occupation but such a conception of this position is extremely erroneous. Any bright girl who readily applies herself to the handling of the checking problem can have a very pleasant time with it and fill the week with happy moments and memorable occasions. The most important point to remember in checking is that the writer is your natural enemy. He is trying to see how much he can get away with. Remember that when people write letters about mistakes it's you who will be screeched at. So protect yourself."

When The New Yorker was founded the year after Time, it was initially quite sloppy with the facts and it was only in 1927, after publishing an inaccurate profile of Edna St. Vincent Millay that the magazine started fact-checking in earnest, largely because its founders realized that if it was going to make fun of other publications for being inaccurate in its "newsbreaks" column, it had better not be guilty of the same.

By the time The New Yorker's first big mistake occurred, in 1983, the magazine had an esteemed fact-checking department. Janet Malcolm, an intellectual and respected writer who was well ensconced at The New Yorker, where her husband, Gardner Botsford, was an editor, wrote two long pieces about Jeffrey Masson, a psychoanalyst and former projects director of the Sigmund Freud Archives. Malcolm made her subject look like a buffoon, quoting him comparing himself to an "intellectual gigolo" and saying that he wanted to turn Anna Freud's home into "a place of sex, women and fun." Masson claimed he'd never said such things, and sued for libel. Malcolm couldn't produce notes or tapes to support the quotations, and the trial went on and on, through various courts, until 1994 – eleven years after the pieces had been published in the magazine. The costs were staggering.

In retrospect, this particular horror was the result of a confluence of factors working together to create a big problem. The first factor was an unreliable editorial process. Janet Malcolm was edited by her own husband, Garner Botsford and according to their account, in the course of editing the story, Botsford was satisfied that Malcolm had notes to support the quotations without actually asking to see them. He also changed the locations of one of the conversations with Masson – always a no-no – and chose to use the “sex, women and fun quotation“ even after he discovered it wasn’t on the tapes. So the first element of the editorial process that went badly wrong was for a husband and wife to work this way together – there simply doesn’t seem to have been enough critical distance. Even without a fact checker being involved, the editor should have worried about the quotations that made Masson look like such an idiot, and insisted on seeing the notes and hearing the relevant sections of the tapes. Whenever someone mentioned in a story is portrayed in a derogatory light, watch out—that person will try to undermine the credibility of the piece in any way he can in order to defend himself. It’s a red flag for extra scrutiny.

The second problem with the editorial process in the Malcolm/Masson case was that at that time fact checkers did not routinely look at an author’s notes to confirm quotations or the context in which they were spoken, or listen to tapes for that reason, and they did not discuss material in quotations with the speaker. So although the checker did talk extensively to Masson, and go over biographical details and other facts, the matter of the disputed quotations seems not to have come up. Though the checker was just following what was checking protocol at that time, it was a checking method that left a lot of room for uncertainty. Nowadays, as a direct result of the Malcolm scandal, we expect checkers to go over the content and context of quotations, if not the actual wording, and although it does sometimes lead to a difficult process, at least we usually know before we publish what the source is going to contest, so we can be sure that we can defend our decision to publish. The image I think of is of a bomb ticking away in a piece. You know it will explode sooner or later, so it’s smarter to set it off before you publish – when you can contain the damage. A subject who is portrayed in an unfavorable light is going to get mad and defensive no matter what, but you are safer if you make it happen before the news hits the stands.

The Malcolm/Masson case illustrates what can happen when you publish something career-destroyingly critical, with insufficient confirmation and an editorial process that isn’t asking the right questions insistently enough. It was a perfect storm of sorts and one that could have been prevented by either the checker or the editor, if either of them had really realized how little evidence there was to support Malcolm's assertions.

The Times considers itself the paper of record, and sets a very high standard for ethical journalism. We moved into a new building a few years ago. It is a metaphoric embodiment of the Times's desire for transparency in reporting – you can actually look through the building, straight from one side to the other, and everyone in the building can see what their colleagues are doing most of the time. Even the offices have glass walls. It's a beautiful place to work, and a constant reminder that ultimately there is no hiding mistakes and bad methods—the world sees what we do, and when we get something wrong in print, we hear about it from our readers very quickly. The Times newspaper isn't fact checked, exactly, though writers are responsible for the accuracy of their facts and their editors do what they can to help them out. The New York Times Magazine is, however—we have 4 people who check the magazine front to back each week. It's amazing how many errors checkers prevent going into print, and sometimes embarrassing how many go into print despite their efforts.

"Is Youssouf Malé a Slave?"

Shortly before I was hired by the New York Times Magazine, it had its own perfect storm – in this case a confluence on an unambiguously unreliable author, and an unreliable editorial process. The piece was called "Is Youssouf Malé a Slave?" I find the story of this debacle to be very poignant, because the author, Michael Finkel, was a genuinely good journalist who went temporarily off the rails and didn't get caught in time to be saved. Finkel had written eight stories for the New York Times before, with no known challenges to his facts, but when it came to a story he was reporting on indentured servitude in Africa, he couldn't seem to get it right, and he and his editor couldn't figure out a way to make his reporting hang together in a compelling way. Finally, in despair, he created a composite character based on numerous indentured young men he had encountered in Mali. He gave this composite character the name of one the actual boys he had interviewed, Youssouf Malé, and presented the magazine with a photograph he had taken of the boy. Finkel was himself a photographer on the story. After piece ran in the magazine, the magazine got a call from Save the Children, saying that the child pictured was not Youssouf Malé, but another boy, Madou Traoré. The whole thing fell apart very rapidly.

Finkel's fabrications were the obvious source of this disaster and it would be tempting to think, "Well, how often does that happen? It's a bit like worrying about a man in the dark with an axe – you can worry all you like but it probably won't ever happen to you." Well, it happened twice at the New York Times within a couple of years – the second perpetrator was Jason Blair, who made up anonymous sources in his reporting for the paper – so I think that rate is actually quite high for a single institution. But more usefully, there were institutional problems that allowed Finkel's story, and Jayson Blair's, to go to print with their fabrications intact. And note that the paper does not fact check but the magazine does, and they both failed to catch these guys.

In the case of Jayson Blair, the newspaper wasn't aggressive enough in questioning his use of unnamed sources. In the enormous brouhaha that followed Blair's exposure (including the departure of Howell Raines, the paper's executive editor) the Times made a policy that at least one editor must know the identity of any unnamed source in a story. This is a good policy, that every magazine should follow, but of course it might not stop a serial fabricator, as in the case of the infamous Stephen Glass of The New Republic, who hoodwinked his fact checkers with fake business cards for his supposed sources and even went so far as to create phony websites for non-existent companies he'd written about. Charles Lane, the editor of the New Republic told the Times that "A frequent tactic of his to elude fact checkers recontacting his source was to provide them with notes saying, "This source is very nervous and specifically asks that you do not call him back, even if there was a phone number." These were enough to satisfy his fact checkers – he had been one of them, so he knew what standard he had to meet, but even if The New Republic hadn't had fact checkers, the fabrications might have been caught if his editor had wondered for a minute if his reporting might be a bit too good to be true.

It's a cardinal rule that you have to listen to your inner skeptic when your vetting a piece, and his editors had earmuffs on – they simply didn't want to believe that his stories were false. In retrospect, another writer from the magazine said, every piece of his began with this really unbelievable sequence or anecdote. What it would have taken to catch Glass would have been an editor – not necessarily a fact checker – who wasn't willing to repeatedly give Glass the benefit of the doubt when it came to verifying the details of his stories. But one can see how tempting it would be to ignore that little skeptical voice when readers were eating up Glass's fictions. He was eventually exposed by Adam Penenberg, a writer at Forbes Digital Tool, who tried to re-report one of his stories and couldn't.

The same warning signs tipped off an editor at The Boston Globe when Patricia Smith, a Metro columnist there, turned in too-good-to-be-true stories that were hard to verify. "I recognized the same pattern," he said. "Someone vaguely identified or not identified at all saying pretty incredible things." It wasn't that her editors didn't try to verify what Smith wrote, but they didn't try hard enough. Smith first claimed that the people she quoted in her columns were too marginal to be traced; they didn't have telephones. Later, worrying about this lack of confirmation, editors tried to find named sources in computer databases and couldn't under this scrutiny, Smith resigned, confessing to having fabricated sources for four columns. The number was later bumped up to 52 – that's 52 columns that contained unverifiable people and quotations. Smith herself later confessed, "From time to time in my Metro column, to create the desired impact or slam home a salient point, I attributed quotes to people who didn't exist. I could give them names, even occupations, but I couldn't give them what they needed most – a heartbeat." Again, in Smith's case I don't think that she lacked a fact checker – she just needed to have a more skeptical editor who would demand to follow up on her repeated use of anonymous, unverifiable sources. To good-to-be-true strikes again...

To get back to Michael Finkel, the New York Times Magazine's fabricator in "Is Youssouf Malé a Slave?", I know a little bit more about the inside story there. The fact checker's couldn't verify much of the piece because of delays in getting email responses from Africa, and of course Finkel himself was the photographer of the boy who later turned out to be someone else entirely. I see both of these as reflecting unreliable editorial practices. If a story is largely unverifiable because of time constraints, then it should be postponed until at least the most basic checking can be done. Believe me, it is very hard, at a weekly magazine, to sub in an alternate story mid week, but it ought to have happened in this case.

As for the author as photographer: this really ought to have worried people, given how little further corroboration there was for this story. It can be challenging to check stories in third world or war torn, distant places. Many people don't have phones, and there can be language barriers, as there was in this case. But in the absence of those normal checks, photographers, translators and fixers can all be useful backup sources. In Finkel's case, the author himself had become the single source for much of the story, including, crucially, the identity of his primary subject. And a single source story is another big red flag to look out for. Even in the most difficult, obscure locations, there is usually someone who can verify the broad outlines at least—an aid organization, a local doctor from Doctors without Borders—someone. If there isn't, you have to ask yourself "Why?"

And the final problem was that the checkers and the editor didn't ask to look at the author's notes. If they had, the editor admitted to me later, it would have been pretty clear what the author had done in conflating several characters into one. So the Finkel case really illustrates that fact-checkers need to be wary of stories for which the author is the sole authority, you need to ask to look at

notes, and then look through them, and you need to give yourself the flexibility of substituting another story if you can't verify enough to go to press with a good conscience. Sadly, the Finkel episode also illustrates that you need to remain skeptical even when you the author has a good track record.
Just as the Malcolm libel case changed the way quotations were handled at The New Yorker and elsewhere, the Finkel disaster led to a change in practices at the New York Times Magazine. Checkers now routinely look at notes, much as it annoys those writers who come to us from other sections of the paper, where notes are still considered very private property. Even if you aren't prepared to fact check a story from top to bottom, asking for a writer's notes, and spending just a few minutes glancing through them can give you a sense of the scope of the reporting and, perhaps, its limitations.

A Woman Named Carmen Climaco

There were three more recent fact-checking problems at the New York Times Magazine, all on a smaller scale. No one went to court, no one lost his job, but in these three cases the magazine got something significantly wrong despite the good intentions of everyone involved. Several ago we ran an article by an established, respected writer from South Carolina, Jack Hitt, on the subject of abortion in El Salvador. Abortions are illegal in El Salvador and women who are discovered to have used illegal methods of abortion are sometimes prosecuted and sent to prison. Hitt wrote that a few women in El Salvador were serving 30 year jail terms for having had abortions in El Salvador, and one these, whom we showed in a photograph, was a woman named Carmen Climaco. Hitt told the story of how she had received the sentence after apparently aborting at 18 weeks of pregnancy, though he acknowledged that it was hard to say what had happened exactly. We thought he was safe hedging his bets when he wrote, "the truth was certainly – well, not in the middle so much as somewhere else entirely." Somewhere like this: She'd had a clandestine abortion at 18 week – something defined as absolutely legal in the United States. It's just that she'd had the abortion in El Salvador." The caption accompanying Carmen Climaco's photograph was less nuanced, and stated flatly that she was jailed for an 18 week abortion that was ruled a homicide. As you know, abortion is a very, very sensitive topic here in the States and because the Times is often portrayed in other media as being excessively liberal, what we publish about abortion often gets more attention from the far right than it might if it were published elsewhere. Even when we get stories about abortion factually right we get criticized, and in this case we got something big wrong. We thought we were being careful when we edited the piece, but it wasn't bulletproofed, which a story on abortion really needs to be. Sure enough, an anti-abortion web site reported soon after our piece ran that Climaco had actually been guilty of infanticide – the murder of a living newborn rather than abortion. The headline read, "New York Times Caught in Abortion-promoting Whopper – infanticide Portrayed as Abortion." The website included a translated court ruling which gave the age of the baby as between 38 and 42 weeks – which is to say full term, and included results of a test on the infant's lungs which showed that they had breathed before death.

Now the author of our piece had gotten much of his information about Climaco from a magistrate who had ruled on an early stage of her case, and she had confirmed the facts as we had printed them. We thought a magistrate was a pretty reliable source, and when she told Hitt, via his translator, that the court documents were archived and unavailable, Hitt took her at her word. Once the pro-life web site had published the court ruling saying that the baby was full term, the Times sent a stringer into the court building to see if he could get an original copy of the ruling, and did so with no problem. Hitt and his translator hadn't tried to do so, which looked terrible in retrospect. Also unfortunate was that Hitt's translator turned out to have been someone that Ipas, an El Salvadoran abortion rights advocacy group, had found for him – and whom Hitt had not paid for the translation services. These factors combined to give our critics the sense that Hitt had been in the pocket of the abortion rights group all along.

Now usually we try to look at court documents from both sides of any legal dispute, and in the case of Carmen Climaco's trial we gave up too easily before we went to press. And we didn't consider how Hitt's choice of translator might look if our readers knew about it, or, more significantly, what impact using a possibly biased translator might have on the reporting. I don't actually think that Hitt or the translator was trying to deceive anyone with the story. I think they were trying to report it accurately and in an unbiased way. But the editorial staff should have worried not just about their actual impartiality, which rightly or wrongly we assumed, but about the appearance of impartiality, which was, in this case, certainly compromised.

And of course we were careless with the caption information which was so much less subtle than Hitt's own description of the Climaco case. Where he had doubted the government's ruling of homicide, the caption flatly contradicted it. Now Hitt himself didn't write the caption, the copyeditors did, but they weren't sensitive enough to the nuances of Hitt's argument. If there's another rule of safety-proofing pieces without fact checkers, it is to make sure that the display type in any piece adheres as closely as possible to the body text. When someone other than the author of the story tries to distill an argument for captions or pull quotes, there's always the risk that the meaning will be distorted. Captions, heds, decks, and pull quotes are the most prominent element of any story – sort of like a press release for the story. For a lot of readers they become the nugget of information they take from a story, so it's a nugget that really needs to be correct. Now our author had the chance to see the caption before we went to press, but under the pressure of closing the story, he probably didn't really scrutinize it himself. It's a good idea to always point out the display type to the author to make sure that they approve it.

The Problem of Quotations

Our weekly question and answer column, which is written by Deborah Solomon, is a very popular part of the magazine and also one that creates a lot of controversy. Deborah is genuinely very liberal, very opinionated, very interested in people's private lives and in getting intimate quotes from famous people. She regularly asks politicians, for example, about their relationships with their mothers, and whether they've ever been in analysis (she has). This makes for a great column, and one that forces the people whom she interviews, many of them masters of the rehearsed sound bite or anecdote, to speak in an unguarded, candid way. She once got the head of the International Atomic Energy Agency to confess that the pressure of worrying about atomic weapons all day at work made him very testy with his wife, and honestly, I doubt I'll ever forget that. But Deborah Solomon gets these amazing quotes from her subjects because she talks to them for hours and hours – all of which she diligently tapes. She has to edit away all but the best bits of the conversations. Now editing conversations gets us into murky water. The Times's Guidelines on Integrity states, "Readers should be able to assume that every word between quotation marks is what the speaker or writer said. The Times does not 'clean up' quotations. No one needs to be reminded that falsifying any part of a news report cannot be tolerated and will result automatically in disciplinary action up to and including termination." So that's clear. But in a conversation that goes on for hours, and sometimes, in Solomon's case, takes place in part via email and in part over the phone, who can say which quotation is the most accurate to use, even if verbatim? And how can the editorial staff make sure that the context in which we put that quote is accurate? With all the condensing that Deborah has to do to get the highlights of these interviews onto a single page, it is a wonder that we don't have more problems than we do. But when we do get something wrong, it's a big deal.
We'd had a few problems in the past as a result of the conflating that Deborah has to do. But recently we really got into trouble when Deborah interviewed Ira

Glass of This American Life, a very popular radio program. Talking about his new TV program on Showtime, Deborah quoted Glass making two comments that were less than wholeheartedly enthusiastic about the network. First, in our printed version of their conversation, we had Deborah ask Glass, "What do you think of the network," to which we had Glass reply, "I don't meet many people who are talking about shows on Showtime." He also was quoted as saying "Here are the advantages of Showtime: They came to us, and at first we said no, and they persevered. We had good experience with the pilot." Now after the piece ran, a journalist from the New York Press named Matt Elzeig spoke to Glass and other interview subjects about how the process had gone with Deborah. Glass, among others, was ready to talk about what he felt had gone wrong. For one thing, he said, Deborah hadn't asked him exactly the question we had printed before his first quotation about Showtime. Another problem, and one that had caused trouble for him with Showtime, was that Solomon had chosen not to use some of the positive things he'd said about Showtime in follow-up interviews. He had gone on to say, "The more I talk to other people who've worked in TV, the more I realize what total sweethearts the Showtime people have been and how rare it is to have such sensible, smart collaborators at the network level. We've been insanely lucky." But rather than seeing that complete response reflected in the magazine, he was left looking critical of the network that was giving him the opportunity to go on TV. Very unfortunate. He didn't dispute that he's said what Deborah quoted him as saying, but felt that it was out of context and that, as Glass put it, Solomon "rewrites her questions and then applies any question to any answer that a person says."

Now I think that both Deborah Solomon and Ira Glass were being self-serving here, as well they might. Glass had indeed been critical of Showtime, but then thought better of it, probably realizing how very impolitic he would sound. And Solomon, understandably, wanted to use the part of their conversation about Showtime that was the edgiest and most newsworthy. She didn't want the PR sanctioned answer because that makes for boring reading. But there is still something troubling about the disproportionate power the interviewer had over the interview. It doesn't seem quite fair, even if it made for juicy reading, that Glass wasn't allowed to give a more complete and nuanced answer about Showtime when he tried to do so first with Deborah and then with the fact checker. And although one could understand why Deborah might reword her question to make it clearer to the reader what she was asking about, that also doesn't seem totally fair, since the subject of the interview isn't permitted the same rights to revise. Ultimately, the Glass problem led the paper to request that we change the byline on every one of Deborah's interviews. Where the byline had previously read, "Interview by Deborah Solomon," we now say, "Interview has been condensed and edited." Solomon and her editors are trying hard to insure that the quotes and questions match and are in context, but we hope that the improved byline will also remind readers of exactly what goes into producing a page of questions and answers. It's a complicated process that necessarily involves a lot of cutting and splicing – there's really no way around it, but we do want people to bear that in mind when they read the column. We want them to be savvier, I guess, while we struggle to be more transparent.

Fact-Checking Without Fact-Checkers

So when journalists are editing publications, probably without fact checkers, but with the best of intentions, I expect, on the part of everyone involved, from writer to editor to copy editor to art and photo editor, they can do some of the most significant and substantial work of fact checkers without fact-checking per se. To go back over the lessons I learned from those horrors at The New Yorker and the New York Times magazines, I would say everyone should be on the look out for the following warning signs:

Warning Signs for Possible Mistakes

Disparaging comments or quotations that make someone look bad
Stories which seem too good to be true
Single source reporting
Anonymous quotations
Lawsuits described by only one party

Disparaging comments about someone in a piece, or quotations that make them look bad – especially professionally, but also personally. People hate to be criticized and if you do so you need to be very sure that the author can back up what she is saying with good sources. It's also a good idea to make sure that the person who is portrayed in an unflattering light knows about it before you go to press and has an opportunity to dispute it – and that his or her arguments against the author's version are taken seriously before going to press.
Second, If a story seems too good to be true – the anecdotes too outrageous, the quotes too word-perfect, you should worry. Your writer may be getting carried away. Anonymous quotations are another tip-off, and are always risky. An editor needs to know the real identity of the person speaking and understand why that person doesn't want his or her name used. You should ask to see the writer's notes, and maybe do a little follow-up reporting yourself.

Third, be very wary of single source reporting. The author should not be the only person who can verify a story, and if he seems to be you should ask him to do further reporting to get corroboration. In the same vein, if you are reporting anything on a lawsuit, the rule of thumb is to contact both sides of any suit, and to make sure you see the most final legal documents related to the suit. Very often, writers will talk to one set of attorneys but not the other – you need too speak to both or you will hear about it post-publication.

We can extrapolate from this that when an author is talking about a non-legal matter, we as her editor want to be sure that she's spoken to opposing views on the issue. If you are publishing a piece about possible causes of autism, for example, you will want to check that the author is quoting not just those people who fear that thimerisol in vaccines is a cause, but also the researchers who argue that they can prove that it isn't. This seems like a very obvious rule, but it is a very essential one if you want to end up with a well rounded and indisputable story.

Interestingly, this problem of one-sidedness comes up quite often in our back page Lives column. This first person essay is sometimes confessional, and often written by a fairly green writer. It's not a reported piece, so we don't expect to see differing opinions or perspectives reflected there. But it is our policy to try to reach any family members, for example, who are characters in the stories, to check names and other facts with them. It's another way of exploding that bomb the paper hits the stands. And sometimes we learn troubling things. In one Lives column I remember a young women described how her father's eating disorder had affected her childhood. He was not named, but the young women had his unusual last name, and she mentioned the state where he lived. Now when we asked her for his phone number, she refused. She told us that she had never discussed her father's eating disorder with him, and she was afraid that he would be embarrassed and upset by her piece. She wanted us to go to press without calling him. I'm still amazed by this. The author comfortable exposing her father's bulimia to his neighbors and colleagues in a national magazine, but she was not willing to talk about it to him directly, or to have us call him as a courtesy. We decided that the piece was not ready to be published and we held it until some later date when we could do the fact-checking to our standard.

Zielsetzung

Zielsetzungen für das „netzwerk recherche“

1. Das „netzwerk recherche“ verfolgt das Ziel, die journalistische Recherche in der Medien-Praxis zu stärken, auf ihre Bedeutung aufmerksam zu machen und die intensive Recherche vor allem in der journalistischen Ausbildung zu fördern.

2. Zu diesem Zweck entwickelt das „netzwerk recherche“ Ausbildungskonzepte für die Recherche-Ausbildung, vermittelt Referenten und berät Institutionen der journalistischen Aus- und Weiterbildung in der Gestaltung und Umsetzung entsprechender Ausbildungskonzepte. Das „netzwerk recherche“ veranstaltet zudem eigene Recherche-Seminare sowie Modellseminare zu verschiedenen Themen.

3. Das „netzwerk recherche“ bietet ein Recherche-Mentoring für jüngere Kolleginnen und Kollegen an, um in einem intensiven Beratungs- und Austauschprozeß über jeweils ein Jahr einen entsprechenden Wissens-Transfer von erfahrenen Rechercheuren zu interessierten Kolleginnen und Kollegen zu organisieren.

4. Das „netzwerk recherche“ fördert den umfassenden Informationsaustausch zum Thema „Recherche“ und bietet seinen Mitgliedern entsprechende Foren an. Im Internet wird durch entsprechende newsletter die Kommunikation untereinander gefördert. Der Austausch über Projekte, konkrete Recherche-Erfahrungen etc., aber auch der Hinweis auf Weiterbildung und entsprechende Serviceangebote soll hier möglich sein.

5. Das „netzwerk recherche“ beteiligt sich am internationalen Austausch entsprechender Journalisten – Organisationen in Europa und in Übersee.

6. Das „netzwerk recherche“ vergibt einmal im Jahr einen Preis für eine aussergewöhnliche Recherche-Leistung, die Themen und Konflikte beleuchtet, die in der Öffentlichkeit bislang nicht oder nicht ausreichend wahrgenommen wurde. Der Leuchtturm – Preis für besondere publizistische Leistungen.

7. Die Mitglieder des Netzwerkes setzen sich dafür ein, dass die Möglichkeiten der Recherche nicht eingeschränkt werden.
Das „netzwerk recherche“ äußert sich öffentlich zu Fragen der Recherche und der Bezüge zur journalistischen Qualität, wenn Begrenzungen oder Einschränkungen der Pressefreiheit festgestellt werden.

8. Das „netzwerk recherche“ arbeitet mit anderen Journalisten Organisationen und Gewerkschaften zusammen, die im Grundsatz ähnliche Ziele verfolgen und ebenfalls dazu beitragen, den Aspekt der Recherche im Journalismus stärken um so die Qualität der Medien insgesamt zu verbessern.

9. Das „netzwerk recherche“ trifft sich einmal im Jahr zu einem Jahres-kongress und erörtert jeweils aktuelle Tendenzen im Umfeld des „Recherche-Journalismus“ und setzt sich hier mit zentralen Themen im Zusammenhang mit der journalistischen Recherche und konkreten Fallbeispielen auseinander.
Jedes Jahr wird ein „Infoblocker“ aus Politik oder Wirtschaft mit der „Verschlossenen Auster“ ausgezeichnet.
Regionale Untergliederungen ermöglichen den Austausch in bestimmten Regionen.

10. Das „netzwerk recherche“ ist politisch unabhängig und verfolgt ausschließlich gemeinnützige Zwecke. Der Zusammenschluß der Journalisten hat den Status der Gemeinnützigkeit erhalten. Die laufende Arbeit und die Projekte des „netzwerkes“ werden durch Spenden und Mitgliedsbeiträge (mindestens 60 Euro im Jahr) finanziert.

www.netzwerkrecherche.de
info@netzwerkrecherche.de

nr netzwerk recherche

Craig Silverman

The Rise of External Fact-Checking

Craig Silverman ist ein kanadischer Journalist und Buchautor. Er ist Kolumnist des Columbia Journalism Review und schreibt etwa für die New York Times, Globe And Mail, The Gazette (Montreal), Toronto Star und Harvard's Nieman Reports. Mit seinem Buch „Regret the Error: How Media Mistakes Pollute the Press and Imperil Free Speech", aus dem der folgende Text entnommen ist, gewann er den „Arthur Rowse Award" für Medienkritik. Auf der Webseite www.RegretThe Error.com berichtet Silverman regelmäßig über Fehler in der englischsprachigen Presse.

As the sun sets on the proofreader and seemingly begins to descend on the magazine fact-checker, there is a new class of checkers rising - a motivated, opinionated, public cadre of checkers who exist outside the press. You would be hard-pressed to believe, after you'd visited a newsroom, that there's an unprecedented amount of fact-checking going on - though it doesn't follow that there's a high level of accuracy. Today facts are gathered to be wielded like weapons, like artillery shells in the battle of ideas and ideologies. Some of the "new checkers", as I'll call them, try to discover true facts; others use fake facts to push their cause.

This culture of checking that has emerged primarily online in recent years focuses largely on holding the press to account and pointing out its errors. Fact-checking - once exclusively the province of magazines such as the New Yorker—is now an industry of NGOs, a hobby for engaged citizens, and standard operating procedure for bloggers. At times, though, it's also a blood sport. Facts are used to expose the perceived bias and inaccuracy of journalists and media outlets, to reveal the incompetence of organizations, to cut people down. In some hands, fact-checking in pursuit of the truth has become weaponized; spotting a factual error is proof of your enemy's folly, ammunition for partisan hackery, and fodder for blogs (I plead guilty), columns, and books (again). We have a culture that is pulsating with warring facts: facts from different sources; facts from endless polls, surveys, NGOs, experts, studies, political parties.

Prior to the American invasion of Iraq, Ambassador Joe Wilson went on a fact-finding mission to Niger to see about some yellow cake uranium for the CIA, the agency that publishes the famous World Fact Book. He would later feel that the Oval Office had twisted the facts he found, so he took to the op-ed page of the New York Times to set the record straight. The facts in his op-ed piece then came under intense scrutiny, and on and on it went.

The current obsession with facts has not necessarily elevated the level of truth or accuracy, though evidence of the power and skill of the new checkers to do so occurs on a regular basis. They have had many remarkable successes. At the core of this new upsurge of checking is the fact that, through Internet searches, information databases, and their own individual expertise, members of the public as well as organizations can gather information from a wide variety of sources and easily question what they read and see in the press. They can then share what they've learned with others via comment postings on blogs and news Web sites, or through their own Web sites, blogs, and social networks. As a result, news stories never die. They fork and fragment. They spark new narratives. The conversation continues outside the realm of the press, and is frequently about the press itself.

There is also a growing list of media-monitoring organizations whose sole purpose is to check up on the press. For example, Media Matters for America checks the facts for the Left, while Accuracy in Media checks them for the Right. FactCheck.org checks the facts of major political players, while the Committee for Accuracy in Middle East Reporting in America (CAMERA) and Honest Reporting check the facts on reporting about Israel. The Media Research Center, a conservative organization, funds a Web site called Newsbusters.org, a name that speaks for itself.

Nonpartisan Web sites such as NewsTrust.net have also emerged to enable readers to rate the accuracy and authority of a given news article. Another, called StinkyJournalism.org, enables readers to send comments and requests for correction to news outlets, and to rate the perceived "stinkiness" of a particular story.

"We start with the facts instead of starting with the assumption that the story is inherently biased," said Jeremy Miller, the editor of the site. "We are interested in factual errors and how they contribute to the thesis of an article being skewed."

In conjunction with these organizations, readers themselves have become more active, more demanding of the press. Feedback is no longer ghettoized in the letters page of newspapers. It explodes onto the Internet on blogs, message boards, and Web sites belonging to news organizations. Journalists can't just publish and then move on without another thought to yesterday's news. They must engage and, frequently, defend themselves and their work. This culture of checking can at times be personal and vindictive, but it can also be revelatory, impassioned, and highly effective. Most of all, it simply cannot be ignored by the press.

"For a writer, this huge, suddenly vocal audience has some significant advantages," wrote Gary Kamiya in an essay for Salon.com. "For one thing, it serves as an enormous fact-checker. If you make a mistake in a piece, some eagle-eyed reader will let you know, often within minutes. But a far more important effect of the reader revolution is that it has forced writers to immediately deal with substantive arguments and critique."

When I accessed Kamiya's article in early June 2007, six months after it was first published, Salon's own metrics showed that it had generated more than three hundred letters from readers, and 120 posts on different blogs. "A writer privileged enough to publish has to be thick-skinned to accept fair criticism, no matter how harsh," wrote Kamiya. He went on:

> Bloggers's denunciation of the "imperial media" can be overblown and paranoid, but it's legitimate to expect journalists to accept criticism. Once you write something and send it out into the world, you don't own it anymore: You

> offered it to the reader, and the reader has the right to respond as he or she wants. Before the Internet, it was easy for a journalist to behave like a sniper, rising furtively out of a foxhole, firing off a shot, then ducking back down to safety. Now, people are shooting back, and it's a bit much for the sniper to complain.

At their worst, this new breed of checker can be blinded by ideology and fail to stick to the facts; at their best, however, they are forcing the press to engage with the public more than ever before, to meet a higher standard of accuracy, and to put an end to what one U.S. newspaper editor called the "fortress newsroom." It has also given rise to "citizen journalism," the product of an informal body of readers who have become reporters, fact-checkers, and contributors in all forms of media.

"Fortress newsroom was the walled enclave where journalists practiced their craft in a 'just the facts' environment, using selective notions of objectivity and artificial forms of balance to shield themselves from many consequences of their work," wrote Steven A. Smith, the editor of the Spokane Spokesman-Review, in a commentary published on PressThink, the influential blog operated by New York University journalism professor Jay Rosen. "In fortress newsroom, readers are something of a necessary inconvenience. We need their business, but not their ideas. In fortress newsroom, objectivity means independence defined by separation from." Smith's paper bulldozed its fortress by inviting members of the public to attend its daily news meeting. It gave blogs to active citizens to have them write about their areas of interest and expertise, and it began Web casting its news meetings and inviting readers to watch and join the conversation in chat rooms. His paper, the Spokesman-Review, has opened up to the public and asked them to be involved. There are today many outside forces banging at the fortress gate, demanding to be let in. Often, their weapon of choice is facts, or claims of error. In this, the age of the fact-checking reader and well-funded media monitor, press outlets that do not dedicate themselves to a high level of accuracy can expect to be called to account.

Distributed Fact-Checking

In a now famous an infamous 60 Minutes II report aired on September 8, 2004, Dan Rather detailed what he and his team of producers believed to be important evidence regarding the National Guard record of U.S. president George W. Bush. The report aired just two months before the presidential election, and Rather said the piece was based on "new documents and new information on the President's military service."

It relied primarily on six documents relating to Bush's service that were provided by Lieutenant Colonel Bill Burkett, a former Texas Air National Guard officer. They apparently showed that Bush was given preferential treatment while in the Guard, and that his commanding officer had recommended he be suspended, among other seemingly damaging information. The documents were said to have been written by the late Lieutenant Colonel Jerry B. Killian, who had been Bush's commander when he was in the Texas Air National Guard during the 1970's.

The story also relied on comments by Ben Barnes, a man actively raising money for Bush's opponent, who said he had helped land Bush a cushy placement in the National Guard to keep him from going to Vietnam. In the story, a spokesperson for Bush was given airtime to deny the charges as being totally false. It was a big story, big enough to potentially impact the results of the upcoming election. As soon as it aired, other media outlets picked up on its claims. But so too did many right-leaning blogs and Web sites including FreeRepublic.com, Power Line.com, and LittleGreenFootballs.com. Commenters and writers questioned the authenticity of the documents, the research done by CBS News, and the overall claims of the story. They were at first driven by their political views, but soon they began to delve into the story's facts and background.

The day after the report, Power Line published a post, "The Sixtyfirst Minute," that initially passed on some of the questions raised in comments posted on Free Republic. But as the day progressed, the Power Line post was updated with more information from readers, other bloggers, and experts who stepped forward to add elements to the story. People from all over were engaging in a form of distributed fact-checking. Each dug in different areas—evaluating the authenticity of the documents, revealing background on the sources—until a clearer, more troubling picture began to emerge.

One Power Line reader identified himself as a "clerk/typist for the US Navy at the Naval Underwater Systems Center (NUSC) in Newport RI for my summer job in 1971" and proceeded to list several points backing up why the memos had to have been forged. "From 1973 until late 1982 I was a repairman for the Office Products Division of IBM," wrote in another reader, offering his expertise. Questions about the type and lettering style on the CBS documents abounded. As the blogosphere cranked up the heat on CBS and its story, the mainstream press worked to stay on top of it, but it seemed as though the blogs were one step ahead of them, driving the narrative and turning up new evidence. By the end of the day, on September 9, less than twenty-four hours after the story had aired, CBS felt compelled to issue a series of statements to defend its reporting.

The first read,

As is standard practice at CBS News, each of the documents broadcast on 60 Minutes was thoroughly investigated by independent experts and we are convinced of their authenticity. In addition to analysis of the documents themselves, CBS verified the authenticity of the documents by talking to individuals who had seen the documents at the time they were written. These individuals were close associates of Colonel Jerry Killian and confirm that the documents reflect his opinions at the time the documents were written.

It was later changed to:

As is standard practice at CBS News, the documents in the 60 Minutes report were thoroughly examined and their authenticity vouched for by independent experts. As importantly, 60 Minutes also interviewed close associates of Colonel Jerry Killian. They confirm that the documents reflect his opinions and actions at the time.

The major shift was that the story was being driven by blogs and average citizens, and not by the mainstream media. Commenters and writers from Free Republic, Power Line, and other blogs raised questions about whether a typewriter made in the 1970s could have produced the documents used by CBS. Two days after the story aired, news organizations had taken up the charge and found world-renowned typewriter experts to comment on the documents. This added a layer of professional authenticity to the fact-checking, but it was in large part just a follow-up to the story being dug up by the blogs. The new checkers were leading the field.

For more than a week, CBS News stood behind its reporting. In the meantime, the media began to pick up the trail of the bloggers and readers who had seemingly broken the story wide open. As journalists worked to unpack the series of events that led to the questioning of the documents, they keyed in on one person who went by the name "Buckhead" and had posted a comment on Free Republic at 11:59 p.m. on the evening of the 60 Minutes II broadcast. He appeared to be patient zero of the fact-checking epidemic. His post was lengthy and seemed to imply a high level of technical expertise. "I am saying these documents are forgeries, run through a copier for 15 generations to make them look old," he concluded. "This should be pursued aggressively." From there, it was.

Power Line put the comment up on its Web site the next morning, and soon former naval officers, typewriter mechanics, and others began weighing in. They were like a group of reporters pursuing a hot story - except that they weren't, at least not professionally trained ones. Later that day, September 9, Little Green Footballs compared the CBS documents to one prepared on a basic word processor and marveled at the seeming similarities. For Matt Drudge, that was enough.

Just before 3 p.m. on that day he updated his hugely trafficked Web site to read, '60 minutes' documents on Bush might be fake.

> 32-year-old documents produced Wednesday by CBSNEWS 60 MINS on Bush's Guard service may have been forged using a current word processing program typed using a proportional font, not common at that time, and they used a superscript font feature found in today's Microsoft Word program, Internet reports claim . . . Developing . . .

That led CBS to issue its statements supporting its story. It also brought an even larger audience to the blogs."The server hosting Power Line crashed as hundreds of thousands of Drudge readers tried to learn about the 60 Minutes scandal," reported the Weekly Standard. "By 5:00 P.M., CBS was spooked enough to release a statement saying the memos were 'thoroughly investigated by independent experts, and we are convinced of their authenticity.'"

Not all of the action was happening on the right leaning blogs. Liberal sites such as Daily Kos were also looking at the documents. A writer named "Hunter" did a point-by-point takedown of the claims on the other blogs. In a follow-up post to his first entry, Hunter wrote, "My point (...) was simply to prove that the argument being proposed and propagated - that MS Word and original version of the documents were 'mostly identical' - was a red herring, and that the denizens of LittleGreenFootballs are intellectual half-wits in a very large pond of right-wing half-wits."

There's no denying that the fact-checking taking place on various blogs was largely ideologically driven. And yet the warring posters attempted to do battle with facts. They dug and researched like any journalist would, and they turned up reams of evidence. Some worked to confirm the documents; others worked to debunk them. Aside from the occasional sniping at each other, they chose to pursue their respective agendas by fact-checking CBS and each other.

Charles Johnson of Little Green Footballs later said the success was all due to "open-source intelligence gathering." He told the Washington Post, "We've got a huge pool of highly motivated people who go out there and use the tools to find stuff. We've got an army of citizen journalists out there." Howard Kurtz, the Post's respected media writer, noted, "Many sites are seething with partisan passion, often directed at the media." And yet he couldn't help but acknowledge that "they are also two-way portals for retired military officers, computer techies, former IBM Selectric salespeople and just about anyone else to challenge and factcheck media claims."

By September 20, the pressure finally got to CBS's main source, Bill Burkett. That day, CBS reported, he admitted "that he deliberately misled the CBS News producer working on the report, giving her a false account of the documents' origins to protect a promise of confidentiality to the actual source." CBS president Andrew Heyward released a statement. "Based on what we now know, CBS News cannot prove that the documents are authentic, which is the only acceptable journalistic standard to justify using them in the report. We should not have used them. That was a mistake, which we deeply regret."

That evening, Dan Rather gave an on-air apology:

> I no longer have the confidence in these documents that would allow us to continue vouching for them journalistically. I find we have been misled on the key question of how our source for the documents came into possession of these papers. That, combined with some of the questions that have been raised in public and in the press, leads me to a point where—if I knew then what I know now—I would not have gone ahead with the story as it was aired, and I certainly would not have used the documents in question. But we did use the documents. We made a mistake in judgment, and for that I am sorry.

RatherGate, as many have come to call this episode, is today seen as a watershed for the power of blogs and the potential for average citizens to take part in reporting and acting as external fact-checkers on the press.

It should be noted that the documents themselves remain in dispute, which supports the idea that they shouldn't have been presented as totally reliable evidence. Mary Mapes, the top producer on the story, who was fired by CBS, later wrote a book that laid out her case for why they are genuine. Today, most believe that the documents are not trust-worthy. The bottom line is that, in the end, there are too many questions and uncertainties about the documents' authenticity to make them the basis for any reporting.

In the years that have passed since RatherGate, more and more blogs have engaged in "distributed fact-checking" by encouraging readers to hunt for information and facts to support or debunk a story or theory.

Talking Points Memo, a left-leaning blog operated by Joshua Micah Marshall, is credited with breaking the story about the questionable firings of U.S. prosecutors by the Bush administration in 2007. When the mainstream media failed to pursue the issue, he and his readers and contributors kept digging and eventually blew it wide open. Resignations and Senate hearings followed their work.

In 2006, Charles Johnson of Little Green Footballs raised doubts about photos taken by Reuters contributing photographer Adnan Hajj. He said they had been manipulated, and it turned out he was right. Hajj was then fired by Reuters.

In October 2006, I was introduced to one dedicated independent fact-checker via e-mail. The subject line of the message seemed spamlike enough: "Perhaps the most important inquiry you could get." I came close to deleting it before having a quick read. "I'm just getting familiar with your site," it read. "Bravo for highlighting the errors, egregious and/or just silly, that big papers make and admit. But at my first glance, you don't seem to deal in a yet-moreimportant issue: the uncorrected errors constantly and permanently disinforming the public." The writer, Mark Powell, then outlined his months of work fact-checking one U.S. newspaper. His conclusion was

> This is the biggest un-/underreported scandal in U.S. journalism
> While the chattering class ever harps on so-and-so's political bias, real and imagined, sheer topical and journalistic incompetence is destroying print's last hope in the electronic age, viz. acknowledged credibility/authority superiority.

Powell lives in Virginia and his paper of choice is the Washington Post. As far as he is concerned, the paper's corrections "represent a very tiny fraction of the paper's 'correctable' errors. Fact is nearly none of the thousand-odd errors I've cataloged—probably less than 2 percent— were ever corrected." While most people might scoff at someone claiming to have cataloged roughly a thousand uncorrected errors in a single newspaper, I had to admit that if I could spend countless hours reading tens of thousands of corrections over the past couple of years, chances were good that my uncorrected-errors doppelgänger existed somewhere in the world.

Powell is a writer who has been published in many different U.S. newspapers. He had taken it upon himself to track the number of errors he could spot in each day's edition of the Post. He was in the process of looking for a publication that would publish his reams of daily and monthly reports about what he perceived to be the Post's litany of errors. (Powell had applied for a job as a copy editor at the Post and had been rebuffed.) He was as focused and dedicated an external fact-checker as I've come across, and no doubt a thorn in the Post's side since he regularly e-mailed editors with his findings. I told him he struck me as the kind of person who would have been well suited to the job of proofreader. Too bad it no longer exists.

Holding the Press to Account

The examples of blogs and individual citizens engaged in fact-checking the press are now legion. It has become routine, expected. Even before RatherGate, many in the press and the online world saw it coming.

"Keep an eye on bloggers," suggested a U.S. News & World Report article in 2002. "The main arena for media criticism is not going to be books, columns, or panel discussions, and it certainly won't be journalism schools. It will be the Internet." "Web diarists are calling the print media's bluff," concluded the writer.

In a post about the U.S. News & World Report story on his personal blog, Nick Denton, a former journalist turned successful blog publisher, noted, "I have a friend who is doing a piece on weblogs for New York Magazine. She's terrified. Good." Some in the profession see this new level of press scrutiny as troublesome. They view bloggers and the other new checkers as nothing more than amateur partisan critics hammering away at stories they don't like. But examples such as RatherGate and the Reuters photomanipulation scandal demonstrate the public's newfound ability to participate in the reporting process and hold the press to account. It has also raised the stakes for press mistakes.

Errors are being turned up more frequently than ever before. Specific reporters are facing increased, and sometimes unfair, scrutiny. New pressure is being exerted on the press, and though bias is usually the charge that follows an error, the error frequently relates to accuracy. Get something wrong or report something questionable and, as Ken Layne put it in a widely quoted blog post from 2002, "This is the Internet, and we can fact check your ass." This makes accuracy within newsrooms all the more important and urgent. If journalists don't find and eliminate errors, there are plenty of outside citizens and organizations itching for the chance to do so.

News organizations such as the Spokesman-Review that embrace the power and wisdom of the crowd can leverage this new environment of checking and reader engagement to forge a stronger connection with their community. It can open doors to new stories and add expertise to reportorial work that can improve overall accuracy. Press outlets that continue to fortify their crumbling fortress walls will continue to be checked and prodded. Their errors will be held up as examples of their arrogance and incompetence.

The best solution for the press today is to raise its level of accuracy and embrace the legions of checkers and citizen reporters clamoring to take part in the news process. Improve the quality of reporting, and there will be less of a need for bloggers to act as fact-checkers. Better yet, invite them into the news process and harness their expertise to do better reporting. The new checkers represent a threat, but they are, more than anything else, an opportunity. They are passionate about the news; all they ask is that they be able to participate in a meaningful way and not be shut out or ignored.

Ralph Berthel

Journalistisch arbeiten und kriminalistisch denken?

Ralph Berthel ist Diplomjurist und Leitender Kriminaldirektor. Er lehrte Kriminalistik an der Polizei-Führungsakademie in Münster und führt seit 2005 als Rektor die Hochschule der Sächsischen Polizei (FH) in Rothenburg/OL. Berthel ist Gründungsmitglied der Gesellschaft für Kriminalistik und publiziert zu den Themen Kriminalstrategie und kriminalistisches Denken sowie Wirtschafts- und Jugendkriminalität. Er ist Mitautor des Buches „Grundlagen der Kriminalistik/Kriminologie".

Recherchetrainer behaupten oft, der gute Rechercheur müsse „kriminalistisch denken“ – um Fehler zu vermeiden oder Sachverhalte aufzudecken. Gerade für ein erfolgreiches Fact-Checking erscheint es mitunter unerlässlich. Aber was bedeutet das eigentlich? Für Kriminalisten ist dieser Ausdruck mehr als eine Phrase, die an Detektive mit hochgeschlagenem Kragen und Lupe gemahnt. Kriminalistisches Denken lässt sich wie folgt definieren: Kriminalistisches Denken ist ein auf Problembewältigung gerichteter Prozess der geistigen Verarbeitung kriminalistisch relevanter Sachverhalte unter Anwendung logischer, psychologischer und anderer natur- und geisteswissenschaftlicher Gesetzmäßigkeiten sowie der Sprache unter Berücksichtigung kriminalistischer Möglichkeiten. Diese Definition lässt erahnen, dass sich hinter den Begriffen ein ganzes Gedankengebäude verbirgt, das vor allem in der Polizeiausbildung, aber auch in der journalistischen Arbeit, nützlich sein kann.

Kriminalistisches Denken als Problemlösung

Kriminalistisches Denken ist zunächst ein Prozess der Problembewältigung. Es ist das Wissen um Methoden und Gesetzmäßigkeiten zur Lösung kriminalistischer Probleme. Es hat nichts mit Intuition und nur bedingt etwas mit Erfahrungen zu tun. Ziel des kriminalistischen Denkens ist sowohl die Wahrheitsfindung im konkreten Einzelfall (Mikroebene) als auch die Problemlösung hinsichtlich der Bekämpfung von Kriminalität als gesellschaftliche Erscheinung (Makroebene) (vgl. Berthel 2007: 736).

In der kriminalistischen Praxis dient es zum Beispiel dazu, den Aufenthaltsort eines flüchtigen Täters oder einer entführten Person zu ermitteln, die Gefahr einer Erpressung einzuschätzen oder die Beziehung zwischen Täter und Opfer zu verstehen. Aber auch für die Probleme und Fragen der journalistischen Praxis ist es hilfreich. Denn auch dort geht es ja vor allem um eines: Versteckte oder unzugängliche Informationen zu finden.

Grundsätzlich unterscheidet der Ermittler „Daten“ und „Informationen“. Daten sind einfache, isolierte Fakten (etwa Messwerte), die einer Interpretation bedürfen. Erst eine Bewertung verwandelt die Daten in Informationen, die bei der Lösung einer bestimmten Aufgabe hilfreich sein können. Dafür ist „Wissen“ nötig – also die Fähigkeit, Daten zu interpretieren und somit Informationen zu erzeugen (vgl. Becker/Kugeler/Rosemann 2000: 308).

Eine Fülle an Daten und Informationen, Problemen und Fragen wirkt auf die Ermittler ein. Wie könnte, wie sollte man mit einer derartigen Daten- und Informationsfülle umgehen? Ist sie überhaupt beherrschbar? Können oder müssen wir bestimmte Informationen einfach vernachlässigen? Und falls ja, welche?

Wenn ich die in den Tagungsunterlagen enthaltene E-Mail des dpa-Chefredakteurs an die Mitarbeiter von dpa richtig interpretiere, ist das Thema „Beherrschen des Informationsaufkommens“ auch für Rechercheure von großer Brisanz. Es liegt mir fern, an dieser Stelle ein Patentrezept vorzustellen. Aber alltägliche Erfahrungen und Erkenntnisse aus spezifischen Konfliktsituationen, brachten mich zu der Überzeugung, dass es eine wesentliche Voraussetzung zur Bewältigung dieser Flut an Aufgaben gibt. Und zwar unabhängig davon, ob bei der Aufklärung eines Verbrechens oder bei der Berichterstattung über eine Aufsehen erregende Entdeckung oder eine nicht vorhergesehene politische Entwicklung. Ich bin überzeugt, dass der Weg zum Ziel nur über eine einzige Mühe verlaufen kann. Diese Mühe heißt: Beschreibe das Problem!
Albert Einstein formulierte es wie folgt: „Die Formulierung eines Problems ist häufig wesentlicher als die Lösung, die nur eine Frage mathematischer oder experimenteller Fertigkeiten sein kann. Das Problem zu erkennen ist wichtiger als die Lösung zu erkennen, denn die genaue Darstellung des Problems führt zur Lösung.“

Denken in Modellen

Um ein Problem zu erkennen und zu lösen, wenden Kriminalisten logische, psychologische und andere natur- und geisteswissenschaftliche Gesetzmäßigkeiten an. Dabei ist ein wesentliches Element das Denken in Modellen. Zunächst entwickelt der Ermittler auf der Grundlage von Daten und Informationen Hypothesen oder so genannte Versionen, zum Beispiel vom Ablauf eines Tötungsverbrechens. Dabei geht es nicht um Spekulationen oder das bloße Übertragen von anderweitig gewonnenen Erkenntnissen auf einen neuen Fall, sondern um die plausible Verknüpfung der jeweiligen Daten und Informationen.
Gelegentlich überprüfen Ermittler ihre Hypothesen durch so genannte Ermittlungsexperimente. So überprüfen sie etwa, ob sich eine Person tatsächlich zu einem bestimmten Zeitpunkt an einem angegebenen Ort befunden haben kann, wie schnell sich ein Brand ausgebreitet haben kann oder wie bestimmte Spuren entstanden sein können. Nicht selten haben solche Experimente bereits ergeben, dass sich ein vermeintliches Opfer Verletzungen selbst zugefügt haben muss – und damit ein ganz neues Bild des Geschehens erbracht.
Wie weit derartige Untersuchungen und Experimente reichen können, will ich an einem anderen Beispiel zeigen: Im Rahmen eines kriminalistischen Problems kann sich etwa die Frage stellen, wann genau eine Tat begangen wurde. Das ist oft bei Tötungsdelikten der Fall, bei denen die Leichname im Zustand der Verwesung (Zerfallsprozess von Organismen bei Anwesenheit von Sauerstoff)

oder Fäulnis (Fehlen von Sauerstoff) aufgefunden werden. Dann stellen entweder Rechtsmediziner, die Ermittler oder Kriminaltechniker Experimente an oder beziehen sich auf solche, die bereits zu einem früheren Zeitpunkt stattgefunden haben. In den USA existiert am Forensic Anthropology Center der Texas State University sogar eine spezielle „Bodyfarm", auf der postmortale Veränderungen an Leichen untersucht und die Ergebnisse dokumentiert werden. Eine ganze Wissenschaftsdisziplin, die kriminalistische oder forensische Entomologie, also die Lehre von der Leichenbesiedelung durch Insekten, befasst sich mit dieser Thematik und liefert wertvolle Hinweise zur Liegezeit eines Leichnams – und damit zur Bestimmung des Tötungszeitpunktes.

Meine Botschaft soll nicht lauten: Beschaffen Sie sich Gutachter, die Experimente durchführen, um die bestehenden Zweifel auszuräumen. Aber der Rechercheur sollte sich wie der Kriminalist stets fragen, ob es zu dem Problemfeld wissenschaftliche Untersuchungen oder gar experimentelle Erfahrungen gibt. Das hilft in jedem Falle zu entdecken, wie plausibel ein Sachverhalt ist, den man wiedergeben möchte.

„Denken in Modellen" bedeutet für den Kriminalisten also, eine nachvollziehbare Vorstellung von Geschehensabläufen aus einer Vielzahl von Hypothesen zu erlangen. Einmal entwickelte Hypothesen muss der Ermittler bis zum Beweis ihrer Wahrheit (Verifikation) ständig auf Richtigkeit überprüfen. Das gilt ebenso für den journalistischen Rechercheur. Beide sollten sich bei neuen Erkenntnissen immer wieder die Frage stellen, ob eine einmal aufgestellte Hypothese noch Bestand hat – sie sollten zweifeln!

Zweifeln als Grundhaltung

Der Zweifel wird als die Grundhaltung des kriminalistischen Denkens bezeichnet (vgl. Reichertz 1998: 51). Denkt man den Ansatz des Zweifelns konsequent weiter, führt er zwangsläufig zu den Fragen: Wann gilt etwas als gesichert, wann gilt etwas als wahr? Und in die Sprache der Ermittler übersetzt: Wann gilt etwas als bewiesen? Das kriminalistische Denken ist auf das Erlangen „wahrer", das bedeutet beweisbarer Erkenntnisse gerichtet. Und Informationen oder Daten gelten eben so lange als „unwahr", wie sie nicht zweifelsfrei bestätigt sind.

Auch hier kann Einstein als „Zeuge" zitiert werden: „Eine neue Frage aufzuwerfen, neue Möglichkeiten oder alte Fragen aus einem neuen Blickwinkel zu betrachten, erfordert kreative Vorstellungskraft und kennzeichnet wirklichen Fortschritt in der Wissenschaft." Denn beim Zweifeln geht es nicht um ein pauschales Infragestellen jeglicher Daten oder Informationen. Vielmehr bedeutet im kriminalistischen – also vielleicht auch im journalistischen – Sinne zweifeln:

Eine permanente Bewertung auf Stichhaltigkeit, Nachvollziehbarkeit, ein Prozess des ständigen Falsifizierens und Verifizierens, des kritischen und strukturierten Hinterfragens erlangter Erkenntnisse.
Eine der großen Hürden beim ergebnisorientierten Zweifeln ist der so genannte gesunde Menschenverstand. Diesen bezeichnete René Descartes als „die am besten verteilte Sache in der ganzen Welt, denn ein jeder fühlt sich damit angemessen ausgestattet. So pflegen sich auch jene, die sonst in allen Dingen sehr schwierig zufrieden zu stellen sind, von diesem nicht mehr zu wünschen, als sie bereits haben." Und Einstein bezeichnet ihn als die „Anhäufung von Vorurteilen, die man bis zum 18. Lebensjahr angehäuft hat".
Vielfach werden mit dem Begriff schlichtweg plausible Erklärungen verbunden, die (auch) dem Nichtfachmann einleuchten. Das darf aber dem Kriminalisten - und sollte auch dem Journalisten - als Begründung keinesfalls ausreichen. Der kriminalistische Zweifel, das kriminalistische Denken insgesamt, und der gesunde Menschenverstand stehen einander also mitunter im Weg. Denn suggeriert uns doch dieser im wesentlichen von Gesetzmäßigkeiten freie und meist nur schwer objektivierbare „gesunde" Verstand, dass etwas allein schon unumstößlich, also wahr sei, weil es oft und von vielen Menschen behauptet und ebenso oft wiedergegeben wurde. Besonders deutlich führt diesen Aspekt die englische Entsprechung des gesunden Menschenverstandes vor Augen: der „common sense".
Anhänger der „Common Sense Theorie", etwa Thomas Reid (1710-1796), betrachten die gemeinschaftliche Überzeugung gar als Grundlage der Erkenntnis. Doch Kriminalisten dürfen sich bei der Wahrheitsfindung nicht auf gemeinschaftliche Überzeugungen ohne die Möglichkeit der Objektivierung verlassen. Ermittler fragen daher bei der Aufklärung von Straftaten nicht danach, ob jemand üblicherweise an einem bestimmten Wochentag eine Kneipe aufsucht oder ob es nach Ansicht vieler üblich sei, dass diese Person dort war, und leiten daraus ab, ob der Betreffende dies auch am Tattag getan hat. Sie fragen vielmehr, welche Beweise es gibt, dass jemand tatsächlich an einem bestimmten Tag die Kneipe aufgesucht hat. Häufig liefert in einem solchen Fall bereits die Definition des Tatzeitpunktes den Schlüssel zur Tataufklärung. Gerade die exakte Beschreibung von Zeitabläufen oder Zeitpunkten ist für die Ermittlungsarbeit von großer Bedeutung – und ein geeigneter Weg, um Fakten beweisbar zu machen.

An einem Beispiel soll verdeutlichet werden, wie etwa der Tatzeitpunkt oder der Zeitpunkt einer Beobachtung möglichst zweifelsfrei festgestellt werden kann: Oft schwören Zeugen Stein und Bein, eine Beobachtung genau so und nicht anders und genau zu einer bestimmten Uhrzeit gemacht zu haben. Ein unprofessionell handelnder Ermittler wird in dem Wissen, dass Zeugen irren können, fragen, ob sich der Zeuge bei seiner Aussage wirklich sicher sei. Was erwarten wir dann vom Zeugen? Doch nicht ernsthaft, dass er seine eben gemachte Aussage revidiert, sich also als unglaubwürdig hinstellt! Der gute Ermittler wird stattdessen versuchen, die Aussage des Zeugen mit objektivierbaren Fakten entweder zu belegen, also zu verifizieren, oder zu widerlegen, also zu falsifizieren. Belegbare, weil nachprüfbare Fakten sind zum Beispiel Aussagen des Zeugen, die anhand der Wetteraufzeichnungen des Deutschen Wetterdienstes nachvollzogen werden können. Dazu gehört etwa der Zeitpunkt des Sonnenaufganges oder eines Regenschauers. Andere Zeitpunkte, die nachgeprüft und somit objektiviert werden können, sind der Beginn einer Fernsehsendung, das Ende eines Fußballspiels oder der Sirenenton beim Auslösen eines Feueralarms.

Der wissenschaftliche Blick

„Nichts geschieht ohne Grund“, heißt es. Das ist keine Binsenweisheit, sondern eines der klassischen logischen Denkgesetze: dem „lex rationis determinantis sive sufficientis“, dem „Gesetz vom zureichenden Grund“. Nach Gottfried Wilhelm Leibniz sagt dieses Gesetz, „dass keine Tatsache als wahr oder existierend und keine Aussage als wahr betrachtet werden kann, ohne dass ein zureichender Grund vorhanden wäre, warum es so ist und nicht anders.“

Für den Kriminalisten wie auch für den Journalisten bedeutet dies nicht weniger, als dass er eine Feststellung nur von einer als wahr bewiesenen Aussage ableiten kann. Oder anders gesagt: Die Tatsache, dass eine Behauptung nur oft genug wiederholt wird oder mit einem Autoritätsbeweis versehen wird („Der Professor hat gesagt ...!“), macht sie zunächst einmal nicht zur Wahrheit. Dazu bedarf es objektivierbarer Hinweise. Kriminalistisches Denken kann daher weder mit irgendeinem Aberglauben noch pseudowissenschaftlichen Erklärungsansätzen in Verbindung gebracht werden. Aussagen wie „es grenzt an ein Wunder, dass ...“ dürften sich also in keinem Ermittlungsbericht finden. In journalistischen Texten wird der Begriff des Wunders dagegen leider häufig strapaziert, etwa bei Berichten über Erdbeben.

Kriminalisten sind der Wahrheit verpflichtet und Kriminalistik ist wesentlich geprägt durch die Beweislehre. Diese besagt, dass jede „entscheidungserhebliche Tatsache", die der Angeklagte (im Prozess) nicht glaubhaft eingesteht und jeder „Erfahrungssatz" (Indiz), der nicht allgemeingültig ist, eines Beweises bedarf. Für die Arbeit des gewissenhaften Journalisten, der sich um die Richtigkeit der Fakten bemüht, könnte dies bedeuten: Jeder Umstand einer Berichterstattung, der von der betreffenden Person oder Institution nicht nachvollziehbar bestätigt wird oder nicht durch eine anerkannte Gesetzmäßigkeit belegt wird, bedarf der Überprüfung – bedarf eines Beweises.

Nach den Grundsätzen der Kriminalistik gelten als Beweise: der Augenschein, der Zeuge, der Sachverständige, Urkunden und die Aussage des Beschuldigten. All dies kann auch für den Journalisten bei der Recherche als Beweis gelten. Am kompliziertesten aber dürfte dabei die Beweisführung mittels eines Sachverständigen zu übernehmen sein. Während vor Gericht sehr hohe Maßstäbe an eine Sachverständigen angelegt werden, habe ich manchmal den Eindruck, dass sich in den Medien heute jeder als Experte bezeichnen darf und es Journalisten wie Publikum sehr schwer fällt, den Spezialisten vom Scharlatan zu unterscheiden. Auch bei Urkunden ist natürlich – spätestens seit den Erfahrungen mit den gefälschten Hitlertagebüchern – Vorsicht und Sorgfalt geboten.

Fazit: Kriminalistisches Denken in der journalistischen Faktenkontrolle

Diese Hinweise sollen lediglich Anregungen geben und keinesfalls als Checkliste dienen. Obwohl solche in vielerlei Bereichen Konjunktur zu haben scheinen, stehen Kriminalisten mit ihnen auf Kriegsfuß. Denn Checklisten vermitteln eine trügerische Sicherheit. Sie sind Algorithmen und folgen als solche dem Muster eines Kochrezepts: Nimm dies und tue jenes – und alles wird gut!

Kriminalistik dagegen geht an die Suche nach Wahrheit kreativ heran - oder anders gesagt: heuristisch. Damit ist die beständige Suche nach Wahrheiten, mithin ein stetiges Hinterfragen von vermeintlich sicheren Aussagen und Erkenntnissen gemeint. Heuristische Prozesse sind anstrengend, da sie vermeintlich gesicherte Erkenntnisse bis zum endgültigen Beweis der Wahrheit in Frage stellen. Am Ende dieses heuristischen Erkenntnisprozesses steht die Überzeugung von der Wahrheit. In einem kriminalistischen Standardwerk heißt es dazu: „Überzeugt sein, heißt aber nichts anderes, als etwas für wahr halten, ohne zu zweifeln oder nach überwundenem Zweifel" (Walder/Hansjakob 2006: 195).

Kriminalisten legen die Ergebnisse ihrer Ermittlungen im Regelfall einem Staatsanwalt oder Richter vor. Journalisten legen ihre Rechercheergebnisse letztlich den Betroffenen, insbesondere jedoch der Öffentlichkeit vor. Art und Form der Ergebnisse der Recherchen oder Ermittlungen, Zielgruppen und natürlich auch Intentionen mögen sich unterscheiden. Aber auf dem Weg zum Ermittlungs- oder eben Rechercheergebnis müssen sich beide Berufsgruppen immer wieder die Frage nach der Validität, ja letztlich der Wahrheit ihrer Arbeitsergebnisse stellen. Kriminalistisches Denken liefert sowohl für den Ermittler als auch den Journalisten ein handhabbares Instrument, um überzeugt – also zweifelsfrei – zu überzeugenden Ergebnissen zu gelangen.

Literatur

BECKER, Jörg; Martin Kugeler; Michael Rosemann (2000): Prozessmanagement. Ein Leitfaden zur prozessorientierten Organisationsgestaltung. Heidelberg: Springer Verlag.

BERTHEL, Ralph (2007): Kriminalistisches Denken neu denken. In: Kriminalistik, S. 732.

REICHERTZ, Jo (1998): Expertensysteme in der Kriminalistik. In: Kriminalistik, S. 51.

WALDER, Hans; Thomas Hansjakob (2006): Kriminalistisches Denken. Heidelberg: Kriminalistik Verlag.

„Unser Wissen ist nicht vorhanden, wenn es nicht benutzt wird.“

Igor Strawinski (1882-1917), russisch-US-amerikanischer Komponist

Theo Dersjant bei der nr-Fachkonferenz beim SPIEGEL in Hamburg

Leif Kramp / Theo Dersjant

Fact-Checking in der Journalistenausbildung

Leif Kramp ist Medien- und Kommunikationswissenschaftler und Historiker. Er arbeitet als Journalist, Dozent und Medientrainer sowie wissenschaftlicher Mitarbeiter an der Macromedia Hochschule für Medien und Kommunikation in Hamburg. Im Herbsttrimester 2009 leitete er das Fact-Checking-Seminar an der Hamburg Media School.
Theo Dersjant ist Dozent und Mitglied der Studiengangsverwaltung der School of Journalism im niederländischen Tilburg. Seit September 2008 ist er dort mitverantwortlich für eine Seminarreihe, in der sich Studierende als Fact-Checker üben. Dersjant ist seit etwa 20 Jahren Medienjournalist.

Eine junge Frau namens Sophie hastet durch den New Yorker Central Park, ihre blonde Mähne im Wind, das Handy am Ohr. Sie beschäftigt nur eine Frage: Ist das berühmte Foto jenes Paares, das sich bei der spontanen Feier zum Kriegsende im Jahr 1945 auf dem Times Square küsst, gestellt oder Ausdruck leidenschaftlicher, wahrer Liebe? Sophie ist Fact-Checkerin bei einem Magazin. Und ihr Chef drängt, denn die Antwort soll schon in der nächsten Ausgabe erscheinen. Schließlich findet Sophie einen Augenzeugen, der beobachtet hat, wie sich ein ausgelassener Matrose in einem Wirbel von Konfetti eine flanierende Krankenschwester griff und sie küsste, als gäbe es kein Morgen. Nein, sagt der Zeuge, es habe keine Anzeichen für eine künstliche Inszenierung gegeben. Es habe wie ein authentischer Gefühlsausbruch gewirkt, gar wie Liebe auf den ersten Blick.
Diese Episode im Film „Briefe an Julia“ zeichnet ein eigentümliches Bild von jenen Journalisten, deren alleinige Aufgabe es ist, die Beiträge ihrer Kollegen zu verifizieren – oder zu falsifizieren. Denn augenscheinlich steckt die schöne Sophie in einem Dilemma: Zwar ist sie ungeheuer gut darin, Texte anderer Autoren zu überprüfen; doch eigentlich träumt sie davon, selbst mit Informanten sprechen und darüber Artikel veröffentlichen zu dürfen. Ihr innigster Wunsch: „Stop checking and start writing“.
Der populäre Filmbetrieb hat ein ums andere Mal ein Bild des Berufs der Fact-Checker gezeichnet, das höchst ambivalent erscheint: Mal gelten Fact-Checker als Hemmklötze, mal als Zeitdiebe oder Spielverderber. Entweder sind die Recherchespezialisten unbeliebt, engstirnig und kompromisslos wie in „Almost Famous“, Cameron Crowes Hommage an den Musikjournalismus der 1970er Jahre, oder sie fristen ein Schattendasein und sind leicht an der Nase herumzuführen wie in „Shattered Glass“, der Verfilmung des Reporterskandals um den Fälscher Stephen Glass. Oder ihre Arbeit wird veralbert wie in der Farce „Fact Checkers Unit“, die bereits weit über 600.000 Mal bei YouTube angeklickt wurde.
Die wechsel- und klischeehaften Filmportraits haben deutliche Spuren bei der nachrückenden Journalistengeneration hinterlassen: Das Profil professioneller Faktenprüfer im Journalismus könnte unschärfer nicht sein, zumal in deutschen Redaktionsgefilden, wo sich die lange US-amerikanische Tradition der gewissenhaften wie peniblen Fehlerjäger („The New Yorker“, „The New York Times“) bisher kaum durchsetzen konnte. Es nimmt sich kaum Wunder, dass Nachwuchsjournalisten ein stark verzerrtes Verständnis davon haben, was sich hinter der Aufgabe von Fact-Checkern verbirgt – und wie essentiell ihre Arbeit insbesondere dann ist, wenn in angespannter Wirtschaftslage an allen Ecken und Enden gespart wird und die Qualität journalistischer Berichterstattung leidet.
An der Fontys Hogeschool Journalistiek im niederländischen Tilburg wurde daher im September 2008 ein Seminarkonzept erprobt, das zum Ziel hatte, das

Bewusstsein für die Notwendigkeit des Fact-Checkings bei Journalistik-Studenten zu schärfen – auch um ihre hehren ethisch-moralischen Vorstellungen vom Journalistenberuf mit den tatsächlichen Arbeitsverhältnissen abzugleichen.
Der Ansatz: Indem angehende Journalisten die tagtägliche Berichterstattung in Presse, Radio, Fernsehen und Online-Medien kritisch verfolgen und die Inhalte solcher Beiträge nachrecherchieren, die ihnen verdächtig oder nicht plausibel erscheinen, gewinnen sie eine differenziertere Vorstellung davon, welchen Störfaktoren die alltägliche Redaktionsarbeit unterliegt und welchen Fehlerquellen selbst erfahrene Journalisten aufsitzen können. Darüber hinaus übernehmen sie Verantwortung für ihre eigenen Rechercheergebnisse, weil sie angehalten sind, über ihre Erkenntnisse in einem Web-blog (fhjfactcheck.wordpress.com) zu berichten und die betreffenden Journalisten mit ihren Fehlern zu konfrontieren.
Mittlerweile ist das Fact-Checking-Seminar fester Bestandteil des Curriculums: Jedes Jahr durchlaufen circa 100 Studierende an der Tilburger Hochschule das Recherchetraining. Schon heute kann eine wichtige Lehre aus den ersten Erfahrungen gezogen werden: So hoch die Studierenden die journalistischen Ideale von Sorgfaltspflicht und Aufrichtigkeit halten, so fest ist anfangs auch ihr Vertrauen in die Berichterstattung ihrer zukünftigen Arbeitgeber. Und dieses ist nur schwer zu erschüttern. Das mag ein wenig naiv sein, doch umso eindrucksvoller ist der Aha-Effekt, wenn die eigenständigen Recherchen ergeben, dass nicht alles wahrheitsgetreu ist, was ehrbare Medienmarken verbreiten.
Fact-Checking in der Journalistenausbildung setzt daher in erster Linie voraus, dass Überzeugungsarbeit in einem sensiblen Terrain geleistet wird: Misstrauisch zu sein gegenüber der eigenen Profession, ja gegenüber den eigenen Vorbildern. Ähnlich verhielt es sich bei der Master-Klasse 2011 der Hamburg Media School, wo das Seminarkonzept in leicht abgewandelter Form erstmals im Herbst 2009 aufgegriffen wurde und auch im Jahr 2010 wieder angeboten wird: Hier mussten 21 Studierende ebenfalls erst vom Wert des akribischen Faktenprüfens überzeugt werden, um mit kritischem Blick die aktuelle Tagespresse, Online-Medien und Fernsehnachrichtensendungen zu verfolgen.

Der lange Weg zum Aha-Effekt

Es ist freilich keine triviale Angelegenheit, Studierende, die sich nichts inniger wünschen als in der schreibenden oder sendenden Zunft endlich durchzustarten, für die Fallstricke des Journalistendaseins zu sensibilisieren. Möglicherweise ist dies auch ein Grund dafür, dass Fact-Checking als effektive Vorbereitung von Nachwuchsjournalisten für die Tücken des Berufsalltags noch lange nicht ausreichend in der Journalistenausbildung verankert wurde, sei es an Hochschulen, Journalistenschulen oder selbst im innerbetrieblichen Volontariatswesen. Die ersten Erfahrungen in Tilburg und Hamburg haben gezeigt, dass der Fact-Checking-Ansatz ein geeignetes Mittel ist, um angehenden Redakteuren und Reportern die Illusion zu rauben, der Journalismus sei eine unfehlbare Glaubwürdigkeitsmaschinerie – und außerdem einen Dialog zwischen Redaktionen und nachrückenden Journalistengenerationen anzuregen, der idealerweise zu mehr Selbst-Bewusstsein und Selbst-Reflexion auf beiden Seiten führen kann und sollte.

Gefragt nach ihren Erwartungen, äußerten die meisten Seminarteilnehmer die Vermutung, dass sich Fehler in überwiegendem Maße oder fast ausschließlich in der Boulevardberichterstattung finden ließen. Konfrontiert mit der These, dass die Fehleranfälligkeit medien- und ressortübergreifend erschreckend hoch sei, regten sich in nicht wenigen Studierenden Zweifel, ob sie der Aufgabe gewachsen seien, inkorrekte Inhalte in Qualitätsmedien falsifizieren zu können. Für viele gestaltet sich die Seminarteilnahme wie ein Sprung ins kalte Wasser: Die Studierenden haben die Aufgabe, jeden Tag nicht selbst journalistische Beiträge zu produzieren, sondern bereits veröffentlichte Nachrichtenbeiträge aller Darstellungsformen und Mediengattungen nachzurecherchieren. Während das Intensivseminar in Tilburg für die Studierenden in ihrem letzten Jahr des Bachelor-Studiums verpflichtend zu belegen ist, findet es für die Hamburger zu Beginn ihres Aufbaustudiums mit Master-Abschluss statt.

Überprüft wird das Klein-Klein des Nachrichtenoutputs ebenso wie das große Ganze: Ist das Thema eines Berichts tatsächlich faktengetreu? Sind die Quellen seriös? Was bleibt von einem Beitrag übrig, wenn sämtliche Fakten noch einmal gecheckt werden? Hält er dem Check stand oder löst sich sein Nachrichtenwert in Luft auf? Oder aber handelt es sich um eine Fälschung?

In Tilburg wurden in eineinhalb Jahren mehr als 180 größere News-Stories einer systematischen Prüfung unterzogen. Die meisten davon erwiesen sich als fehlerhaft. Für die Studierenden war dies ein herber Dämpfer, schließlich hatte sich ihr unerschütterlicher Glauben in die Wahrhaftigkeit journalistischer Arbeit aufgelöst. Gewichen ist er aber der wichtigen Erkenntnis, dass Fehler in Nachrichtenmedien an der Tagesordnung sind. Dazugelernt hat bereits derjenige, der nicht mehr alles, was in der Zeitung steht, für bare Münze nimmt.

Nicht wenige der ersten Seminarteilnehmer hofften auf eine große Enthüllung, wie sie 1998 dem jungen Journalisten Adam Penenberg vom Online-Ableger des „Forbes Magazine" gelang. Penenbergs Erfolg wurde im Jahr 2003 unter dem Titel „Shattered Glass" verfilmt und damit zu einem illustren Lehrstück über die Schwierigkeiten und blinden Flecken des Fact-Checkings – in und außerhalb von Redaktionen. Der Film, der sich im Übrigen als Einstieg in die Materie eignet, unterstreicht zwar die Bedeutung von redaktionellen Kontrollinstanzen, zeigt den Fehlerdetektiven aber auch klare Grenzen auf: Wenn ein Journalist seine Redaktion und das Publikum bewusst hintergehen will und entsprechende Verschleierungstaktiken anwendet, dann können auch Fact-Checker im Regelfall nichts dagegen ausrichten.

Bisher konnten weder in Tilburg noch in Hamburg große Fälschungsskandale aufgedeckt werden. Das ist auch nicht das Ziel. Zwar zeigt die Affäre rund um den Kulturjournalisten Ingo Mocek und das Magazin „Neon", dass sich der Borderline-Journalismus à la Tom Kummer (ehemals „SZ Magazin") offenbar immer wieder zweifelhafte Geltung verschaffen kann. Doch hat sich in überwältigender Vielfalt gezeigt, dass der Fehlerteufel im Alltag und Detail sein Unwesen treibt. Es beginnt bei Kleinigkeiten, zum Beispiel häufig in Berichten verwendeten Floskeln wie „immer mehr", die einen kontinuierlichen Anstieg suggerieren, dies aber in den seltensten Fällen tatsächlich zutrifft, und reicht bis zur ungeprüften Übernahme von PR-Informationen. Dazwischen tummeln sich Nachlässigkeit und bewusste Irreführung, etwa durch Sensationalisierung. Übertreibungen, Superlative, Verkürzungen, Verwechslungen, Suggestionen, Ungenauigkeiten wie die Falschschreibung von Namen, Missverständnisse bei der Faktenwiedergabe oder aus dem Zusammenhang gerissene Inhalte, aber auch lausige Belegführung sind nur einige wichtige Fehlerkategorien, die von Studierenden entdeckt wurden. Verwunderung, aber auch Enttäuschung griff mitunter um sich, weil die Analysen ein ernüchterndes Bild vom Zustand des praktizierten Journalismus zeichnen und im Widerspruch zu den Vorgaben international anerkannter Richtlinien für die journalistische Arbeit stehen, wie sie auch im deutschen Pressekodex festgehalten sind: Die wahrhaftige Unterrichtung der Öffentlichkeit, die Prüfung von Informationen auf ihren Tatsachengehalt, die Richtigstellung sich als falsch erwiesener Beiträge, keine Beeinflussung journalistischer Beiträge durch Geschäftsinteressen jeglicher Art und die Unzulässigkeit unbegründeter Behauptungen, Beschuldigungen und sensationalisierter Darstellungen.

In Hamburg umfasste das Themenspektrum lokale Ereignisse wie die Entgleisung einer S-Bahn, Einzelhandelsprognosen, überregionale Nachrichten wie Brandanschläge in Berlin oder Wettmanipulationen im Fußball bis hin zu internationalen Belangen wie Berichten über Ausschreitungen in Athen oder über naturwissenschaftliche, historische, politische und Lifestyle-Themen. Ungefähr jeder zweite Beitrag war in Teilen fehlerhaft. Speziell bei der Überprüfung von Fakten in einem plausibel erscheinenden Beitrag sind die Studierenden mit der Herausforderung konfrontiert, einzelne Tatsachenbehauptungen in ihrer Relevanz für den Nachrichtenwert zu gewichten und mit zusätzlichen Quellen abzugleichen. Mancher Seminarteilnehmer musste mit Mühe lernen, dass jeder Quelle,

auch den nachträglich befragten Interviewpartnern eines bereits erschienenen Beitrags, mit Vorsicht und Skepsis zu begegnen ist; Meinungen können sich bekanntlich ändern. Umso schwieriger lassen sich Missverständnisse herausarbeiten. Wesentlich ist hierbei die Dokumentation des Faktenchecks in Form eines Rechercheprotokolls, das den Prüfprozess nachvollziehbar macht.
Einige skurrile Meldungen konnten die Studenten in Tilburg schnell als Blödsinn entlarven: Schädigen Schnarcher die Wirtschaft? Nein. Werden mehr Katzen und Hunde durch die Wirtschaftskrise von ihren Herrchen und Frauchen verstoßen? Quatsch. Manche Fälle waren jedoch diffiziler: Einige holländische Zeitungen berichteten beispielsweise, dass Eltern bei der Erziehung ihrer Kinder verzweifeln würden. Die Journalisten beriefen sich dabei auf die große niederländische Nachrichtenagentur ANP. Die Meldung basierte auf einer Umfrage, die vom nationalen Familienministerium durchgeführt worden war. Die zentrale Frage lautete: Waren Sie jemals unsicher, wie Sie Ihre Kinder aufziehen sollen? Die Mehrheit der Befragten bejahte. Von Verzweiflung aber war keine Rede. Auch gab es keinerlei Hinweise darauf, dass es sich um einen Trend handele. Das (PR-)Ziel wurde dennoch erreicht: Die fragwürdige Medienresonanz sorgte für ein positives Klima zu einer Gesetzgebungsinitiative des Ministeriums.

Die Frage nach dem Warum

Was aber steckt hinter dem laxen Umgang mit Informationen, der allzu oft der wichtigen Aufklärungs- und Vermittlerfunktion von Journalisten entgegensteht? Woher kommen all die Flüchtigkeitsfehler und Verständnisprobleme? Und was können angehende Journalisten davon lernen? Die Studierenden in Tilburg und Hamburg erkannten bei ihren Recherchen zahlreiche besorgniserregende Determinanten journalistischer Arbeit: Zeitdruck, fehlende Ressourcen, personelle Überlastung, Wettbewerbszwänge, Exklusivitätsdruck und die trügerische Leichtigkeit der Internet-Recherche wurden als hauptsächliche Störfaktoren identifiziert. Die Gründe für eine gewisse Verlotterung der journalistischen Arbeit wurden ausgiebig in einer Fact-Checking-Kooperation zwischen den Hochschulen in Tilburg und Leiden erforscht. Dabei wurden verschiedene Problemfelder herausgearbeitet, die zum Teil auch bei den Hamburger Untersuchungen zum Tragen kamen: Journalisten, deren untersuchte Beiträge Fehler aufwiesen, arbeiteten bisweilen mit unzuverlässigen Quellen. Häufig stellte sich heraus, dass Journalisten sich nicht für Originaldokumente wie zum Beispiel Studien interessieren, weil ihnen die Zeit fehlt, sich in die Materie einzuarbeiten. Deshalb greifen sie auf Pressemitteilungen zurück und hinterfragen nicht die Hintergründe (Intentionen/Methodik) des Quellenmaterials.

Journalisten sind keine Blitzmerker, wenn es um fachbezogenes Methodenwissen geht. Selbst Rechercheprofis müssen gemeinhin passen, wenn sie damit konfrontiert werden, Statistiken auszuwerten oder Kalkulationen anzufertigen, um akkurat berichten zu können. So werden die methodischen Ansätze einer Untersuchung oftmals geflissentlich überlesen und Umfrageergebnisse nicht hinterfragt – und damit Fehlinformationen Tür und Tor geöffnet. Auch der redaktionelle Prozess kann eine Fehlerquelle sein. Häufig stellten die studentischen Fact-Checker eine starke Diskrepanz zwischen der Überschrift eines Artikels und dessen Inhalt fest. Gleiches ist bei Bildunterschriften festzustellen, die wie die Headline von Redakteuren eingefügt werden, die üblicherweise keine Detailkenntnis über den Beitrag haben und im Produktionsstress Fehler machen.
Die Studenten entdeckten darüber hinaus: Plausibilität hat nicht selten Vorrang vor Akkuratesse. Journalisten erfinden sogar manchmal Erklärungen, um eine Story veröffentlichen zu können. Das kann an Unwissenheit, Gutgläubigkeit oder einer allzu freudigen Kombinationsgabe liegen: Manche Journalisten lieben es offenbar so sehr, Phänomene oder Trends zu entdecken, dass sie zwei vollkommen getrennte Sachverhalte aufeinander beziehen, um etwas zu beweisen.
Es mag nachvollziehbar erscheinen, dass sich das Verständnis von Journalistik-Studierenden für solche Fehltritte in Grenzen hält - schließlich wollen sie es besser machen. Doch das Fact-Checking-Konzept hilft ihnen, potenzielle wie reale Missstände im Journalismus zu reflektieren und Lösungsstrategien (auch in der Gruppe) zu erarbeiten.
Nach Ansicht der Studierenden selbst hat Fact-Checking in der Journalistenausbildung das primäre Ziel, zur Stärkung der journalistischen Identität als unabhängige Rechercheure beizutragen (siehe Kasten). Diese Selbstvergewisserung in Zeiten unsicher gewordener Journalistenidentitäten und eines unter Druck geratenen Berufsbildes wird flankiert von einem effektiven, praxisbezogenen Training von Recherchefähigkeiten (Online, Datenbanken, Telefon etc.), das gezielt die Fehleranfälligkeit des journalistischen Arbeitsalltags in den Blick nimmt.

Zitate von Studierenden der Hamburg Media School zum Seminar „Fact-Checking":

„Bevor ich an diesem Seminar teilnahm, habe ich mir nicht allzu viele Gedanken um die Wichtigkeit des Fact-Checkings gemacht. Mir war bewusst, dass viele Artikel in der Tagespresse unter erhöhtem Arbeitsdruck entstehen und die Recherchequalität der Journalisten deshalb bisweilen leidet. Wie gravierend allerdings die einzelnen Fehler sein können, hätte ich mir zuvor nicht vorstellen können."

„Selbst die am wahrhaftigsten erscheinenden Artikel, bei denen Quellen möglicherweise direkt verlinkt sind, können sich bei genauerem Hinsehen als falsch entpuppen. Ich hätte mich im Nachhinein gern öfter getraut, den verantwortlichen Redakteur mit meinen falsifizierten Fakten zu konfrontieren, doch hatte ich bei meinem ersten und einzigen Anlauf den Eindruck, dass die Tätigkeit des Fact-Checkings nicht nur als nicht notwendig, sondern vor allem auch als nicht erwünscht angesehen wird."
„Ein manifestes Resultat ist nicht zuletzt das neu gewonnene Instrumentarium an Zugangswegen für die Überprüfung von Fakten. In erster Linie ist es die Sensibilisierung des Journalisten für Fehler und potenzielle Fehlerquellen, die nur in solch intensiver Projektarbeit ermöglicht werden kann."

Die Unbelehrbarkeit der Erfahrenen

Die Resümees der Hamburger Seminarteilnehmer waren angesichts der Erfahrungen aus Tilburg zu erwarten gewesen: Die Reaktionen der mit ihren Fehlern konfrontierten Journalisten fielen zumeist unbefriedigend aus. Nur selten wurde die Kontaktaufnahme der Studierenden mit den Redaktionen als Kooperationsangebot wahrgenommen, sondern vielmehr als Vorwurf oder unberechtigte Kritik seitens unwissender Journalistenschüler, die nur glauben, es besser machen zu können als die alten Hasen des Nachrichtengeschäfts. Dies äußerte sich zum einen durch Ignoranz und Abwehr, zum anderen durch abfällige Bemerkungen über die „Kollegenschelte". Holländische Redakteure entgegneten sogar erbost, sie bräuchten keine Studenten, um sich erklären zu lassen, wie sie ihre Arbeit zu erledigen hätten. Andere ließen sich verleugnen.
Dabei geht es beim Fact-Checking nicht darum, Journalisten zu reizen oder in ihrer Berufsehre zu kränken, sondern ihnen bei ihrer Arbeit behilflich zu sein. Gleichwohl die Hamburger Studierenden angehalten waren, bei der persönlichen Kontaktaufnahme mit der Redaktion Konflikte zu vermeiden und den Kontext ihres Anliegens transparent zu schildern, nahmen sich nur wenige Journalisten die Zeit, die Fragen zu ihren Beiträgen am Telefon oder per E-Mail in der gebotenen Ausführlichkeit zu beantworten und ihre Fehler zu rechtfertigen. Eben dies gehört aber zum Lernprozess auf beiden Seiten: Die Jungen bekommen einen wichtigen Eindruck von den Nöten und Beweggründen erfahrener Berichterstatter, und die Veteranen erhalten die seltene Gelegenheit, ihr eigenes Handeln zu überdenken. Natürlich gehört Einiges dazu einzuräumen, man habe seinen Job nicht gut gemacht. Eine derartige Courage bewies aber die Nachrichtenagentur ANP, als sie ihre Richtlinie zum Umgang mit Meinungsumfragen änderte, nach-

dem sie die Tilburger Fact-Checker mit ihren Ergebnissen konfrontiert hatten. Die Abwehrhaltung vieler Redaktionen trug bei den Studierenden signifikant zur Unsicherheit über das eigene journalistische Rollenverständnis in der Funktion des externen Fact-Checkers bei – mit der Konsequenz, dass einige Vorbehalte entwickelten, fehlerhafte Beiträge öffentlich (wenn auch konstruktiv) zum Beispiel in Form eines Web-blog zu kritisieren. Die Furcht vor der Missgunst überführter Redakteure, die sich bei der späteren Jobsuche rächen könnten, ist keineswegs zu unterschätzen. Dieses Risiko lässt sich nur durch die Ausweitung und weitere Professionalisierung studentischer Fact-Checking-Projekte minimieren.

„Trainees Train the Trainer"

Aus Sicht altgedienter Nachrichtenprofis mag der Gedanke obskur erscheinen, dass sie etwas von jenen lernen können, denen es an eben jener Arbeitserfahrung fehlt, die sie im Überfluss vorzuweisen haben, zumal in klassischen Recherchedisziplinen. Doch das um den Dialog zwischen Journalistenschülern und Journalistenveteranen ergänzte „Train the Trainer"-Prinzip zielt weit darüber hinaus: Verlags- und Senderleitungen gegenüber lässt sich eindrücklich belegen, wie sinnvoll externes, retrospektives Fact-Checking in die redaktionellen Prozesse eingebunden werden kann.

So überprüften die Tilburger Seminarteilnehmer für eine Regionalzeitung sämtliche Artikel über einen Zeitraum von zwei Wochen. Im Anschluss präsentierten die Studierenden den Redakteuren die Ergebnisse und arbeiteten die schwerwiegendsten Fehlerquellen heraus. In Kooperationen mit sechs weiteren regionalen Tageszeitungen wurden überdies gezielt Fehler in der Schreibweise von Namen gesucht. Außerdem wurden im Auftrag eines Buchverlags alle Rezensionen zu einem Band aus dem Verlagsprogramm auf ihre Faktentreue hin analysiert.

In Deutschland stehen solcherlei Kooperationen noch aus. Dabei fehlen auch hierzulande in den meisten Redaktionen – ob nun bei tagesaktuellen, wöchentlich oder monatlich erscheinenden Medien – Konzepte für eine verlässliche journalistische Qualitätssicherung. Die Ansicht, die Tradition des Fact-Checkings sei bei großen Qualitätsmedien nicht so wichtig, weil die Redakteure auf ihrem jeweiligen Fachgebiet eine hohe inhaltliche Kompetenz auszeichne, trägt nicht sehr weit. Zumindest dann nicht, wenn es um die Mehrheit an Redaktionen geht, welche das Nachrichtenaufkommen – gerade auch im Lokalsektor – mit weniger luxuriösen Ressourcen und personeller Ausstattung zu bewältigen haben.

Wie können Redaktionen also auf den zunehmenden Zeit- und Kostendruck reagieren, um die Fehleranfälligkeit ihrer publizistischen Produkte zu minimieren? Die Einrichtung von Redaktionsabteilungen, die sich ausschließlich der

Überprüfung von zu veröffentlichenden Beiträgen widmen, ist nicht immer die effizienteste Alternative. Mitunter reichen auch schon kleine Eingriffe in die Redaktionsroutine, um Maßnahmen für eine zuverlässige Kontrolle zu initiieren. Journalisten sollten gegenüber anderen Medienmarken skeptischer sein und nicht alles für wahr befinden, was in einem anerkannten Blatt gestanden hat. Nur weil ein vermeintlicher Fakt im Guardian, bei der BBC, von der dpa oder AP veröffentlicht wurde, bedeutet das nicht automatisch, dass er tatsächlich korrekt ist und nicht überprüft zu werden braucht. Jeder Journalist sollte sich bei seinen Geschichten oder der Übernahme von Agenturmaterial selbst und eigenständig vergewissern, dass es sich um akkurate Inhalte handelt.

Wo Expertenwissen fehlt, sind Fehler beinahe vorprogrammiert. Jeder Newsroom braucht Allrounder, aber genauso Spezialisten, die sich auf thematischen und methodischen Feldern besonders gut auskennen. Keine Redaktion kommt zum Beispiel ohne mindestens einen Experten aus, der ressortübergreifend prüft, wie seriös extern angefertigte Umfragen, Studien oder Kalkulationen sind. Allzu oft wird Repräsentativität bloß vorgegaukelt, werden wichtige Hintergrundinformationen über die Entstehung von Statistiken verschwiegen. Wer sich mit Kriminalitätsraten beschäftigt und versucht, einen Trend zu beschreiben, der braucht nicht nur die aktuellen Daten und jene von vor zehn Jahren, sondern auch von sämtlichen Jahren dazwischen.

Journalisten sind keine Kinder von Schüchternheit. Da sollten sie auch bei der Anforderung von originalem Quellenmaterial keine Zurückhaltung üben. Recherche braucht Zeit, und doch ist sie in den seltensten Fällen so zeitaufwendig, wie üblicherweise behauptet wird. Wer sich auf Pressemitteilungen verlässt, hat im Geiste des Sorgfaltsdiktums schon verloren. Jedes Unternehmen, jeder Verband, jede Partei, jeder gemeinnützige Verein hat ein starkes Interesse, wenn er sich an einen Journalisten wendet. Wer sich auf die vorbereiteten PR-Häppchen verlässt, die appetitlich portioniert ihren Weg in die Redaktion finden, macht sich zum Erfüllungsgehilfen. Die Anfertigung von Rechercheprotokollen ist eine vergessene Tugend, die wieder mehr Beachtung verdient: Journalisten sollten sich ehrlich fragen, wie sorgfältig sie gearbeitet haben.

Schlussendlich ist es auch niemals verkehrt, einen unabhängigen Experten um Rat zu fragen. Nicht ohne Grund gibt es so hilfreiche Einrichtungen wie den Informationsdienst Wissenschaft, der mit einem sogenannten „Expertenmakler" als verblüffend zeiteffiziente Schnittstelle zwischen Berichterstattern und Fachleuten aus allen nur erdenklichen Wissenschaftsbereichen fungiert. Manchmal reicht eine kurze Frage zur Vergewisserung. Journalisten müssen sich ihrer partiellen Unwissenheit nicht schämen; schließlich ist es ihr Job, Fragen zu stellen.

Beziehen sich diese Ratschläge aus der Fact-Checking-Praxis eher auf die Bereitschaft des einzelnen Berichterstatters, sich selbst und seine Arbeit kritisch zu hinterfragen, so können auch Redaktionen als organisierte Einheiten mit einigen einfachen Schritten Sicherheitsvorkehrungen treffen, um die Fehlerquote niedrig zu halten. Etabliert hat sich hier das Vier-Augen-Prinzip, das sich in der Praxis indes noch nicht überzeugend bewähren konnte: Jeder Journalist, der die Arbeit seines Kollegen kritisch bewerten soll, steckt in einer Zwickmühle. Nicht von ungefähr arbeiten die Fact-Checker beim US-Magazin „The New Yorker" oder die Dokumentarjournalisten beim Hamburger Nachrichtenmagazin „Der Spiegel" getrennt von ihren schreibenden Kollegen.

Die innerbetriebliche Weiterbildung sollte hier ansetzen, um einheitliche Formen und Kriterien zu finden, wie Redaktionskollegen gegenseitig ihre Beiträge konstruktiv kritisieren können. Kommunikationstraining und erlernbare Regelstrukturen können sicherstellen, dass keine Missverständnisse entstehen. Eine weitere Maßnahme hat sich bereits im studentischen Umfeld in Tilburg als ungeheuer effektiv erwiesen, um alle Beteiligten für die gemeinsame Sache zu disziplinieren: Wem nachweislich ein Fehler unterläuft, der muss dem Betroffenen auf eigene Kosten einen Kuchen kaufen und persönlich überreichen. Übertragen auf das professionelle Redaktionsumfeld könnte dies beispielsweise bedeuten, dass Journalisten im Falle eines Fehlers 100 Euro in einen Topf einzahlen müssen, der am Ende des Jahres symbolisch einem wohltätigen Zweck zukommt. So repressiv dieses Vorgehen auch wirken mag, könnte es doch das Bewusstsein für die gute journalistische Sache schärfen.

Das Lehrkonzept in Tilburg und Hamburg

Das Fact-Checking-Projekt basiert auf dem Konzept eines Intensivseminars. In Tilburg dauert ein Kurs drei Wochen. Die Studierenden arbeiten in dieser Zeit jeden Tag (außer mittwochs) an ihren Fällen. Das Seminar umfasst damit insgesamt 12 Sitzungen, jeweils von 9:30 bis 17 Uhr. Vormittags und nachmittags findet jeweils eine Lagebesprechung zur Koordination und zum aktuellen Stand der Recherchen statt. Nach Abschluss eines Falls wird der verantwortliche Journalist kontaktiert und um eine Stellungnahme gebeten. Die Ergebnisse werden schließlich in einem Web-blog (fhjfactcheck.wordpress.com) veröffentlicht. In Hamburg umfasst der Kurs zehn Sitzungen in zwei Wochen.

Mathew Rose

Von der Behauptung zur Tatsache: Erfahrungen eines Rechercheurs

Mathew D. Rose konzentriert sich als investigativer Journalist seit Mitte der 1990er Jahre besonders auf White Collar Crime. Nach etlichen Jahren der Spezialisierung auf Korruption und Filz in Berlin, war er an der Untersuchung des Berliner Bankenskandals beteiligt. Danach wechselte er seinen Schwerpunkt auf bundespolitische und politikfreie organisierte Wirtschaftskriminalität. Rose studierte an der University of California in Berkeley moderne Geschichte.

Freie Journalisten wie ich kommen selten in den Genuss der Unterstützung oder Kontrolle durch eine Dokumentationsabteilung. Das kann auch von Vorteil sein. Denn die beste Methode, Fehler zu vermeiden ist aus meiner Sicht nicht, auf andere zu zählen, sondern selbst stringent und überlegt vorzugehen.

Phase 1: Die Recherche

Ein Journalist ist und soll am Anfang nicht objektiv sein. Man stellt eine Hypothese oder Meinung auf, die es zu überprüfen gilt. Der renommierte britische Journalist Andrew Jennings hat einmal sinngemäß gesagt: Man stellt sich bei seiner Hypothese das schlimmste Szenario vor und geht davon aus, dass es noch schlimmer sein wird. Um die Hypothese zu überprüfen, muss man streng empirisch vorgehen. Wir brauchen dafür Dokumente und Zeugen, die eine Handlung oder einen Zusammenhang beweisen oder widerlegen. Mit jeder neuen Information relativiert sich das alte Wissen, verflüchtigt sich eine Hypothese. Aber auch wenn eine Information die Hypothese zu wiederlegen scheint, schließe nicht vorschnell aus, dass gar nichts dran ist. Auch Intuition spielt eine wichtige Rolle. Traue deinen Gefühlen, so absurd sie dir zunächst auch vorkommen.
In einer Recherche zu einer städtischen Wohnungsbaugesellschaft hatte ich einmal den Verdacht, der Geschäftsführer habe seinem besten Freund eine Immobilie kostenlos überlassen. Im Grundbuch fand ich zwar einen Kaufvertrag, doch keine Auflassungsvormerkung oder Eintragung als Eigentümer zu Gunsten des Freundes. Sehr seltsam, denn kein seriöser Geschäftsmann bezahlt für ein Grundstück, ohne sich mit einer Eintragung im Grundbuch abzusichern. Und: Der Freund bezahlte keine Miete an die Wohnungsbaugesellschaft für die Immobilie. Die Hypothese lautete also: Der Mann nutzt die Immobilie kostenlos. Als ich den Geschäftsführer mit dieser Annahme konfrontierte, legte er einen Brief einer Bank vor, der besagte, der Kaufpreis sei an die Wohnungsbaugesellschaft gezahlt worden. Einige Monate später fand ich in der Bank einen Informanten, der die Zahlung kontrollierte. Sie stimmte. Doch ich wollte die Hypothese nicht aufgeben und recherchierte weiter. Es zeigte sich: Das Vertrauensverhältnis zwischen den beiden Freunden war so groß, dass sie auf einen Grundbucheintrag verzichtet hatten – ein Beweis dafür, dass es nicht um eine normale Geschäftsbeziehung ging.
Wichtig in dieser Phase war die Archivierung des Materials. Jeder sollte dafür sein eigenes System finden. Es gibt kein Patentrezept. Ob elektronisch oder auf Papier - es soll für den jeweiligen Bedarf einfach gut funktionieren. Denn was nützen die besten Recherchen, wenn man die Dokumente hinterher nicht finden kann?

Das Internet ist schön und gut für eine Recherche. Aber das wichtigste sind die Informanten. Treffe dich mit so vielen Personen wie möglich. Denn Menschen liefern nicht nur Fakten und Dokumente, sondern Hintergründe und Atmosphäre. Und über sie bekommt man Kontakt zu weiteren Informanten. Der Umgang mit Informanten hat viel mit der zwischenmenschlichen Chemie zu tun. Oft treten wir als absolut Fremde an diese Menschen heran. Es hilft, wenn Fremde kurz über uns recherchieren können: Dafür lohnt es sich, einen Eintrag bei Wikipedia anzulegen oder im Vorfeld auf ein paar Artikel im Internet hinzuweisen.
Aber auch abseits der Informanten gibt es Quellen, die nach meinem Eindruck viel zu selten ausgeschöpft werden: Das Handelsregister etwa ist eine meiner wichtigsten Quellen (im In- und Ausland). Wenn möglich geht persönlich hin. Im Handelsregister ist ein Reichtum an Informationen, die weit über das Internetangebot oder Creditreform hinausreichen. Kaum ein Journalist weiß, dass wir laut §10 Handelsregisterverordnung ein Recht auf Einsicht in Hauptbände der Archivbestände haben. Das wird man kaum erkennen, wenn man den Paragrafen liest. Doch schlägt man im Kommentar von Melchior und Schulte nach, findet man unter „Presserechtliche Informationsansprüche" diesen Hinweis. Eine Kopie kann beim Handelsregister vor Ort mitunter Wunder bewirken!
Ebenso wichtig und nützlich wie das Handelsregister sind die Grundbücher. Seit zehn Jahren haben Journalisten auch dort Einsichtsrecht. Und: Beim Bundesanzeiger kann man unter anderem die Jahresberichte von Unternehmen umsonst einsehen (https://www.ebundesanzeiger.de/ebanzwww/wexsservlet).
Wo möglich, sollte man alles von zwei verschiedenen Quellen bestätigen lassen. Ab und zu muss man einen Einfachbeweis hinnehmen. Doch meist lassen sich diese durch andere Belege zumindest flankieren. Bei möglichst vielen Unterlagen sollte man sich bei der eigenen Auslegung von einem Experten kontrollieren lassen und bei der Interpretation mit anderen beraten.
Nach der Recherche-Phase muss man zum größten Kritiker und Zweifler der eigenen Ergebnisse werden. Für mich war der Fall „Die Bestatter" eine Epiphanie (http://www.zeit.de/2007/22/Bestatter): Die Recherche, die sich zum großen Teil auf Dokumente aus dem Handelsregister bezog, war abgeschlossen. Ich hatte zu einer Gesellschaft drei Unterlagen auf dem Schreibtisch vor mir. Mit einem Mal merkte ich, dass die Unterschriften des Geschäftsführers alle unterschiedlich waren. Bald stellte ich fest, dass die meisten Unterlagen gefälscht waren. Die Recherche konnte neu anfangen – mit der Hauptaufgabe, meine bisherigen Dokumente als Fälschungen zu dokumentieren.

Phase 2: Die Kontrolle

Wenn ein Beitrag fertig ist, stelle ich einen Ordner für die Dokumentation zusammen. Jede Behauptung im Text bekommt eine Fußnote, dazu bis zu drei Dokumente. An diesem Punkt ist man hoffentlich mit der Arbeit nicht ganz allein. Vielleicht steht einem ein Dokumentar oder ein Justiziar zur Seite, zumindest ein Redakteur. Diese Personen sind (hoffentlich) auf der Seite des Autors und wollen nur das Beste. Leider ist das gelegentlich nicht so. Das Wichtigste für die Arbeit im Team ist: Bleibe offen für Kritik. Die größte Illoyalität der Kontrollierenden ist, den Autor nicht in Frage zu stellen. Es ist nicht unfreundlich, sondern notwendig.

Fragen, die die Kontrollierenden in jedem Falle stellen müssen: Sind alle Fakten vorhanden? Stimmen die Fakten? Sind die Dokumente und Aussagen logisch? Hätte ein Aspekt weiter verfolgt werden müssen? Fehlt ein Aspekt? Geht der Autor kritisch genug an sein eigenes Material heran? Gab es eine gründliche Konfrontation? Sind die Fakten präzise zusammengefasst? Die Dokumentation muss darauf beharren, alles Schwarz auf Weiß zu sehen oder wissen wer die Quelle für eine Behauptung ist! Aber das gilt auch für den Autor: Alle Recherche- oder Kontrollergebnisse der Dokumentation sollten dem Autor vorgelegt werden. Er betrachtet das Material vor einem anderen Hintergrund als die Dokumentation, die sich womöglich nicht allzu tief in das Thema einarbeiten konnte. Aber es kann sein, dass die Dokumentation neue, wichtige Informationen aufgetan hat. Ebenso ist es möglich, dass der Autor ein Dokument missverstanden, übersehen oder falsch interpretiert hat.

Meine letzte Erfahrung beim Spiegel war ein hervorragendes Beispiel dafür, wie es nicht geht. Die Spiegel-Redakteure wollten die Unterlagen nicht vollständig haben, sondern nur Auszugsweise. Das Material haben sie nicht beherrscht, da sie ständig mit anderen Artikeln beschäftigt waren. Als der Artikel vor der Veröffentlichung in die Spiegel-Dokumentationsabteilung wanderte, haben die Fact-Checker nicht unmittelbar mit dem tatsächlichen Autor die Kontrolle durchgeführt, sondern mit den Redakteuren. Es entstand eine Art „Stille Post“: Die Spiegel-Dokumentation fragte den Spiegel-Redakteur, der Spiegel-Redakteur fragte mich, der Spiegel-Redakteur bekam die Information von mir und gab sie an die Spiegel-Dokumentation weiter. Auf solchen Wegen entstehen zwangsläufig Fehler.

Workshop von Albrecht Ude auf der nr-Fachkonferenz.

Herbert Staub

„Korrigieren Sie das bitte vorher!“: Ein Bericht über die nr-Fachkonferenz

Herbert Staub ist Stellvertretender Leiter der Dokumentationen und Archive des Schweizer Fernsehens. Er studierte Kunstgeschichte, Geschichte und Filmwissenschaft und ist Vorstandsmitglied im Fachverband „Bibliothek Information Schweiz“ (BIS). Als Dozent engagiert er sich für die berufliche Grundausbildung im Bereich Information und Dokumentation.

Die Nachfrage war enorm: Rund 130 Vertreterinnen und Vertreter aus Journalismus und Dokumentation haben an der von netzwerk recherche in Kooperation mit „Der Spiegel" in Hamburg organisierten Konferenz zum Thema „Fact-Checking" teilgenommen. Es musste gar eine Warteliste für weitere Interessenten eingerichtet werden. Die mehr als 40 Referentinnen und Referenten aus Deutschland, den Niederlanden, der Schweiz und Nordamerika staunten nicht schlecht über das Interesse, das ihren Untersuchungen und Praxisberichten entgegengebracht wurde. Zur Sprache kamen dabei natürlich auch jene gravierenden Fälschungen, die normalerweise bei der Tätigkeit eines Fact-Checkers die Ausnahme sind, zum Beispiel die Hitler-Tagebücher im „Stern", die fingierten Interviews von Tom Kummer im Magazin der „Süddeutschen Zeitung" oder aktuell von Ingo Mocek in „Neon".

Theo Dersjant, Dozent an der School of Journalism im niederländischen Tilburg, stellte eine Untersuchung lokaler Printmedien vor, die angehende Journalisten während drei Wochen in Tilburg und in Hamburg durchgeführt hatten. Sie brachte – zum leichten Bedauern der Studierenden – keine Fälschungen ans Tageslicht. Dafür Fehler über Fehler! Durchschnittlich zehn bis zwanzig Fehler wiesen die Artikel auf; und dabei handelte es sich nicht um orthografische Schnitzer. Laut Dersjant waren sieben von zehn Artikel sogar „im Herzen falsch". Es wurden also nicht nur Namen falsch geschrieben oder Zahlen verdreht, sondern auch Meldungen in Umlauf gesetzt, die einer näheren Prüfung schlicht nicht standhielten. Zum Beispiel: Dass bei einer Stromunterbrechung mit Blackout in ein paar niederländischen Dörfern neun Monate später markant mehr Kinder geboren wurden. Das ist eine nette Geschichte, die in geografischen Varianten immer mal wieder in den Medien auftaucht. Die Studierenden in Tilburg überprüften die Fakten. Die Geschichte entpuppte sich als falsch. Das Fazit des dreiwöchigen Kurses war für die angehenden Journalisten denn auch ziemlich ernüchternd: Selten stimmt, was in der Presse steht.

Die Untersuchung von Scott Maier, Professor an der University of Oregon, bestätigt dieses Resultat. Er ließ in den USA 7600 Artikel aus 22 Tageszeitungen überprüfen: 50 Prozent der Artikel wiesen Fehler auf. Es wurde falsch zitiert, die Titel stimmten nicht mit dem Inhalt überein, es wurden unrichtige Zahlen genannt und Begriffe falsch geschrieben. Hinzu kamen so genannte „subjektive Fehler": Fakten wurden ausgelassen, Zitate entstellt, der Inhalt sensationalisiert oder die Geschichte banalisiert. Scott Maier nannte folgende Gründe für die Fehler, soweit diese ermittelt werden konnten: Die Schreibenden hatten keine Fachkenntnisse, der Zeitdruck war zu groß, es wurde ungenügend recherchiert oder zu wenig nachgefragt. Ein Vergleich mit ähnlichen Untersuchungen der letzten 70 Jahre ergab, dass die Qualität der journalistischen Produkte stetig sinkt. Es erstaunt daher nicht, dass bei einer Umfrage in den USA nur noch 29 Prozent der Befragten die Presse als glaubwürdig bezeichneten. Eine von Maier begleitete Studie der Universität Lugano über Tageszeitun-

gen in Italien und in der Schweiz ergab noch bedenklichere Resultate – wobei der Fakt nicht unterschlagen sei, dass die Zeitungen in der Schweiz noch schlechter abschnitten als die italienischen.
Eine andere Untersuchung aus der Schweiz, vorgestellt von Vinzenz Wyss, Professor an der Zürcher Hochschule für Angewandte Wissenschaften, zeigte, dass die Qualitätsüberprüfung in Medienunternehmen sehr unterschiedlich gehandhabt wird. Die gebührenfinanzierten öffentlich-rechtlichen Sender lassen sich die Gegenrecherche von Geschichten und die Abnahme von Beiträgen einiges kosten. Tageszeitungen und private Radio- und Fernsehstationen haben dagegen in diesem Bereich zum Teil starke Defizite. Das mag neben finanziellen Gründen auch damit zusammenhängen, dass die Öffentlich-rechtlichen in der Schweiz per Gesetz zu Qualitätsmanagement verpflichtet sind. Für Wyss ist konsequentes Fact-Checking ein geeignetes Mittel der Qualitätssicherung. Der Fact-Checker soll sich aber nicht nur um die Fakten per se kümmern, sondern um deren korrekte Einbettung und Verkettung in der Geschichte. Das wiederum bedingt eine enge Zusammenarbeit von Fact-Checker und Storyteller. Wyss plädierte deshalb dafür, das Fact-Checking vollumfänglich ins Qualitätsmanagement zu integrieren. Das heißt auch: Fact-Checker raus aus der Dokumentation, rein in den Newsroom!
In den USA wird in den Medien bereits seit Jahrzehnten Qualitätssicherung durch Fact-Checking betrieben. Der „New Yorker" war eines der ersten Magazine, das in der ersten Hälfte des 20. Jahrhunderts eigens Spezialisten einstellte, um Reportagen und Berichte vor der Publikation zu überprüfen. Wie Sarah Smith, heute Managing Editor beim „New York Times Magazine" und Autorin des Sachbuchs „The Fact Checker's Bible", aus ihrer Zeit beim „New Yorker" berichtete, war ein falsches Zitat, das 1983 veröffentlicht wurde und einen elf Jahre dauernden Prozess zur Folge hatte, Auslöser für eine Verschärfung des Fact-Checkings in der Redaktion. Peter Canby, Senior Editor beim „New Yorker" und seit 1994 Chef der Fact-Checking-Abteilung, schilderte eindrücklich, wie sein Team daran arbeitet, möglichen Sprengstoff in den Artikeln vor der Publikation zur Explosion zu bringen. Dabei gehe es nicht darum, brisante Artikel zu entschärfen, sondern Fehler, die zum „Rohrkrepierer" werden könnten, auszumerzen. Als Beispiel für die Kooperation von Fact-Checker und Storyteller nannte er die Zusammenarbeit mit Seymour Hersh, einem der renommiertesten Autoren des Heftes, der u. a. 1969 das Massaker von My Lai in Vietnam und 2004 den Folter-Skandal im Abu-Graib-Gefängnis in Irak an die Öffentlichkeit brachte. Canby, der „Personal Fact-Checker" von Hersh, arbeitet aufs Engste mit dem Investigativjournalisten zusammen, hat Zugang zu allen Unterlagen und fragt auch bei Informanten nach, ob deren Aussagen wirklich stimmen.
Fehler können jedoch nicht nur in hochbrisanten politischen Geschichten auftauchen. Es kann auch ein Cartoon sein, in dem sich zwei Pinguine politisch korrekt als

„arctic american" ansprechen lassen wollen. Ein guter Fact-Checker merkt: Pinguine gibt's nur in der Antarktis.
Pinguine in der Arktis lösen zwar keine langjährigen Prozesse aus, aber Lawinen von Leserzuschriften. Das bestätigen auch die Fact-Checker vom „Spiegel": Falsche geografische oder regionale Bezüge dürfen nicht sein. Eine Elbe, die durch Prag fließt, erschüttert die Glaubwürdigkeit eines Titels fundamental. Fact-Checking hat beim „Spiegel" eine dementsprechend lange Tradition. Schon 1947 beim Erscheinen der ersten Nummern beschäftigte das Blatt fünf Archivare. Als Rudolf Augstein in den 50er-Jahren von einem Dokumentar auf einen Fehler in der gedruckten Ausgabe hingewiesen wurde, konterte er: „Dann korrigieren Sie das bitte vorher!" Mittlerweile kontrollieren 70 Dokumentare, alle mit Hochschulabschluss, jeden Artikel, der ins Blatt kommt. Ist ein Artikel verifiziert, verantwortet die Dokumentation die Richtigkeit des Inhalts. Für Hauke Janssen, seit 2000 Leiter der Dokumentation und Mitgastgeber der Konferenz, ist Fact-Checking eine der Grundvoraussetzungen für Qualitätsjournalismus. Uneingeschränkt dieser Meinung ist auch „Spiegel"-Chefredakteur Mathias Müller von Blumencron: Ohne Fakten keine guten Stories. Fakten seien ein Mittel, um der in vielen Medien verbreiteten Kolportage von Halbwahrheiten und Gerüchten entgegenzuwirken, sagte er zu den Gästen der Konferenz.
Fact-Checking ist aber nicht nur Verifikation, sondern hat auch kollaterale Auswirkungen wie Thomas Leif, Vorsitzender des netzwerk recherche, betonte: Die interdisziplinäre Arbeit zwischen Journalist und Fact-Checker führt zu neuen Themen. Leif forderte denn auch einen „Fakten-TÜV" für jedes Medienunternehmen. Davon sind die Medien in Deutschland (wie in den meisten Ländern der Welt) noch weit entfernt. Immerhin, es ist nicht nur der „Spiegel", der Fact-Checking als wesentlichen Qualitätsfaktor erkannt hat. Auf der Konferenz referierten auch Vertreter des Medienhauses Gruner+Jahr und der Redaktionen von „Focus" und „Brand Eins".
Craig Silverman, kanadischer Journalist und Autor des Sachbuchs „Regret the Error", beschwor die Nützlichkeit von Check-Listen. Wenn selbst hochspezialisierte Berufsleute wie Piloten und Chirurgen Check-Listen führten, um ihre anspruchsvollen Aufgaben fehlerfrei zu erledigen, sollten sich auch Journalisten dazu durchringen können. Da Fehler meist situationsbedingt und nicht individuell seien, gelte es, diese fehlerverursachenden Situationen zu erkennen. Zudem warnte Silverman davor, das menschliche Gedächtnis zu überschätzen: „Der Mensch ist schlicht nicht gut genug, um auf Check-Listen verzichten zu können."
Bei großem Produktionsdruck weichen kleine Fact-Checker-Crews auf freie Mitarbeiter aus. Diese Form des Outsourcing, bedingt auch durch immer größeren Kostendruck, wurde während der Tagung ebenfalls diskutiert. Die Referentinnen und Referenten waren jedoch fast einhellig der Meinung, dass der integrative Prozess des Fact-Checkings in der redaktionellen Arbeit, die nötige Erfahrung und das Ver-

trauensverhältnis, das zwischen Fact-Checker und Autor aufgebaut werden muss, eine Auslagerung des sensiblen Bereichs nicht zulassen.
Für eine in den USA sehr populäre Form des externen Fact-Checking mittels „crowdsourcing“ im Internet plädierte Craig Silverman in einem weiteren Referat. Silverman geht davon aus, dass sich einerseits immer weniger Medienhäuser ein professionelles Fact-Checking leisten können, andererseits Fact-Checking zu einem Freizeitvergnügen des Internet-Zeitalters werde. Schon jetzt gebe es Medien-Watchblogs, in Deutschland etwa bildblog.de, die eine starke Wirkung zeigten. Medien-Watchblogs arbeiten jedoch korrektiv und nicht präventiv. Sie übernehmen die Funktion des „Korrigendum“ in den klassischen Printmedien, also das Offenlegen und Eingestehen von Fehlern, die bereits gemacht und veröffentlicht sind. Die „New York Times“ pflegt diese offene Deklaration und Richtigstellung von Fehlern seit 1972 auf der zweiten Seite. Auch der „Spiegel“ hat eine Rubrik „Korrekturen“ in der Printausgabe eingeführt – trotz vorbildlichem Fact-Checking können sich Fehler ins Heft schleichen.
In einer Hinsicht ist das „crowdsourcing“ dem hausinternen Fact-Checking aber möglicherweise überlegen: Im Aufdecken von bewussten Manipulationen, von gezielten Plagiaten und Fälschungen. „Professionelle“ Fälscher wie Ingo Mocek oder Tom Kummer setzen gezielt interne Kontrollinstanzen außer Kraft, indem sie auch ihre Quellen fälschen. Gefälschte Websites und fingierte Wikipedia-Einträge ließen vergangenen September die „dpa“ eine Falschmeldung über einen angeblichen Terroranschlag verbreiten. Dieser „Bluewater“-Fall wurde bei einer Podiumsdiskussion auf der Konferenz des netzwerk recherche ausführlich diskutiert. Konsequentes Fact-Checking, das zeigte die Hamburger Konferenz eindrücklich, hätte diesen Fehler verhindert. Auch bei ständig steigendem Produktionstempo bleibt Glaubwürdigkeit ein äußerst wertvolles Gut. Der Grundsatz aus dem Spiegel-Redaktionsstatut von 1949, dass im Zweifelsfall auf eine Meldung verzichtet wird, behält gerade im Internet-Zeitalter seine Richtigkeit, weil das World Wide Web eine völlig neue Dimension von Fälschungen ermöglicht. Wie Martin Welker, Professor an der Macromedia Hochschule für Medien und Kommunikation in München, in seinem Schlußreferat betonte, geht es beim Fact-Checking um mehr als Qualitätsjournalismus und Glaubwürdigkeit: Fact-Checking bietet letztlich die Grundlage für politische Meinungsbildung und Demokratie. Wenn das kein Auftrag ist ...

Bemerkung des Autors: Wegen Zeitdrucks konnten nicht alle Fakten dieses Artikels überprüft werden.

Martin Welker

„Proletarier des Journalismus": Ein Bericht über die nr-Fachkonferenz

Prof. Dr. Martin Welker lehrt Journalistik an der Macromedia Hochschule für Medien und Kommunikation in München. Nach einem Studium der Politologie, Anglistik, Philosophie und Volkswirtschaftslehre arbeitete Welker als Journalist, u. a. für die dpa. Einer seiner Forschungsschwerpunkte ist die journalistische Informationsbeschaffung im Internet. Er ist Vorstandsmitglied der „Deutschen Gesellschaft für Online-Forschung" sowie Gründer und Reihenherausgeber der „Neuen Schriften zur Online-Forschung".

Wie leicht sich Fehler einschleichen, musste ausgerechnet die Süddeutsche Zeitung erkennen, die in ihrem Online-Angebot über die Hamburger Fact-Checking-Konferenz des netzwerk recherche berichtete („Wie wahr sind Fakten?", 19. April 2010): In einem Satz über Peter Canby, Senior-Editor von The New Yorker und Chef einer 16-köpfigen Fact-Checker-Abteilung, hieß es im dritten Absatz des Beitrags: „Er arbeitet für das Magazin The New Yorker." Ein Leser des Online-Angebots schrieb daraufhin über das Kommentartool der Seite: „Die Bewunderung der Autoren der Süddeutschen für ihre Kollegen des New Yorker ist absolut berechtigt. (...) The New Yorker ist jedoch ein Wochenmagazin." Die Online-Redaktion hatte den Fehler allerdings zu diesem Zeitpunkt bereits korrigiert. Er war entstanden, weil der noch nicht ganz redigierte Artikel aus der Print-Ausgabe unter Zeitdruck ins Online-Angebot übernommen worden war.[1] Auch dieses eher harmlose Beispiel zeigt: Fehler lauern überall! Den Computer runterfahren und entspannt Feierabend machen? Nicht im Fact-Checking-Geschäft! „Dokumentare gehen nie beruhigt nach Hause", lautete einer der Kernsätze dieser Konferenz, ausgesprochen haben ihn Dr. Eckart Teichert und Klaus Falkenberg, Dokumentare des Spiegel. Denn Fehler, Begriffsverwirrungen oder Widersprüche lauern ausnahmslos in jedem redaktionellen Text. Der Prüfende kann und sollte sich nie sicher sein ob er doch nicht einen Fehler übersehen hat – die professionelle Skepsis gehört zur Grundausstattung eines jeden Fact-Checkers, betonte auch Peter Canby vom New Yorker: „Unser Job ist es, skeptisch zu sein!" Irrtümer und Fallgruben beginnen nicht erst beim „japanischen" Springkraut und enden leider auch nicht bei der „Prinzessin von Wales". Zeitdruck ist dabei der ständige Begleiter und gleichzeitig eines der größten Probleme des Fact-Checkers, auch in personell noch gut ausgestatteten Redaktionen. Denn durch die Beschleunigung redaktioneller Prozesse verkürzt sich der Zeitabstand bis zur Veröffentlichung heute drastisch. Fact-Checker stehen somit ständig unter Druck.

Macht also Fact-Checking „krank bis zur Anstaltsreife", wie Rudolf Augstein bereits Ende der 50er-Jahre die Arbeit seiner „Archivleute" nicht ohne Hintersinn in einem Brief an John Jahr charakterisierte, oder kann der Redakteur auch „Spaß am Fact-Checking" haben, wie Craig Silverman, kanadischer Journalist und Autor, die Zuhörer motivierte? Diese Frage bewegte auch die Teilnehmer der Fachkonferenz, die organisationsbedingt zwischen Räumen im Erdgeschoss und dem 12. Stock des Spiegel-Hauses pendelten: Himmel oder Hölle? Wohl eine Mischung aus beidem wie sich im Verlauf der Tagung zeigte.

Denn einerseits wächst der Druck auf die Dokumentare, wie sie hierzulande immer noch vielfach heißen. Es müssen daher stärker Prioritäten gesetzt wer-

[1] *Telefonische Auskunft der Online-Redaktion, Ressort Medien, an den Autor, vom 26. April 2010.*

den, wie Dr. Hauke Janssen, Leiter der Spiegel-Dokumentation, einforderte: „Stimmen die Namen und Zahlen, sind die Fakten richtig, stimmen die Zitate?" Dabei bedeutet eigentlich „Fact-Checking gar nicht ausschließlich Verifikation, sondern auch die Einführung neuer Themen und einer breiteren Perspektive", betonte Dr. Thomas Leif, nr-Vorstand. Beim Magazin Brand Eins wirkt die Dokumentation permanent an den Themenvorschlägen mit. Andererseits soll aber auch der Spaß am Fact-Checking nicht zu kurz kommen. Und der kommt laut Silverman vor allem beim Einsatz neuer, kollaborativer Formen des Fact-Checkings. Innovation der Verifikation heißt heute vielfach über das Internet Publikum am Fact-Checking zu beteiligen. Die korrigierende Kraft des guten alten Leserbriefes kann heute mit ganz neuen Methoden erweitert werden, schneller und mit höherer Reichweite als in Vor-Internet-Zeiten.

„External Fact-Checking" heißt nun nicht zwangsläufig, dass Jobs aus der Redaktion „crowdgesourced" werden müssen. Silverman erläuterte, dass es eher um zusätzliche Aufgaben geht, die in der Redaktion normalerweise gar nicht erledigt werden können. Als Beispiel zeigte der Kanadier das Projekt „Control your MP's expenses" des Guardian aus dem Jahr 2009, ein typisches „Pro-Am" (Professional-Amateur)-Projekt. In diesem Fall waren die Leser aufgerufen, in einer großen Datenbank die Ausgaben des Abgeordneten ihres Wahlkreises auf Unregelmäßigkeiten zu überprüfen. Auf diese Weise könnten internetgestützte Projekte auf der Basis von Freiwilligkeit helfen, die Qualität der Recherche und letztlich der Berichterstattung zu steigern. Die Spielfreude und der Spaß der Leser würden somit in Qualität umgewandelt.

Was das Internet angeht – auch das zeigte diese Konferenz – waren nicht alle Fact-Checker so positiv eingestellt wie Silverman: Gerade die investigativ arbeitenden Journalisten wie Mathew D. Rose schwören nach wie vor auf papierbasierte Informationen wie Handelsregisterauszüge oder eidesstattliche Erklärungen. Auch Janssen beklagte, dass er bei unklarem Material von Redakteuren immer öfter den Satz zu hören bekomme: „Das habe ich aus dem Internet". Recherche und vor allem die Verifikation von Fakten müssten sich aber auf verlässliche Quellen stützen, die Online-Enzyklopädie Wikipedia gehöre nicht dazu. Hinzu komme: In Zeiten von Weblogs und Facebook „glauben wir eher dem Tipp eines Freundes als einer Redaktion", sagte Spiegel-Chefredakteur Mathias Müller von Blumencron und betonte, dass sich alle journalistischen Produkte heute in einer Art Glaubwürdigkeits-Wettbewerb mit den Inhalten sozialer Netzwerke befänden. Wenn dann etablierte Agenturen und Medien Falschmeldungen, die mit Hilfe des Internets verbreitet worden sind, übernehmen, gerät Journalismus in Verruf. Gerade deshalb sei „richtig" so wichtig, sagten auch die Teilnehmer des Podiums am zweiten Tag der Konferenz, die sich mit Fakes und den dar-

auf aufbauenden Falschmeldungen á la „Bluewater“ auseinandersetzten. Die Versendung einer solchen Falschmeldung bereite ihm „körperliche Schmerzen“ bekannte denn auch Jens Dudziak, Chef vom Dienst der dpa.
Ob offline oder online: Fact-Checking sollte in mehr Redaktionen eine Rolle spielen. Doch die Realität sieht leider anders aus. Das zeigte der Vortrag von Prof. Scott Maier, Medienforscher der University of Oregon, der das redaktionelle Angebot von 22 US-amerikanischen Zeitungen systematisch untersucht hatte. 50 Prozent aller untersuchten Artikel enthielten Fakten-Fehler, im Schnitt traten 3 Fehler pro Artikel auf. Maier nannte dieses Ergebnis „shocking“ und meinte: „Irgendetwas läuft falsch.“ Die häufigsten Fehlerarten waren übrigens die üblichen Verdächtigen: falsche Zitate, falsche Überschriften, falsche Zahlen. Maier strich heraus, dass es in Europa nicht viel besser aussähe, im Gegenteil: Untersuchungen seiner Kollegen in Italien und der Schweiz zeigten einen höheren Fehleranteil als in den USA. Die Fehlerarten seien interessanterweise jedoch gleich. Der Spiegel begegnet dem Fehlerteufel mit der mutmaßlich größten Fact-Checking-Abteilung der Welt: Rund 100 Dokumentare sorgen für möglichst wenig Falschangaben im Heft und zunehmend auch in der Online-Ausgabe. Dokumentations-Chef Janssen zitierte eine kürzlich angefertigte Diplomarbeit, der zufolge die Spiegel-Dokumentare in einer einzigen Heftausgabe über 1.150 Änderungen auf Basis von mehr als 550 Fehlern und 400 Ungenauigkeiten vorschlugen. Mehr als 85 Prozent waren nach Meinung der Fact-Checker relevant. Der jeweilige Redakteur lehnte nur jeden achten Änderungsvorschlag ab. Wichtigstes Werkzeug ist heute der Computer, aber auch das Papier-Archiv gibt es noch. Im Spiegel-Archiv lagern 30 Millionen Dokumente, aber „so genau weiß das keiner“, sagte Janssen.
Insgesamt zeigte die Konferenz, mutmaßlich die erste in Deutschland, die sich ausschließlich dem Thema „Fact-Checking“ widmete, dass es vier Haupt-Begründungen für Fact-Checking gibt, die in der einen oder anderen Weise in den einzelnen Workshops aufschienen:

Vier Gründe für Fact-Checking
Moralisch-ethische: Wir dürfen unsere Leser nicht betrügen
Juristische: Wir sind gesetzlich zur Sorgfalt verpflichtet
Ökonomische: Fact-Checking ist Qualitätsmanagement
Technologische: Wir müssen in Zeiten des Internets und der Konvergenz besonders aufmerksam sein

Die Welt sei kompliziert, also seien auch die Sachverhalte kompliziert, betonten mehrere Referenten. Jedes Wissen sei unsicher. Deshalb gelte: Zweifel müsse der ständige Begleiter sein. Besonders schwierig sei die Lage aber bei tages- und stundenaktuellen Medien, da hier der Zeitdruck besonders hoch sei. Dabei gehe es nicht um „Wahrheit“, viel eher um „Unstrittigkeit“. Nur Fakten können überprüft werden, insbesondere die W-Fragen. Interpretationen und Meinungen seien problematisch.
Die Referenten der Konferenz näherten sich auf ganz unterschiedliche Weise dem Fact-Checking. Sie beschrieben es wie folgt:

Fact-Checking ist ...
... Kontrolle und Vorbeugung
... Aufwand und Anstrengung
... „Checks and Balances“
... Vertrauensaufbau, insbesondere zu den Autoren
... Teamwork zwischen Autoren, der Dokumentation und dem Justiziar
... ein Prozess der Bewusstmachung

Insbesondere der letzte Punkt fehle in vielen Redaktionen. So appellierte Autor Silverman: „Schreiben Sie Ihre Fehler auf!“ Ehrlich sein, das sei der erste Schritt. Journalisten müssten Fehler-Selbstbewusstsein entwickeln. Denn journalistische Fehler könnten genauso schlimm sein wie Fehler im Bereich Medizin oder in der Nukleartechnik, sagte Silverman. In den USA werde nach dem Prinzip der „kontrollierten Explosion“ geprüft, sagte Sarah Smith, Autorin des Fachbuches „The Fact Checker's Bible“ und Mitarbeiterin des New York Times Magazine. Probleme, auch juristischer Art, müssten vor der Veröffentlichung entschärft werden, indem sie notfalls „kontrolliert“ zur Explosion gebracht würden.
Wie wichtig das Fact-Checking ist, hat diese Konferenz gezeigt. Kompakt und konzentriert konnten die etwa 130 Teilnehmer erfahren, was Journalismus im Innersten zusammenhält: Faktentreue und damit verbunden auch Glaubwürdigkeit. Denn „ohne Fakten auch keine großen Storys“ wie es Müller von Blumencron formulierte. Weil Fact-Checker und Dokumentare als „Proletarier unter den Journalisten“ (Canby) gelten, hat die Konferenz bestätigt, dass ohne diese proletarische Basisarbeit kein guter Journalismus möglich ist. Abschließend bleibt die Hoffnung, das Thema stärker in die Redaktionen und vor allem in die Ausbildung tragen zu können. Auch Janssen betonte die Notwendigkeit für qualifiziertes Fachpersonal. Dr. Jochen Murken, Leiter der Dokumentation des Stern, sprang ihm bei: Gute Fact-Checker brauchten eine gute Einarbeitung - „Es geht ja auch um Vertraulichkeit.“

Einige Kommentare von Teilnehmern zur nr-Fachkonferenz

„Ich fand die Organisation schlicht und diskret (auch wenn man um die enorme Arbeit weiß, die das verlangt) wie es sein soll. Großes Lob“

*

„Gute Organisation mit Blick für`s Detail, super“

*

„sehr gut organisierte und abwechslungsreiche Konferenz“

*

„Danke für die exzellente Idee“

*

„Enorm viele praktisch verwendbare Informationen“

*

„Gute, teilweise sehr erhellende Veranstaltung mit teilweise guten bis sehr guten Tipps für die Recherche“

*

„Super, ein toller Einblick in die Welt des Fact-Checking“

*

„Die Tagung war phantastisch – inhaltlich wie organisatorisch. Vielen Dank!“

*

„sehr gute Zusammenstellung und Organisation. Angesichts des so kleinen Teams eine tolle Sache. Bitte gerne in dieser Form, auf diesem Niveau, wiederholen!“

*

„Vielen herzlichen Dank für die phantastische Konferenz. Ich war selten bei einer inhaltlich durchweg so konzentriert-spannenden Veranstaltung (okay, ich bin noch keine 30, trotzdem).“

„Ich bin nicht bekannt für meine* Großzügigkeit, wenn es um Lob geht. Doch ich fand die Veranstaltung die beste, die ich je in Deutschland besucht habe. Der pragmatische Ansatz der Vorträge und Workshops war höchst ungewöhnlich. Ich fand die meisten ausländischen Referenten hervorragend.“

*

„Fazit: Es war eine sehr interessante, lehrreiche und gut organisierte Veranstaltung mit fast durchgängig gut ausgewählten, tollen Referenten. Vielen Dank für dieses Wochenende!“

*

„Sehr positiv war der Blick „über den Teich“ nach Amerika“

*

„Ein dickes Plus für die spannende und tolle Auswahl der Referenten.“

*

„Die Länge der Beiträge der und Pausen war passend, die Fülle des Programms ebenfalls. Die Pausen hätten nicht kurz genug sein können.“

*

„Teilweise gab es Überschneidungen, dies ist sicherlich nicht auszuschließen.“

*

„gute Materialien zum Mitnehmen“

*

„sehr gute Unterlagen, Flyer“

*

„professionelle Moderation“

The
Fact

netzwerk
recherche
alismus lebt von Unabhän-
ngt Mut, Urteilskraft und
Integrität. Wer schreibt,
hes Temperament, eine
t, eine Freud

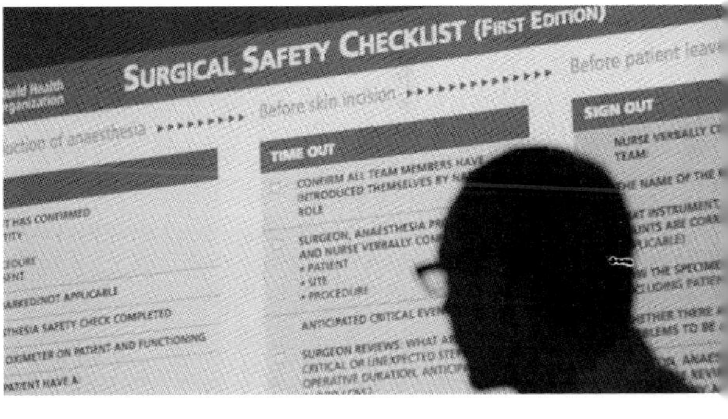
SURGICAL SAFETY CHECKLIST (FIRST EDITION)
Before skin incision
TIME OUT
SIGN OUT
SURGEON, ANAESTHESIA PROFESSIONAL AND NURSE VERBALLY CONFIRM
• PATIENT
• SITE
• PROCEDURE

nr
netzwerk recherche

Peter Canby

Fact-Checking at "The New Yorker"

Peter Canby ist Senior Editor des Magazins The New Yorker und leitet dort seit 1994 die Fact-Checking-Abteilung. Er verfasste das Buch „The Heart of the Sky: Travels Among the Maya." Sein Essay „The Forest Primeval: a Month in Congo's wildest jungle", veröffentlicht im Harper's Magazine, wurde 2003 ausgewählt für die Anthologie „Best American Science Writing".

"The New Yorker" was founded in 1925. And, remarkably, over that time it's had only five editors. The original editor was Harold Ross. When he started the magazine, it was light, somewhat gossipy, funny, and urbane. But it gradually became more serious, and this particularly happened in the early fifties. The second editor, William Shawn, who everybody knew as Mr. Shawn, took over in 1952, turned the magazine into a more serious direction, and really began the reporting tradition for which "The New Yorker" is known today. In the late 1960's a writer named Jonathan Schell did a series of pieces on the destruction of a village in Vietnam. The piece starts with a description of Ben Suc, a relatively small agricultural village, and leads up through military and political logic to its complete eradication. At around that time, the magazine came out against the war in Vietnam and developed a reputation as the thoughtful, politically liberal publication that it has today.

I'm proud to say that under our current editor David Remnick we're continued and in some ways enhanced this reporting tradition. I guess the most famous investigative journalist is Seymour Hersh whom we know as "Sy". He is a very likeable, very eccentric man. And he wrote a number of pieces about the Bush administration's build up to the Iraq war, and also, crazy as it may sound, about plans that he found inside the Bush administration, notably in the Vice-President's office, to extend that war into Iran. We also have another famous investigative reporter, Jane Mayer, who wrote a series of pieces for us, really remarkable pieces, on the genesis of the torture programme post 9/11.

But beside all this "The New Yorker" continues to run its humour pieces, its memoirs, its fiction, its poetry, all the things it's also been famous for, and you'll keep in mind that we do things as crazy as check cartoons and covers and fiction and poetry and many people say, "How can you check poetry?, and many poets say, "How can you check poetry?". But if we have a botanical name or you have a city name or something like that you want to make sure that it's either correct or it's deliberately incorrect. And then we do make space in fiction for a deliberate departure from the journalistically real world that we know.

There are sixteen checkers including myself at "The New Yorker". I would say most of them are in their upper 20's or mid-20's. We have people for the most part who've had a job or two before they come to us, or have a graduate degree. And we do care a lot about languages. I'm not really sure what the logic of that is because we could easily hire translators. But we presently have nine languages that people speak fluently, and many of these are languages that several people speak.

Two Traditions in Fact-Checking

There are two traditions in fact-checking in the United States. "Time" and its rival "Newsweek" had a tradition of what they call reporter-researchers who helped the reporters put their stories together and sometimes conducted interviews and occasionally contributed writing or got reporter credits. The second tradition, which we use at "The New Yorker", consists of a system of checks and balances where we get the piece as a completed manuscript, then take it apart and we chase it down to its details. So we don't really help the writer put it together, although it's not completely unheard of for us to look up things for people. But there's a more or less infinite appetite for that, so if you start doing favours to writers helping them put their stories together, there's probably no end to it because they'll think, "Oh my gosh, there's this very smart people who can tell me how to find out things". And we wind up having no time to do the work that we're supposed to be doing.
There is a kind of a directive that "The New Yorker" sends out to its writers about what to expect from the fact-checking department. It sounds very ferocious and very draconian, and it tells them what they need to provide for us. We ask them for their newspaper clips, their magazine stories, the websites they consulted, the telephone numbers of their sources, Wikipedia files which we find very often – simple things. But we also ask writers for their notebooks and their tapes, their transcripts – and telephone numbers, because our fact checkers call the writer's sources. This can be sensitive. Writers can get nervous that their sources may disavow what they told the reporter. But if you have the notebook and you've read the notes or you've heard the tape or you've looked at the transcripts, you basically know what the person said. And if the person starts backing off and saying, "I never said that, that's completely untrue", well, then you are in a position to say, "I have the notebooks, I know what you said, I'm inviting you to fix anything sort of factually wrong, but not to rewrite the interview". My term for that is "yanking the chain". But if you're a newly hired 26 year old fact checker, 18 months out of graduate school, and you are talking to an Under-Secretary of Defense who is trying to intimidate you, it is not that easy. But we never read quotes verbatim to sources. We go over the substance of quotes and not the actual quotes, unless there is some quote approval arrangement.

Blind Sources

Blind sources are a special problem for us. There are a couple of things that we have be especially careful of with blind sources. One is we want to make sure that we're not being manipulated into getting into a story where there's a sort of a personal vendetta or rivalry between some factions or interests in Washington. We also want

to make sure that it's a really substantial story that the person is telling us and this information is consistent with other information. We always look for ways that we can confirm this information on the record. We also have to be careful that we don't say something about people that will identify who they are, and that's something we negotiate with them directly. Inside the magazine there are maybe five or six people who know who the blind sources are. But of those, the only ones who actually speak with them and really cross-examine them on what they were saying are the fact checkers. So they have a considerable responsibility.
That is the standard that we use pretty much throughout the editorial process. And if we get writers who say, "I don't want you to talk to this person, that person is too fragile or too nervous or too scared", then that's an issue for us, because we kind of figure that by working systematically through all the sources and speaking and listening to them all, we get a fairly firm idea about what's going on.

Fact-Checking Allegations

We also follow of rule of thumb that if someone actions are attributed to someone in one of our pieces, then we want to speak with that person. If the reporter never spoke to that person, we typically urge him to do so first. We often follow up. By an extension of this same logic, when we run investigative pieces about things the government is doing wrong, we want to give the government – or its spokespeople – the chance to explain themselves. On late-breaking pieces, that's often a complicated process. For example: we might get a first draft of a Sy Hersh piece on a Monday that will go to press on Friday of that same week. We usually get some kind of a warning that a Sy piece is coming, but often not much since Sy is always working on something. It's only when Sy's work gets to a certain level of fruition that it taxis up to the runway for take off. At that point, we start thinking about contacting the Pentagon or the CIA or whoever it might be to check whatever we're alleging about them. But we really don't want to do that until we have a complete list of questions. And because the piece evolves over the course of the week, that's complicated.
As I mentioned, these kinds of investigative pieces typically close late in the week – on a Friday. In the beginning, we would hold off with our questions for the White House or the Pentagon until Wednesday or Thursday. They start complaining saying we can't answer these questions on one day's notice forgetting the fact that they answer newspaper questions on one day's notice all the time, but then they would go to the editor in chief and send a message to his office and call him and say, "Your fact checkers are ambushing us, we can't respond to these things." Mind you, we boil these questions down so it's like nine or ten questions of a fairly general nature that if they put their minds to them and they wanted to answer these questions, they

could do it very quickly. But the fact is that they often don't really want to answer. There was a Deputy Assistant Secretary for Public Affairs at the Defense Department who would frequently respond to our questions. We learned through the grapevine that he aspired to be a writer. He was responding to one of my favorite checkers and he said, "not surprisingly we are requested to respond to yet another series of questions poorly disguised as facts to be verified for another Seymour Hersh creation. Once again Mr. Hersh returns to his formula of presenting as fact a litany of unsubstantiated claims culled from a variety of unnamed sources. The United States government remains committed to a diplomatic solution to the problem of Iran's clandestine nuclear weapons program. The President and the State Department are working are working with the international community including the European Union, the IAEA and the United Nations to put a halt to this dangerous problem. (...) The assertions and assumptions in all of these questions clearly indicate that another act of journalistic fraud is about to be committed, and ‚The New Yorker' continues to be an accessory to that crime."
It's easy to laugh at this, but we take such letters very seriously. They make us go back to our sources and be double sure thay're solid. We also always try to quote from these letters, although there's often little to quote from, there's so little substantial, so little substance in these letters that there's not a lot we can use, but we always take at least one strong refutation and denial and include it in the piece.

Letters to the Editor

"The New Yorker" has a dangerously high reputation, I think, for accuracy. What is true is that the checkers are extraordinarily dedicated and that we take accuracy very seriously. But its not as if we never make mistakes. We work under impossible deadlines and in each issue there are typically one or two small mistakes. Naturally, we'd prefer not to have any, but as long as they're small and peripheral and the checker has a good record, I try not to get too excited about them. Inside the department, we try to look at the mistakes we make as opportunities to learn how to avoid the same or a similar mistake in the future. These days, we fix most things online without fanfare.
Typically, the fix is marked with an asterisk. There used to be whole dedicated person at "The New Yorker" to answer reader queries, but in our trimming down our editorial process that person left and it essentially falls to me. The tone of the letters we receive is often surprisingly indignant. For example there are a couple of art letters we received a year or two back that struck me as completely hilarious. There was a cartoon in which two penguins were sitting in somebody's living-room and they have their legs crossed and it's a very kind of urbane scene, and the caption is, "Actually

we prefer to be known as Arctic Americans." We got numbers of angry letters pointing out that penguins don't live in the Arctic, they only live in the Antarctic – and "did you fire all your fact checkers? What's wrong with your magazine?" Of course, as the checker pointed out to me, neither do penguins sit in people's living rooms conversing in English.

The Sceptical Eye

You might wonder what the point of all this is, what the value of all this fact-checking is. The problem is, from the end point of reader you never see the things that we fix. Fact-checking can be an extremely thankless job. The fact checkers are kind of the proletariat of the editorial world. But there's a certain kind of a proletarian camaraderie among the people in my department. I tell checkers sometimes that they're only distinguished by their mistakes, they can have a perfect record for six months or eight months, and then they can make one mistake, and that's all anybody remembers them for. But, you know, we fix a lot of things, we avoid law-suits, we avoid embarrassment, we try to keep people's focus on the magazine rather than on the mistakes in the magazine.
But, in a way, I think that the effect of fact-checking is really more significant than that. All who have written what we call long-form journalism will recognize the moment when you've been surprised by the facts that you're looking at, by the stories that you're writing, and you discover new things, and it takes you beyond the sort of rehearsed tropes that you already have in your mind, the understandings that you already have of a subject you are writing about, it takes you into new territory, and ultimately into a place where the world seems fresh and new and you're doing something honest, and really that's what journalism is about. By essentially sort of forcing the writers to stick to something like that standard I think that we've really been part of a symbiotic process that's contributed to "The New Yorker's" evolution as a place where long-form reporting has flourished.
Our original editor Harold Ross once wrote of about one of our most famous editors, that before the writing she worked on was presented to the public she brought to it a "skeptical not a cynical eye." In some ways, in my mind, that's the most useful function that checkers perform — we really look at things sceptically, we try to get them right and I think that's central to the whole editorial process at "The New Yorker".

Dieser Text ist eine kurze Zusammenfassung der weit ausführlicheren Reden, die Peter Canby auf der nr-Fachkonferenz hielt. Er berichtete über Redaktionsinterna, die er nicht publizieren möchte.

Dr. Hauke Janssen, Leiter der SPIEGEL-Dokumentation

Fact-Checking beim „SPIEGEL“

Über die Arbeit der Dokumentation des Nachrichtenmagazins DER SPIEGEL berichteten auf der nr-Fachkonferenz die Dokumentationsjournalisten Jörg-Hinrich Ahrens, Almut Cieschinger, Klaus Falkenberg, Dr. André Geicke, Nadine Markwaldt-Buchhorn, Dr. Andreas Meyhoff, Dr. Eckart Teichert und Peter Wahle. Dr. Hauke Janssen hielt den Eingangsvortrag der Tagung. Er leitet seit dem Jahr 2000 die SPIEGEL-Dokumentation in Hamburg. Er studierte Volkswirtschaftlehre und war von 1986 bis 1990 als Assistent an der Universität Hamburg mit dem Schwerpunkt „Geschichte der Volkswirtschaftslehre“ tätig. Janssen promovierte mit dem Thema „Nationalökonomie und Nationalsozialismus“ und ist seit 1991 – zunächst im Referat Wirtschaft – in der SPIEGEL-Dokumentation tätig. Der vorliegende Text ist eine Zusammenfassung der verschiedenen Beiträge.

Journalisten machen Fehler, ob unbeabsichtigt oder gar beabsichtigt. Solche Fehler schädigen das größte Kapital des Qualitätsjournalismus: die Glaubwürdigkeit. Also genau das, womit man sich von den vielen subjektiven Blogs und No-Name-Newslettern im Internet abgrenzen will. Eine Methode, die Wahrscheinlichkeit von Fehlern zu verringern, ist die Verifikation (oder Fact-Checking), also die Überprüfung der Fakten vor der Veröffentlichung. Die ist allerdings in Deutschland nicht weit verbreitet. Bei einer Befragung von 259 deutschen Redaktionen gaben lediglich sechs an, dass eine Abteilung ihre Beiträge auf Richtigkeit prüft.1 Das war 2006. Es dürften heute eher weniger geworden sein. Beim SPIEGEL ist Verifikation seit Jahrzehnten Standard und wird im Vergleich zu anderen Häusern mit sehr großem Aufwand betrieben. Doch auch beim SPIEGEL hat dies klein angefangen – im Archiv.

Die Geburtsstunde der SPIEGEL-Dokumentation

Im April 1965 stellte Heinz Klatte, der damalige Leiter der SPIEGEL-Dokumentation fest: „Sicherlich gibt es keinen zweiten Verleger in der Bundesrepublik, der von der Bedeutung und dem Wert eines Archivs so überzeugt ist und der diese Überzeugung zugleich so sehr in die Tat umgesetzt hat wie der Herausgeber des Spiegel.“ Denn den Anstoß zum Aufbau der Dokumentations- und Verifikationsabteilung gab Rudolf Augstein selbst, der schon als Schüler und Soldat ihm wichtig erscheinende Presseartikel gesammelt hatte. Bereits Monate bevor der erste SPIEGEL am 4. Januar 1947 erschien stellte er einen Mitarbeiter des Vorläuferblatts „Diese Woche” als Archivar ein. Doch der promovierte Germanist schrieb lieber eigene Artikel.

Als die erste „richtige” Archivarin, Maria Rank, 1946 in Hannover im 6. Stock des Anzeiger-Hochhauses beim späteren SPIEGEL ihre Arbeit begann, „gab es nichts. Keine Ordner und natürlich auch keine Systematik“. Sie beschaffte daraufhin Ordner und führte eine selbst erfundene Beschriftung ein. Es war ein simples alphanumerisch gegliedertes System: K für Kultur, R für Religion, W für Wirtschaft, D für Deutschland, A für Ausland – die SPIEGEL-Systematik war geboren. Firmen- und Personennamen werden gesondert abgelegt und sind in einem eigenen Wörterbuch aufzufinden. Das Ordnungsprinzip spross und verästelte sich, der Bestand weitete sich aus. Bald füllten die Archivalien Hunderte, dann Tausende Regalmeter.

Augstein war zufrieden und lobte die „Rank-Organisation, die die extravagantesten Auskünfte herbeizauberte“ (Heft 41/1952). Der Herausgeber, der in Hannover sein Zimmer neben dem Archiv hatte, kam regelmäßig dorthin und vergab Aufträge: „Wir wollen bald eine große Geschichte über dies und das schreiben, sammelt dazu schon mal Archivunterlagen!“ Die erste Mitarbeiter-Liste des SPIEGEL vom 6. März 1947 führte bereits fünf Personen für die Abteilung Archiv auf, darunter als Chef Dr. Werner Hühne.

Bis Ende der 1980er-Jahre war das SPIEGEL -Archiv ein Papierarchiv. Der Bestand umfasste zuletzt rund 30 Millionen Dokumente. Ab den 1990er-Jahren erweiterte sich das klassische Archiv in einen virtuellen Raum: Es entstanden die ersten kostenpflichtigen Online-Datenbanken. Mit der Umstellung zu elektronischen Satz-Umbruch-Systemen fielen ab Mitte der 1990er-Jahre quasi automatisch digitale Archivversionen von Presseerzeugnissen an. Dies ist die Geburtsstunde des modernen Archivs, in dem heute wöchentlich 60 000 neue Artikel aus über 300 Quellen gespeichert werden. 25 bis 30 Prozent davon sind deskribiert, also nach inhaltlichen Kriterien sortiert und gekennzeichnet. Mittlerweile verzeichnet Digas, das Digitale Archivsystem (Bild 1), 50 Millionen Text- und fünf Millionen Bilddokumente, auf die alle Dokumentare und Redakteure des SPIEGEL jederzeit zugreifen können. Digas ist aber keine reine Pressedatenbank. Gespeichert werden auch Dokumente, die Journalisten und Dokumentare während der Recherche auftun, etwa Studien, Akten, Reden oder Sonderveröffentlichungen.

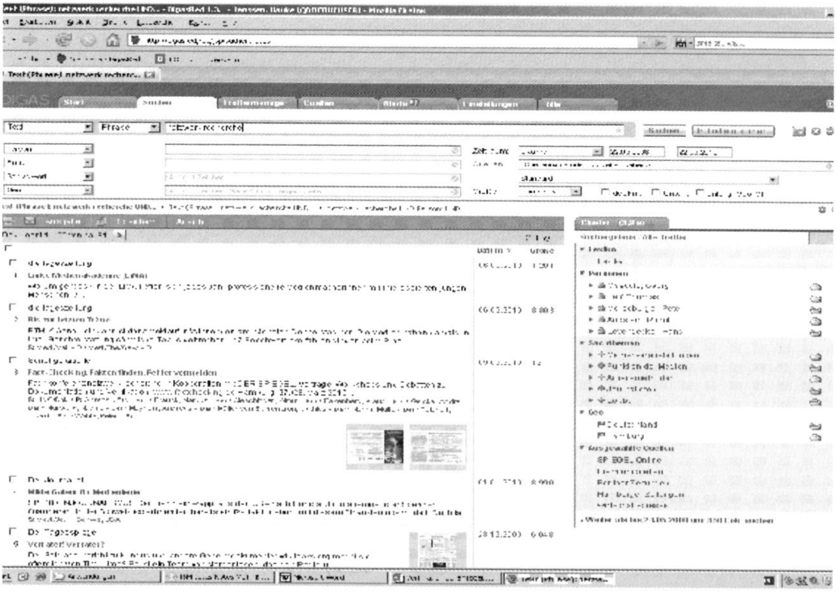

Bild 1: Das Digitale Archivsystem (Digas) verzeichnet wöchentlich rund 60 000 Artikel aus der deutschen und internationalen Presse.

Doch das Archiv dient nicht nur der Recherche und Speicherung. Es ist auch ein unerlässliches Instrument für die Verifikation der Artikel vor der Veröffentlichung. Auf die Idee, diesen Arbeitsschritt einzelnen Mitarbeitern zu übertragen, brachte die SPIEGEL-Redaktion ein dummer Fehler: Die Hafenstadt Basra am Persischen Golf wurde in einem Artikel fälschlich am Roten Meer verortet. Denn „ein Atlas existierte damals weder in der Redaktion, noch im Archiv“, erinnert sich Maria Rank, die Archivarin der ersten Stunde. „Da habe ich dann meinen von zu Hause mitgebracht und den Brockhaus von 1898 gleich dazu.“ Doch die Institutionalisierung des Fact-Checking kam erst mit einer Geschichte über einen Zahnarzt in Gang: Als die Archivarin 1955 auf einen Fehler in dem bereits gedruckten Artikel hinwies, antwortete Rudolf Augstein unwirsch: „Dann überprüfen Sie das in Zukunft doch schon vorher.“

Bald darauf wurde das Fact-Checking zur festen Aufgabe der Archiv-Mitarbeiter. Im SPIEGEL-Statut, das unter der Federführung von Dr. Werner Hühne erarbeitet und im Juni 1949 an alle Redakteure verteilt wurde, hieß es:

Auszug aus dem SPIEGEL-Statut von 1949

„Der SPIEGEL ist ein Nachrichten- (Neuigkeiten-)Magazin. Darum muss der SPIEGEL
1. aktuell sein,
2. einen hohen Nachrichten- (Neuigkeits-) Gehalt haben. Dabei muss er andere, d. h. persönlichere, intimere, hintergründigere Nachrichten (Neuigkeiten) mitteilen und verarbeiten, als sie die Tagespresse darbietet (...)
zu 2: Alle im SPIEGEL verarbeiteten und verzeichneten Nachrichten, Informationen, Tatsachen müssen unbedingt zutreffen. Jede Nachricht und jede Tatsache ist vor der Weitergabe an die Redaktion peinlichst genau nachzuprüfen. Quellen sind in jedem Fall informativ mitzuteilen. In Zweifelsfällen ist eher auf eine Information zu verzichten, als die Gefahr einer falschen Berichterstattung zu laufen.“

Doch erst ab 1952, nach dem Umzug der SPIEGEL-Redaktion nach Hamburg, entwickelte sich das Archiv unter dem Geschäftsführenden Redakteur Hans Detlev Becker von einem Annex der Redaktion zum autonomen Betriebsbereich Dokumentation (Bild 2), der bis heute gleichwertig neben Verlag und Redaktion besteht.

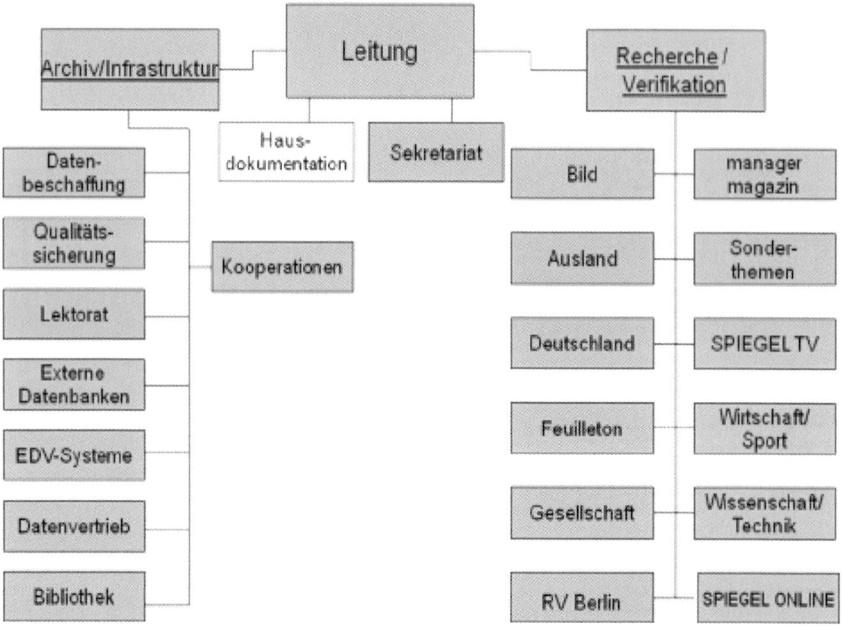

Bild 2: Die Dokumentation des SPIEGEL bildet einen eigenständigen Betriebsbereich mit einer differenzierten Aufgabenverteilung.

Das Fact-Checking entwickelte sich nunmehr zur zentralen Aufgabe der Abteilung – eine augenscheinlich logische Konsequenz der Geschichte des Archivs: „Ursprünglich sollte ein Redaktionsarchiv nur Informationsmaterial (großenteils Presseausschnitte) sammeln“, so Becker. „Aus Sammeln nach Schleppnetzprinzip wird unmerklich Beschaffen durch Recherche. Aus Sammeln und Beschaffen zur Verwertung wird im ‚Chaos des Schlachtfelds‘ (von Clausewitz) der Redaktion unmerklich Verwertung des Gesammelten und Beschafften zum Belegen von Behauptetem.“

Die Arbeit der Verifikationsabteilung

Der Arbeitsbereich „Redaktion/Verifikation“ ist analog den Ressorts in der Redaktion in Referate gegliedert und beschäftigt heute etwa 70 Dokumentationsjournalisten. Sie verifizieren die Artikel vor dem Abdruck und unterstützen die Redaktion bei der Recherche. Bei der Vorrecherche zu einem Artikel stehen für den Dokumentar vor allem drei Fragen im Vordergrund: Wie hat sich das Thema historisch entwickelt (auch hinsichtlich der Rechtslage)? Was hat der SPIEGEL bereits berichtet? Welche Aspekte haben andere Medien bereits thematisiert? Die Dokumentare sind jeweils Experten auf einem bestimmten Themengebiet, etwa Medizin, Biologie, Physik, Militär, Volkswirtschaft etc. (Bild 3). Im Rahmen seiner Fachkompetenz unterhält jeder Dokumentar einen Apparat einschlägiger Literatur an seinem Arbeitsplatz. Die SPIEGEL-Bibliothek hält darüber hinaus auf 500 Regalmetern diverse Nachschlagewerke und Sachbücher bereit. Recherchiert wird aber vor allem in externen Datenbanken (Bloomberg, Datastream, Lexis-Nexis, Factiva, Dimdi, Juris, GBI-Genios etc.), dem Internet und in Digas.

- Dr. Helmut Bott
- Michael Jürgens
- Dr. Petra Ludwig
- Werner Nielsen
- Maximilian Schäfer
- Peter Wetter

- Humanmedizin, Zahnmedizin, Tiermedizin (BSE), Psychatrie, Ärzte (Kunstfehler)...
- Biologie, Tier- und Artenschutz, Gen- und Biotechnik (Stamm-zellen, Klonen), Paläontologie, Ernährung...
- Geologie, Ozeanografie, Meteorologie, Klima, Chemie, Mineralien, Psychologie...
- Umwelt- und Naturschutz, Archäologie, Autotechnik...
- Physik, Atomtechnik, Raumfahrt, Energie, Mathematik...
- Computer, Internet, IuK, Flugzeuge...

Bild 3: Allein im Referat „Wissenschaft und Technik“ der SPIEGEL-Dokumentation arbeiten sechs Experten für bestimmte Wissensgebiete.

Fact-Checking bedeutet für die SPIEGEL-Dokumentationsjournalisten heute die gewissenhafte Verifikation des abgeschlossenen Manuskripts (Bild 4). Dabei wird „jede zur Veröffentlichung bestimmte Tatsache als solche und in ihrem Zusammenhang mit den zur Verfügung stehenden Mitteln und in Abhängigkeit der verfügbaren Zeit auf sachliche Richtigkeit geprüft. Ebenso werden auch alle Bilder und Bildtexte geprüft (siehe Kasten am Ende dieses Textes). Die Dokumentation erwartet im Gegenzug von der Redaktion ausrecherchierte Geschichten und das bei der Recherche benutzte Material. Das Vorgehen bei der Verifikation soll folgendes Beispiel einer dokumentarischen Recherche veranschaulichen, die der Dokumentationsjournalist Klaus Falkenberg durchgeführt hat.

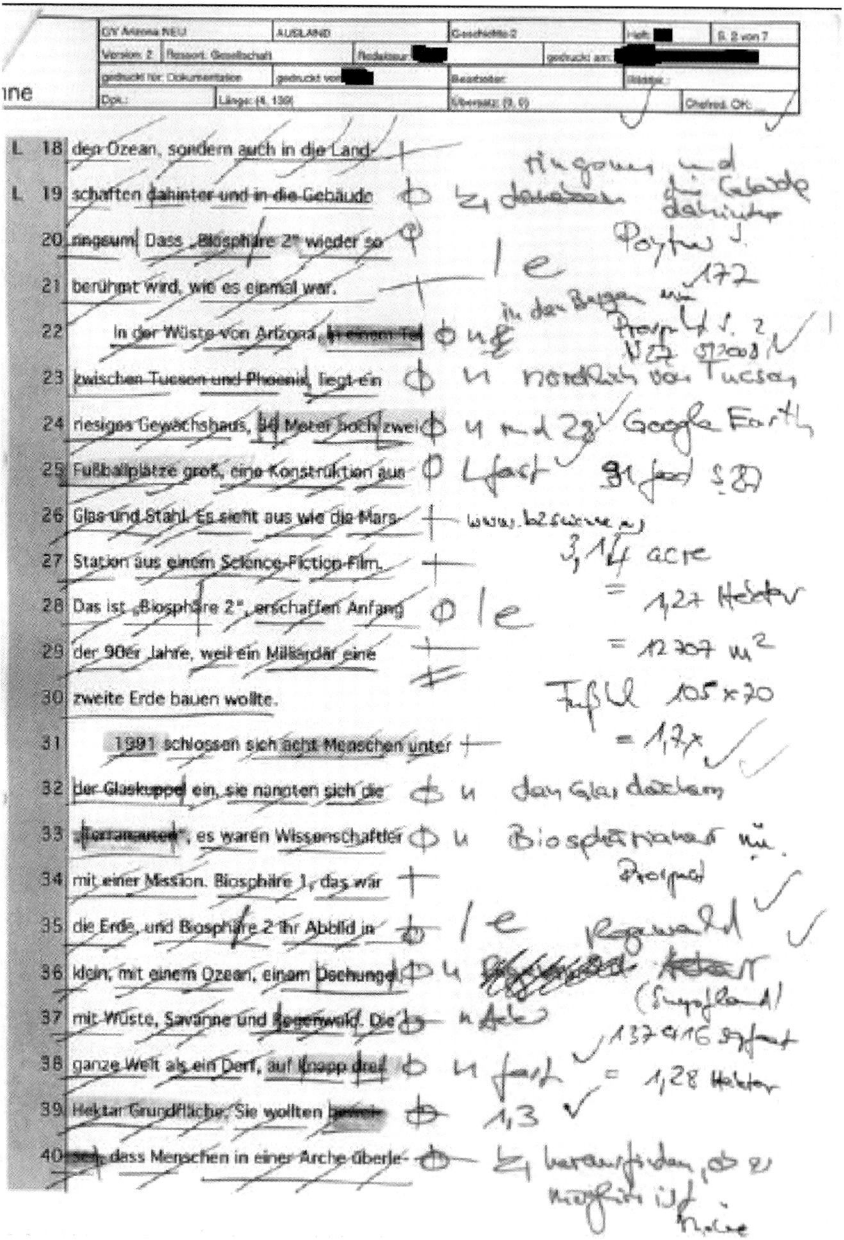

GY Arizona NEU	AUSLAND	Geschichte 2	Heft: [redacted]	S. 2 von 7
Version: 2 / Ressort: Gesellschaft	Redakteur: [redacted]	gedruckt am: [redacted]		
gedruckt für: Dokumentation	gedruckt von: [redacted]	Bearbeiter:	Bildtitel:	
Dpk.:	Länge: (4, 139)	Übersatz: (0, 0)	Chefred. OK:	

den Ozean, sondern auch in die Landschaften dahinter und in die Gebäude ringsum. Dass „Biosphäre 2" wieder so berühmt wird, wie es einmal war.

In der Wüste von Arizona, in einem Tal zwischen Tucson und Phoenix, liegt ein riesiges Gewächshaus, 30 Meter hoch, zwei Fußballplätze groß, eine Konstruktion aus Glas und Stahl. Es sieht aus wie die Mars-Station aus einem Science-Fiction-Film. Das ist „Biosphäre 2", erschaffen Anfang der 90er Jahre, weil ein Milliardär eine zweite Erde bauen wollte.

1991 schlossen sich acht Menschen unter der Glaskuppel ein, sie nannten sich die „Terranauten", es waren Wissenschaftler mit einer Mission. Biosphäre 1, das war die Erde, und Biosphäre 2 ihr Abbild im Klein, mit einem Ozean, einem Dschungel, mit Wüste, Savanne und Regenwald. Die ganze Welt als ein Dorf, auf knapp drei Hektar Grundfläche. Sie wollten beweisen, dass Menschen in einer Arche überle-

Bild 4: Bei der Überprüfung eines Textes verwendet die SPIEGEL-Dokumentation ein spezielles System von Zeichen.

Die dokumentarische Recherche: Ein Beispiel

Zu prüfende Behauptung: „Nach Erdöl ist Kaffee der zweitstärkste Rohstoffmarkt der Welt“

Quelle des Autors: Zeitungsartikel.

Problem: keine Originalquelle.

Ausgangsfrage: Gibt es weitere Quellen für diese Behauptung?

Schritt 1: Das Digitale Archivsystem des SPIEGEL verzeichnet 29 Artikel mit dieser Behauptung. In keinem der Artikel wird eine Quelle angegeben.

Schritt 2: Bei Wikipedia steht unter „wirtschaftliche Bedeutung“ des Kaffees: „Kaffee ist nicht, wie häufig behauptet, das ‚weltweit zweitwichtigste [legale] Handelsprodukt nach Erdöl‘, sondern ist ‚das zweit-wertvollste Handelsprodukt, das von Entwicklungsländern exportiert wird‘. (Quelle: Mark Pendergrast, Fachmagazin ‚Tea and Coffee Journal‘)“ Doch auch ein Fachartikel ist keine Originalquelle.

Schritt 3: Der Artikel von Mark Pendergrast verweist auf drei Quellen: die Welternährungsorganisation FAO, die Welthandelskonferenz UNCTAD, den Weltkaffeeverband ICO.

Schritt 4: Der Weltspitzenverband des Kaffeehandels ist die ICO, in der Kaffeebauern und Kaffeeröster organisiert sind. Zum Rohkaffee steht auf der Webseite der ICO: „The importance of coffee in the world economy cannot be overstated. It is one of the most valuable primary products in world trade, in many years second in value only to oil as a source of foreign exchange to developing countries.” Zahlen werden nur in Mengen des gehandelten Kaffees angegeben. Eine wertmäßige Umrechnung fehlt.

Schritt 5: Die findet sich bei FAOstat, einer verlässlichen Quelle für den Handel mit Landwirtschaftsgütern. Im letzten Berichtsjahr 2007 wurde Rohkaffee im Wert von 13,6 Milliarden USD gehandelt. In der Rangliste reicht das bei agrarischen Rohstoffen hinter Weizen, Soja, Wein, Mais, und Hühnerfleisch nur für Platz 5. Bei der UNCTAD, der Welthandelskonferenz, lässt sich nachprüfen, ob Rohkaffee als Devisenbringer für die Entwicklungsländer noch eine herausragende Rolle spielt. Mit sinkenden Kaffeepreisen und steigenden Getreideerlösen gilt aber auch das seit Jahren nicht mehr.

Schritt 6: Die letzte Möglichkeit, den Superlativ für Kaffee zu retten, wäre seine Bedeutung im Börsenhandel. Eine Google-Recherche ergibt: Das „Commodity Research Bureau“, das jährliche Statistiken über die meistgehandelten Rohstoffkontrakte herausgibt und als Originalquelle gelten kann, verzeichnete Kaffeekontrakte im Jahr 2007 an 18. Stelle, vor lebenden Rindern und hinter Heizöl.

Fazit: Der Satz des Autors ist als „falsch“ einzustufen und wird aus dem Manuskript gestrichen.

Dauer der Recherche: 20 Minuten. Datenbankkosten: keine.

Im Anschluss an die Verifikation einigen sich Dokumentar und Redakteur in einem „Übergabegespräch“ auf die endgültige Version des Manuskripts. Die Korrekturen führt anschließend die Redaktion aus, doch die Dokumentation überprüft diese und andere zwischenzeitlich eingefügte Änderungen erneut. Beim Fact-Checking orientieren sich die Dokumentare an festgeschriebenen Richtlinien, darin heißt es:

Auszug aus den SPIEGEL-Richtlinien für das Fact-Checking:

- Das zu überprüfende Manuskript wird gelesen und jede überprüfbare Sach- oder Personenangabe unterstrichen.
- Für richtig, unrichtig, nicht festzustellen etc. werden bestimmte, normierte Zeichen verwendet.
- Richtige Angaben werden abgehakt. Sind Korrekturen erforderlich, werden sie mit den üblichen Korrekturzeichen (Duden) am Rand in roter Schrift vorgenommen.
- Bei sachlichen Korrekturen und bei Zitaten ist die Quelle anzugeben.
- Von der Redaktion ausgeführte Änderungen werden abgehakt, die anderen als „n. ü.“ (nicht übernommen) gekennzeichnet.
- Zur Verifikation sind auch andere, wenn möglich bessere Quellen, als die vom Autor heranzuziehen.
- Als verifiziert kann nur gelten, was mit zuverlässigen Quellen oder von Experten bestätigt worden ist.
- Widersprechen Quellen den Angaben des Autors, muss dieser bei der Übergabe darauf aufmerksam gemacht werden, ebenso darauf, wenn Fak ten nicht verifiziert werden konnten.
- Informanten der Redaktion, die Objekt einer Geschichte sind, dürfen nur nach Absprache mit der Redaktion befragt werden.
- Schwierige Passagen werden vom fachlich zuständigen Referat gegengelesen.

Aus zeitökonomischen Gründen müssen bei der Verifikation zuweilen Prioritäten gesetzt werden. Es kann dann nicht Zeile für Zeile fortlaufend verifiziert werden, sondern zunächst und bevorzugt die Fakten und Sachverhalte, die erkennbar unter die Verantwortung der Dokumentation fallen. Gerade wenn es schnell gehen muss, hilft auch die Orientierung an drei „Basis-Checks“:

Fact-Checking unter Zeitdruck: Die Basis-Checks

Der Quellen-Check
- Ist es eine gute Quelle? Ist die Quelle belastbar?
- Bin ich an der Originalquelle?
- Gibt es weitere oder abweichende Quellen?
- Der Plausibilitäts-Check
- Kann die Nachricht so stimmen?
- Gab es bereits ähnliche Meldungen?
- Welche Nachrichtenlage lag/liegt zugrunde?
- Wie ist die Nachricht/These einzuordnen?
- Kontext und Wertigkeit: Wie ist die bisherige Berichterstattung zum Thema?

Der Fakten-Check
- Stimmen die einzelnen Informationen?
- Stimmen die Namen?
- Stimmen die Zahlen?
- Stimmen die Bezeichnungen?
- Stimmen die Zeitbezüge?

Wenn selbst die Zeit fehlt, um die drei Basis-Checks systematisch durchzuführen, hilft ein Schluss-Check, um zumindest grobe Fehler zu vermeiden. Dieses Raster von Fragen, die SPIEGEL-Dokumentare sich stellen, kann gerade bei der Arbeit in tagesaktuellen oder Online-Medien nützlich sein:

Der Schluss-Check: An alles gedacht?

Namen checken:
- Alle Vor- und Nachnamen richtig?
- Korrekte Funktion?

Fakten kritisch beäugen:
- Stimmen die Zahlen/Fakten mit der Quelle überein?
- Fachbegriffe und Zeitbezüge gecheckt?
- Orte und regionale Bezüge?

Justitiabilität hinterfragen:
- Habe ich bei Vorwürfen konfrontiert?
- Sind die Sachverhalte wasserdicht dargestellt?

Quellen prüfen:
- Habe ich alle Quellen vorliegen?
- Sind alle Fakten/Quellen belegbar?

Vier-Augen-Prinzip:
- Hat jemand den Text gegengelesen?

Rechtschreibprüfung im Auge behalten

So weit die Theorie. Mitunter erweist sich das Fact-Checking als weitaus komplizierter und weniger übersichtlich, als es die Richtlinien erscheinen lassen. Über die vielen Hürden, denen ein Fact-Checker bei der Arbeit begegnen kann, hilft vor allem eines hinweg: Erfahrung.
Ein Student zählte 2008 in seiner Abschlussarbeit 1153 Änderungen durch die Dokumentation in einer einzigen SPIEGEL-Ausgabe. Lässt man eher schlussredaktionelle Probleme der Rechtschreibung und Stilfragen außer Acht, verblieben immerhin 559 Fehler und 400 Ungenauigkeiten, von denen über 85 Prozent als relevant bzw. sehr relevant eingeschätzt wurden. Knapp drei Viertel der rund 1400 vorgeschlagenen Änderungen wurden übernommen, dazu rund 15 Prozent sinngemäß. Nur jede achte vorgeschlagene Änderung wurde durch die Redaktion abgelehnt. Was wäre also, wenn es keine Verifikation beim SPIEGEL mehr gäbe? Eine Antwort darauf gibt wiederum Hans Detlev Becker, der von 1959 bis 1962 als Chefredakteur die Redaktion und von 1961 bis 1984 als Direktor das Verlagsgeschäft leitete: „Ohne den systematischen Prozess der Verifikation hätte der SPIEGEL nicht werden können, was er ist.“ Und: „Das legendäre SPIEGEL-Archiv hat die Reputation des SPIEGEL mit ausgemacht – aus zwei Gründen: 1. wäre viel Falsches gedruckt worden und 2. hätte vieles nicht geschrieben werden können.“ Denn mit der Sicherheit der Dokumentation im Rücken kann eine Redaktion es wagen, auch einmal heiße Eisen anzufassen, ohne sich zu verbrennen.

Die SPIEGEL-Bilddokumentation

von Catrin Zander

Man könnte sie die „visuelle Dreifaltigkeit“ nennen: Die Bildredakteure, Layouter und Bilddokumentare, die beim SPIEGEL für die Bebilderung zuständig sind. Mitunter wirkt diese Arbeitsteilung kurios: „Nachdem die Bildredakteure Fotos für die Themen ausgesucht und die Layouter davon die schönsten ausgewählt haben, kommen die Bilddokumentare und werfen sie wieder aus dem Heft“, sagt Jörg-Hinrich Ahrens, Leiter der Bilddokumentation des SPIEGEL. Denn während die Textdokumentare jeden Satz überprüfen, nehmen die Bilddokumentare alle Bilder unter die Lupe.

So mussten die Fotoexperten zum Beispiel einmal die Herkunft eines undatierten Bildes klären: Es zeigt einen jungen Mann in Jeans und Wollpulli in einem Strandkorb, irgendwo auf einer grüner Wiese, auf der noch viele andere Strandkörbe stehen. Der Mann ist Mohammed Atta, einer der Männer, die am 11. September 2001 zwei Flugzeuge entführt und in die Türme des World Trade Centers in New York gelenkt haben. Das Foto wurde nach den Anschlägen in einem Schrank der „Islam-AG“ an der Technischen Universität Hamburg-Harburg gefunden, in einer Kiste, zwischen Notizen und Visitenkarten – aber das Datum der Aufnahme ist nicht auszumachen. Doch neben Atta liegt ein Exemplar der Bild am Sonntag. Das Erscheinungsdatum der Zeitung ist nicht erkennbar, dafür aber ein Fußballergebnis: 3:4. Die Vereinsnamen sind zu unscharf, um sie eindeutig zu identifizieren. Aber selbst ein so kleines Detail wie das Ergebnis des Spiels kann manchmal genügen. Eine Recherche im Archiv des Deutschen Fußballbunds zeigte des Bilddokumentaren: Am 15. August 1992 hatte Schalke 3:4 gegen Wattenscheid verloren. Die Ausgabe müsste also vom 16. August 1992 gewesen sein, was sich bei der Recherche im Archiv des Springer-Verlags und dem Abgleich der anderen Titel-Schlagzeilen bestätigte.

Die Arbeitswoche der SPIEGEL-Bilddokumentare beginnt mit der Verifikation von Fotos aus SPIEGEL GESCHICHTE, SPIEGEL WISSEN, UniSpiegel, KulturSPIEGEL oder Dein SPIEGEL. Am Donnerstag und Freitag widmen sie sich dann den Bildern des Nachrichtenmagazins. Pro Ausgabe prüfen sie im Durchschnitt 250 Fotos. 20 bis 30 davon können sie nicht ohne Weiteres durchwinken – es muss nachrecherchiert werden. Zwei oder drei Bilder müssen daraufhin ausgetauscht werden, weil sie schwerwiegende Fehler enthalten.

Die Bilddokumentare unterscheiden zwei grundlegende Kategorien von Fehlern: technische und inhaltliche. Ein technischer Fehler liegt etwa vor, wenn ein Motiv seitenverkehrt abgebildet ist. Um ein solches „gekontertes Bild" zu erkennen, schaut der Bildprüfer etwa auf die Knopfreihen an Kleidungsstücken, die geschlechtsspezifisch unterschiedlich sind. Besonders heikel sind manipulierte Bilder. Denn digitale Tricksereien sind technisch einfach realisierbar, aber manchmal schwer zu erkennen. Eine Vorsichtsmaßnahme beim SPIEGEL: Bilder aus dem Internet sind eher nicht erwünscht.

Das Schwarzbrot der Bilddokumentare ist aber die Suche nach inhaltlichen Bildfehlern. Dafür überprüfen sie zunächst die Fotolegende, die Agenturen oder Fotografen mitliefern: Stimmen die Namen, Orte und Datumsangaben? Kann sie alle W-Fragen beantworten? Entdecken die Dokumentare Ungenauigkeiten oder Fehler in einer Bildlegende, vermerken sie die Korrektur in der internen SPIEGEL-Bilddatenbank. Nicht selten finden sie den gleichen Schnitzer aber später erneut. Denn viele Fotos werden von Nachrichten-Agenturen immer wieder falsch in die Redaktion geliefert.

Im nächsten Schritt überprüfen die Bilddokumentare die Bildunterschrift des Redakteurs: Stimmen auch hier Namen, Orte und Datumsangaben? Ist alles richtig geschrieben? Zeigt das Foto, was in der Bildunterschrift steht? Wenn etwa „Israelischer Luftschlag im Gaza-Streifen" unter dem Foto steht, gilt eine Explosion von Täuschkörpern als inhaltlicher Bildfehler.

Um sicher zu gehen, dass alle Bildinhalte auch plausibel sind, nehmen sich die Dokumentare zusätzlich den ganzen Text vor: Passt das Foto überhaupt zur Geschichte? Ist es zu alt? Oder aus einem anderen Grund unpassend? Fehlt es an Plausibilität, veranlassen die Dokumentare eine Änderung des Bildes – oder des Textes. Wenn in der Geschichte der Abtransport einer Leiche erwähnt wird, ist ein Bild irreführend, das zeigt, wie ein Sarg im Treppenhaus hinauf getragen wird. Eine besonders tückische Falle sind gestellte Szenen auf Bildern: Zum Beispiel stammen Fotos, die angeblich bei Kampfhandlungen im Ersten Weltkrieg aufgenommen wurden, in Wahrheit häufig aus Filmen. Auch diese werfen die Bilddokumentare aus dem Heft, wenn es ihnen gelingt, sie zu entlarven. Denn im Nachrichtenmagazin sollen nur authentische, faktenrichtige Aufnahmen erscheinen.

Catrin Zander studiert am Institut für Journalistik und Kommunikationswissenschaft der Universität Hamburg.

Dokumentationen

Die Dokumentationen

nr-Werkstatt:
Quellenmanagement

nr-Werkstatt:
In der Lobby brennt noch Licht

nr-Werkstatt:
Veränderung der Nachrichtenfaktoren

nr-Werkstatt:
Undercover

können kostenfrei gegen einen adressierten und ausreichend frankierten Rückumschlag (DIN C5, 1.50 Euro) beim netzwerk recherche bezogen werden.

Bezugsadresse:
netzwerk recherche e.V.
Geschäftsstelle
Stubbenhuk 10, 5. OG
20459 Hamburg

www.netzwerkrecherche.de
info netzwerkrecherche.de

nr
netzwerk
recherche

Jochen Murken

Fact-Checking beim „stern“

Dr. Jochen Murken leitet seit 1997 die Dokumentationsabteilung der Stern-Redaktion. Der promovierte Meeresbiologe arbeitete zuvor bereits 13 Jahre in diesem Ressort des Hamburger Wochenmagazins aus dem Verlagshaus Gruner + Jahr.

Der Begriff „Dokumentation” kann im redaktionellen Sinne verschieden ausgelegt werden: Dokumentation bedeutet laut Fremdwörterlexikon „das Zusammenstellen, Ordnen und Nutzbarmachen von Dokumenten und (Sprach-)materialien aller Art”. Diese Definition trifft beispielsweise auf ein Text- oder Bildarchiv zu. Der Begriff bedeutet aber auch „beweiskräftiges Zeugnis, anschaulicher Beweis“. Und dokumentieren heißt nicht nur etwas „zeigen“, sondern auch etwas „(mit Dokumenten) beweisen“. Die Dokumentation des 1948 gegründeten Wochenmagazins „Stern“ ist daher auch kein Textarchiv, sondern bildet zusammen mit dem Lektorat (Schlussredaktion) ein Ressort, das im Redaktionsprozess zwischen den Textchefs und der Schlussgrafik angesiedelt ist. Die Aufgabe der Mitarbeiter der Dokumentation ist es, im Sinne der zweiten Definition alle Texte des Magazins, aber auch grafische Darstellungen zu prüfen und die darin getroffenen Aussagen mit Quellen zu belegen.
Eine einheitliche Ausbildung gibt es für diese Tätigkeit nicht. Üblich ist ein abgeschlossenes Fachstudium und erwünscht ist eine ausgeprägte Allgemeinbildung. Viele der Dokumentationsmitarbeiter haben bereits Erfahrungen in Medienberufen gesammelt, bevor sie in das Ressort des Sterns eintraten. Heute arbeiten in der Stern-Dokumentation acht Mitarbeiter, vertreten sind u. a. die Studienfächer Biologie, Geschichte, Wirtschaftswissenschaften, Amerikanistik, Romanistik und Orientalistik.

Die glaubwürdige Illustrierte

Der Stern ist als klassische Illustrierte entstanden, mit vielen Fotos und Geschichten, die von einem großen Publikum verstanden werden können. Doch ist der Stern schon vor Jahrzehnten aus diesem Genre herausgewachsen. Denn er bietet neben unterhaltsamen Elementen viel Information und fundierte Hintergrundberichterstattung. Um glaubwürdig zu sein, ist eine gleich bleibende, hohe journalistische Qualität notwendig. Die Dokumentation wurde 1960 gewissermaßen als „Qualitätsgarant“ beim Stern eingeführt, um diesen Anspruch gewährleisten zu können. Verantwortlich für den Inhalt eines Textes im Stern ist zunächst der Autor oder die zuständige Ressortleitung. Ist eine Geschichte aber durch die Dokumentation abgesegnet worden, „teilen“ sich Autor und Dokumentationsredakteur die Verantwortung für etwaige Fehler, die erst nach der Veröffentlichung erkannt werden. Die Stern-Dokumentare sind keine Rechercheure für die Redakteure und Autoren. Sie konzentrieren sich ganz auf die Verifikation der Manuskripte. Die Erfahrung der Dokumentare mit unterschiedlichsten Quellen wird aber immer wieder gern von den Autoren genutzt, um Tipps für die eigene Recherche einzuholen.

Der organisatorische Ablauf der Arbeit in der Stern-Dokumentation sieht in der Regel wie folgt aus: Die Mitarbeiter lesen den Text nachdem er von den Textchefs bearbeitet und abgesegnet ist und versuchen zunächst, soweit möglich, alle Fakten ohne Hilfe des Autors zu belegen. Grundsätzlich wird Originalquellen der Vorzug vor Sekundärquellen gegeben, bei medizinischen Themen etwa der Originalveröffentlichung vor dem Zitat in einer nichtwissenschaftlichen Publikation. Die Autoren sind verpflichtet, eine so genannte „annotierte Fassung“ ihres Textes inklusive ihrer benutzten Quellen vorzulegen und der Dokumentation ihr gesamtes Recherchematerial zur Verfügung zu stellen. Nach einem Abgleich mit der „annotierten Fassung“ werden offene Fragen oder strittige Punkte im Gespräch zwischen Autor und Dokumentar geklärt, bei Nichterreichbarkeit des Autors mit dem zuständigen Redakteur oder Ressortleiter.
Im seltenen Fall, dass sich Dokumentation und Autor bei strittigen Punkten (Bewertung von Quellen) nicht einigen können, wird der zuständige Ressortleiter hinzugezogen. Beruht eine Geschichte in wesentlichen Elementen auf faktisch falschen oder nicht verifizierbaren Behauptungen, kann die Dokumentation dafür eintreten, diese nicht zu veröffentlichen. Dieser Fall tritt äußerst selten auf, da derartige Artikel fast immer schon durch frühere Kontrollinstanzen „gekippt“ werden.

Der technische Ablauf der Verifikation

Die Dokumentation arbeitet mit einem Papierausdruck der Texte, auf dem alle Veränderungen mit den Korrekturzeichen des Dudens schriftlich vermerkt werden. Ist der Verifikationsprozess abgeschlossen, so überträgt die Dokumentation die Änderungen in das Manuskript im elektronischen Redaktionssystem. Kleintexte wie Bildunterschriften bearbeitet die Dokumentation im Layoutausdruck nach der grafischen Abnahme. Auch hier werden Korrekturen in das elektronische Dokument übertragen. Die elektronischen Dokumente werden nach der Verifikation dem Lektorat zur weiteren Bearbeitung zugeleitet. Das Lektorat erhält auch die Papierversion, um einen Korrekturabgleich zu ermöglichen.
Die Dokumentation ist in den Räumen der Stern-Bibliothek angesiedelt, die von einer Bibliothekarin gepflegt wird und mehr als 25000 Bände umfasst. Damit verfügen die Mitarbeiter unmittelbar an ihrem Arbeitsplatz über wichtige Hauptwerkzeuge ihrer Arbeit. Neben den allgemeinen Nachschlagewerken enthält die Bibliothek viele Speziallexika, Fach- und Lehrbücher, aber auch klassische Werke der Belletristik. Die zentrale Pressedatenbank des Verlagshauses Gruner + Jahr ist eine weitere wichtige Quelle der Dokumentare. Der Zugriff erfolgt via Internetbrowser, darüber hinaus werden aber auch Rechercheaufträge an die Mitar-

beiter der Pressedatenbank vergeben. Außerdem hat jeder Dokumentar Zugriff auf die Meldungen der Presseagenturen. Einen immer größeren Stellenwert bei der Verifikationsarbeit hat das Internet durch seine vielfältigen Möglichkeiten des Zugriffs auf Originalquellen, wie etwa wissenschaftliche Veröffentlichungen, statistische Datenbanken, Homepages von Firmen, Instituten und Behörden. Darüber hinaus bietet es die Möglichkeit schneller Anfragen per E-Mail, etwa bei Pressestellen von Behörden.
Zunächst richten die Dokumentare ihr Augenmerk auf Schreibweisen, etwa von Personennamen oder geografischen Begriffen, auf Zahlen und Daten sowie die korrekte Wiedergabe von Zitaten usw. Aber auch komplexe Zusammenhänge, chronologische Abfolgen, Plausibilität und Logik werden überprüft. Dabei gilt es, wenn möglich, stets mehrere Quellen zu Rate zu ziehen. Denn eine allein, mag sie noch so glaubwürdig erscheinen, führt leicht in die Irre, wie das folgende Beispiel zeigt:

Das Mehrere-Quellen-Prinzip: Ein Beispiel

In einem Beitrag über den italienischen Unternehmer Giovanni Agnelli verweist der Autor auf dessen Amtszeit im römischen Parlament. Als Quelle gibt der Autor dem Dokumentar das Munzinger-Archiv an, ein ausführliches Personenarchiv zu vielen gesellschaftlich relevanten Bereichen. Diverse Artikel aus der zentralen Pressedatenbank von Gruner + Jahr decken sich nicht mit dieser Angabe, selbst Artikel aus dem betreffenden Jahr erwähnen nicht einmal eine Kandidatur Agnellis. Ein Vergleich mit anderen Artikeln macht deutlich: Giovannis Bruder Umberto Agnelli war Abgeordneter im römischen Parlament. Das von Autoren gern verwendete Munzinger-Archiv macht also eine falsche Angabe, die sich erst durch weitere Quellen entlarven lässt. Inzwischen ist dieser Fehler im Archiv korrigiert.

Einer der wichtigen Aspekte der redaktionellen Verifikation ist das Überprüfen von Zitaten. Zitate aus der Literatur oder Weltgeschichte lassen sich zumeist mit den Handbüchern der Stern-Bibliothek oder den Quellen der Autoren belegen. Für persönlich eingeholte Zitate muss der Autor selbst einen Beleg erbringen, etwa eine Mitschrift oder einen Bandmitschnitt. Üblich ist beim Stern die Autorisierung durch den Zitatgeber. Auch die autorisierten Interviews werden verifiziert. Wichtig ist zunächst die Überprüfung der Fakten in den Fragen des Interviewers. Aber auch die Aussagen der interviewten Person werden, soweit möglich, überprüft. Behauptet der Befragte etwas eindeutig Falsches, so ist es die Aufgabe des Autors, dies mit dem Interviewten zu klären.

Die Zusammenarbeit mit den Autoren schätzen die Dokumentationsredakteure als grundsätzlich gut ein. Sie ist in den meisten Fällen sehr kollegial. Problematisch ist es, wenn neue Mitarbeiter oder Autoren, die nur selten für den Stern tätig sind, von ihrem zuständigen Ressort nicht ausdrücklich auf die Abläufe des Verifikationsprozesses hingewiesen werden. Dann betrachten manche Autoren die Arbeit der Dokumentation als „Überprüfung“ ihrer Arbeit und fühlen sich „kontrolliert“. Überwiegend wird die Arbeit der Dokumentation von den Autoren jedoch geschätzt. Die Verifikation ist für sie eine wichtige Hilfestellung, um die Qualität ihrer Arbeit zu sichern.
Um gelegentliche Konflikte zwischen der „Formulierungsliebe“ eines Autors und der „Faktenliebe“ des Dokumentars aufzulösen ist Erfahrung gefragt, dazu oft Diplomatie und die Geschicklichkeit des Dokumentars, Kompromissformulierungen zu finden, die beiden Anforderungen genügen. So kann dann sogar manche gefährdete Pointe gerettet werden.

Arno Nehlsen

Fact-Checking bei „GEO“

Dr. Arno Nehlsen leitete von 1985 bis 2009 die Abteilung „Dokumentation und Verifikation“ beim Reportagemagazin GEO in Hamburg. Der promovierte Physiker arbeitet heute als freier Autor und Dokumentar.

Herr Nehlsen, was bedeutet Fact-Checking oder Verifikation bei GEO?

Nehlsen: Alle Texte, Bilder und Grafiken, die im monatlichen GEO oder den anderen Titeln der GEO-Gruppe erscheinen, werden vor dem Druck von Verifikateuren in einem eigenständigen Arbeitsschritt auf ihre sachliche Richtigkeit hin überprüft. Das ist der Vorgang der Verifikation. Das bedeutet aber nicht, dass der Verifikateur nur die Dinge in Frage stellt, die ihm seltsam vorkommen. Er recherchiert im Prinzip alles noch einmal neu, was sich objektivieren lässt, was also nicht subjektive Meinung des Autors ist. Aber die GEO-Verifikateure sind keine Philosophen, die wochenlang über der Wahrheit brüten. Das Ziel der Verifikation ist nicht die Wahrheit zu finden, sondern die Übereinstimmung mit einer Quelle, die der Verifikateur für zuverlässig und deshalb für wahr hält. Wahrheit können sich auch Journalisten nicht anmaßen.

Wie gehen die Verifikateure bei GEO vor?

Nehlsen: Die Autoren sind verpflichtet, den Verifikateuren alle verwendeten Quellen zur Verfügung zu stellen. Das gilt auch für externe Autoren. Sie sollten eine so genannte „annotierte Version" erstellen, also alle Fakten wie Namen, Zitate oder Zahlen im Text markieren und die Quellen als Fußnoten angeben. Diese annotierte Version bildet die Basis für die Arbeit der Verifikateure, die bei GEO auch Dokumentare oder kurz „Dokker" genannt werden. Die wesentliche Aufgabe der Verifikateure ist es, die Zuverlässigkeit dieser Quellen einzuschätzen und ihren Inhalt mit dem Manuskript zu vergleichen. Die Verifikateure gewinnen im Laufe der Zeit an Erfahrung, welchen Quellen sie vertrauen können und welchen eher nicht. Darüber hinaus gilt es, zu jeder Information möglichst noch eine weitere, unabhängige Quelle zu finden. Das gelingt nicht immer, weil die Informationen aus sehr speziellen Originalquellen wie wissenschaftlichen Studien stammen oder weil die Geschichten manchmal unter hohem Zeitdruck produziert werden. Beim Kindermagazin GEOlino bearbeitet ein Dokumentar etwa 20 Manuskripte im Monat.

Nach welchen Fehlern halten die GEO-Verifikateure Ausschau – und welche finden sie?

Nehlsen: Am häufigsten sind Fehler in der Schreibweise. Das bedeutet nicht, dass die Schreibweise unbedingt falsch ist – oftmals entspricht sie einfach nicht der Konvention, auf die man sich in der GEO-Redaktion geeinigt hat. Manchmal stammen Angaben aus Quellen, die wir nicht akzeptieren, weil sie notorisch fehlerhaft sind. Dann müssen valide Quellen gefunden werden, oder die Informationen gänzlich gestrichen werden. Auch Verständnisfehler sind nicht selten. Denn die wissenschaftliche Grundlage vieler GEO-Geschichten ist nicht einfach zu verstehen, so dass auf dem Weg der journalistischen Vereinfachung Transformationsfehler entstehen. Bei besonders schwierigen Geschichten holen die Dokumentare externen Rat ein. Denn man kann einen Text vom ersten bis zum letzten Fakt verifizieren, und er kann trotzdem völliger Blödsinn sein. Jedes einzelne Fakt mag richtig sein, doch die Gesamtaussage, der große Zusammenhang, ist falsch. Problematisch sind immer die bei Journalisten so beliebten Superlative. Da heißt es dann etwa: „Keine andere Millionenstadt“ oder „Auch der beste Geometrie-Experte schafft es nicht“. Um einen Superlativ zu verifizieren muss man – im Prinzip – alle denkbaren anderen Fälle ausschließen.

Welche Fähigkeiten sind bei der Verifikation besonders hilfreich?

Nehlsen: Man muss eine gewisse Terrier-Mentalität haben. Man muss die Fakten wirklich recherchieren, dabei hartnäckig bleiben, und, wenn erforderlich, sich in eine Frage verbeißen, nicht nachlassen und nicht einfach glauben, es wird schon stimmen – selbst wenn der Chef vom Dienst mit den Druckterminen im Nacken sitzt. Der Dokumentar ist die letzte Tatsacheninstanz, auf die die Redaktion und der verantwortliche Chefredakteur sich verlassen. Und ein Dokumentar sollte skeptisch sein. Die eigene Skepsis ist das wichtigste Werkzeug dieser Arbeit. Aus der Sichtweise und der Erfahrung des Verifikateurs machen alle, aber auch wirklich alle Menschen Fehler. Natürlich auch er selbst. Diese permanente Skepsis ist psychisch nicht ganz einfach. Es ist leichter zu sagen „Das klingt einleuchtend“, als ständig zu sagen „Das glaube ich nicht.“ Es ist wirklich anstrengend, immer nur „nein“ zu sagen. Um das ein wenig zu kompensieren, empfehle ich jedem in diesem Beruf von Zeit zu Zeit selbst zu schreiben und das Ergebnis verifizieren zu lassen. Ich gebe mein Wort darauf, dass die Verifikateure Fehler finden werden.
Anfänger haben manchmal Furcht, Fehler zu übersehen oder zu machen. Sie neigen deshalb dazu, Geschichten „überzudokumentieren“, also den Blick für Wesentliches und Unwesentliches zu verlieren. Im Laufe der Zeit gewinnt man an Intuition. Man entwickelt ein Gespür dafür, wann es sich lohnt, einem Problem lange nachzugehen. Jeder Verifikateur kann von so einem „siebten Sinn“ für Fehler berichten.

Meinen Sie, dass Verifikateure auch journalistische Kompetenzen benötigen?

Nehlsen: Bei GEO gehört das zum Profil der Verifikateure, denn die Autoren und Redakteure erwarten das. Es reicht nicht nur zu sagen: „Das ist falsch und das wäre richtig.“ Dokumentare müssen auch bereit und fähig sein, notwendige Korrekturen im Kontext und Stil des ganzen Manuskripts zu formulieren. Sie müssen also auch ein Gefühl für Sprache haben, für die Dramaturgie eines Textes, um zu verstehen, warum ein Autor einen Satz genau so geschrieben hat und nicht anders. Und sie müssen ein Gespür dafür haben, wo Journalismus aufhört – wann man bei der Recherche zum Ergebnis kommen muss, weil am Ende ein verständlicher Zeitschriftentext und keine wissenschaftliche Arbeit stehen soll.

Wie gestaltet sich die Zusammenarbeit zwischen Autoren und Verifikateuren?

Nehlsen: Gut, auch wenn man eigentlich erwarten sollte, dass es Konflikte zwischen den Autoren und Verifikateuren gibt, bleiben diese meist aus. Trotzdem ist manchmal Taktik gefragt: Wenn ein Autor einmal nicht besonders einsichtig ist, sollte der Dokker ihn zunächst auf die Dinge hinweisen, die in seiner Geschichte wirklich grob falsch sind. Danach ist der Autor sicherlich etwas zahmer. Aber in der Regel ist das gar nicht nötig. Denn letztendlich ist klar: Die Verifikationsarbeit verbessert die Geschichten, zumindest hinsichtlich ihrer Fakten.

Haben Sie den Eindruck, dass auch die Leser die Verifikationsarbeit wahrnehmen?

Nehlsen: Nein, das muss auch nicht sein. Das verhält sich wie in der Autoindustrie: Da denkt man als Käufer bestenfalls daran, wie das Auto gebaut wird. Aber nicht daran, dass die Endmontage noch einmal überprüft wird.

Katja Ploch (l.) und Victoria Strathon (r.)

Katja Ploch / Victoria Strathon

Fact-Checking bei „brand eins“

Katja Ploch ist Diplom-Kauffrau und absolvierte eine Trainee-Ausbildung in der Spiegel-Dokumentation bevor sie neben freien Aufträgen für verschiedene Verlage im Print- und Corporate-Publishing-Bereich als Dokumentationsjournalistin die Recherche und Verifikation für Econy, den Vorläufer von brand eins, übernahm.
Victoria Strathon studierte Bibliotheks- und Informationswesen und arbeitete in der Informationsabteilung des Hamburger Welt-Weltwirtschafts-Archivs (HWWA) sowie als freie Dokumentarin für verschiedene Verlage. Zusammen bilden Ploch und Strathon seit der Gründung 1999 die Dokumentation des Wirtschaftsmagazins brand eins.

Brand eins ist das Wirtschaftsmagazin, das Veränderungen zum Thema macht. Wir suchen in Wirtschaft, Gesellschaft und Kultur nach Anzeichen einer neuen Zeit, nach Menschen und Unternehmen, die sich der Zukunft stellen. Brand eins will Wirtschaft verständlich machen und sucht nach Zusammenhängen und Hintergründen. Wir werfen einen etwas anderen Blick auf Erfolge und Misserfolge gleichermaßen. brand eins will nützlich sein, nicht durch Tabellen und Checklisten, sondern durch Geschichten, die auf Ideen bringen und die zeigen, was Menschen bewegt. brand eins will die Bruchstellen aufzeigen, die sich beim Übergang vom Informations- zum Wissenszeitalter ergeben, und liefert Vorlagen, Ideen und Konzepte für alle, die diesen Wandel aktiv vorantreiben wollen oder von ihm berührt werden.
Gerade weil wir uns auch erlauben, unternehmerische Leistung gut zu finden, ist die redaktionelle Unabhängigkeit unser höchster Wert. brand eins ist ein unabhängiges Unternehmen mit einer kleinen, aber leidenschaftlichen Redaktion und unabhängigen freien Mitarbeitern, die unsere Werte teilen. brand eins will fair und glaubwürdig sein. Der brand eins-Leser entwickelt eine Beziehung – zum Magazin und zur Redaktion. Der Anspruch, der aus dieser Beziehung erwächst, ist hoch, aber er ist das Fundament, auf dem wir stehen. Deshalb gehört bei brand eins eine verifizierende Dokumentation zum redaktionellen Prozess.
Die Dokumentation arbeitet bereits bei der Ideenfindung eng mit der Redaktion zusammen. Dazu gehört auch die Prüfung von Themenvorschlägen von externen Autoren: Inwieweit wurde bereits über dieses Thema in anderen Medien berichtet? Handelt es sich um ein exklusives Angebot? Zusammenstellungen von Presse-Dossiers zur Vorbereitung auf Themen und Gesprächspartner für die internen und externen Kollegen sind ein wichtiger Bestandteil der Dokumentationsarbeit. Pauschale umfangreiche Dossieranfragen oder unklare Weitwürfe für ein Thema sind aber weder für den Autor hilfreich, noch für den Dokumentar machbar.
Denn die wichtigste Aufgabe der Dokumentation ist die Arbeit am Manuskript. Grundsätzlich ist es die Pflicht der Dokumentation, alle Fakten eines Beitrages einzeln zu prüfen. Dafür stehen der Dokumentation verschiedene Hilfsmittel wie Datenbanken, Internet oder Bücher zur Verfügung. Eine einheitliche Formalie hat sich dabei als sinnvoll erwiesen. Es wird unterschieden zwischen: noch offen, richtig, falsch, wahrscheinlich und nicht festzustellen.
Es wird nicht Zeile für Zeile fortlaufend verifiziert, sondern nach Fakten und Sachverhalten. Dies gilt vorrangig für Namen, Alter, berufliche Funktionen, geografische Angaben oder mathematische Rechnungen. Meinungen, Spekulationen und Schätzungen werden zweitrangig behandelt. Wenn mehrere Sachverhalte in einer Zeile der Manuskript-Fahne stehen, so wird die Zeile als geprüft abgehakt, wenn der letzte Sachverhalt überprüft wurde. Korrekturen sind mit den

üblichen Korrekturzeichen auszuführen. Wenn ein Fakt nicht mit einem „normalen“ Rechercheaufwand zu finden ist, so ist die Quelle anzugeben. In seltenen Fällen sind zusätzliche (erklärende) Randnotizen vorzunehmen. So profitieren auch die Redakteure und Autoren von der Recherchearbeit der Dokumentare. „Journalisten können von der Dokumentation den Wert einer zweiten Quelle lernen und eine professionelle Skepsis gegenüber allem und jedem", sagt Jens Bergmann, Geschäftsführender Textredakteur des Magazins: „Fact-Checking ist wie ein Besuch beim Zahnarzt: Besser man geht regelmäßig hin, denn wie die Zahl der Löcher ist die Zahl der Fehler meist höher als gedacht“.
Grundsätzlich gilt: Zur Erst-Verifikation sind andere (wenn möglich bessere oder aktuellere Quellen) heranzuziehen als jene, die der Autor verwendet hat. Zwar ist es auch Aufgabe der Dokumentation, die Unterlagen des Autors mit den Angaben im Text zu vergleichen. Das bloße Feststellen, ob der Autor richtig gelesen hat, ist aber noch keine Verifikation. Vor allem gilt es dabei, die benutzten Quellen erneut kritisch zu lesen und zu überprüfen, ob in ihnen selbst nicht bereits Fehler enthalten sind. Erst dabei entfaltet sich der Wert der Verifikation, des zusätzlichen Kontrollblicks.
Widersprechen die Quellen des Dokumentars inhaltlich wesentlich denen des Autors, so muss dieses Problem unmittelbar mit dem Autor besprochen werden. Unbestrittene Korrekturen wie falsche Schreibweisen nimmt der Dokumentar jedoch allein verantwortlich vor. In jedem Falle legt der Dokumentar seine Recherchelücken gegenüber dem Autor in einem gemeinsamen Gespräch dar. Dann ist der Autor grundsätzlich in der Pflicht, die offenen Fragen zu beantworten.
Als verifiziert gilt schließlich, was mit zuverlässigen Quellen belegt ist. Dies liegt in der Verantwortung der Dokumentation. Deshalb ist es auch die Aufgabe der Dokumentation, Leserbriefe zu beantworten, die sich auf Fakten oder konkrete Quellen beziehen.
Zeichnet der Autor nach dem Gespräch mit der Dokumentation für einzelne Sachverhalte oder Passagen ausnahmsweise allein verantwortlich, so markiert die Dokumentation diese als „Nicht festzustellen“. Dies kann etwa für Informationen von oder über Informanten und Protagonisten einer Geschichte gelten. Denn die Dokumentation befragt diese grundsätzlich NICHT nochmals. Etwaige Nachfragen obliegen allein dem Autor, genauso die Abstimmung aller Zitate.
Eine fundierte Dokumentationsleistung bedeutet nicht, dass der Dokumentar grundsätzlich alles infrage stellt. Es bedeutet, eine selbstständig denkende und handelnde Arbeitsweise zu entwickeln, sich dabei aber nicht für den „eigentlich besseren Journalisten“ zu halten. Wir Dokumentare wollen die schreibenden Kollegen nicht beim Fehlermachen erwischen, denn das ist das erklärte, gemeinsame Ziel. Es gibt keine Geschichten ohne Fehler. Je nach Art der Geschichte können

es bis zu zehn Fehler pro Seite sein, wobei eine Reise-Reportage aufgrund einer geringeren Faktendichte für die Dokumentation weniger recherchеaufwendig sein kann als ein Branchenreport. Typische Fehler sind falsche (Vor-)Namen, Schreibweisen, Altersangaben, Umrechnungsfehler, Übersetzungen oder Verwechslungen bzw. Zahlendreher. Aber mitunter sind die Fehlerquellen weniger offensichtlich. Daher muss die Dokumentation auch stets fragen: Stimmen die Zeitbezüge innerhalb des Textes? Enthält der Text innere Widersprüche? Stimmen die Zitate nach Wort und Sinn? Wie steht es um die Aktualität und Seriosität der Quellen? Hält ein Superlativ oder ein Vergleich einer Prüfung stand?
Bei Interviews und Gesprächen sind die Fragen sorgfältig zu prüfen. Die Aussagen des Interviewten werden vornehmlich nach Fehlern durchsucht, die aus Fairness berichtigt werden müssen, zum Beispiel wenn sich der Interviewpartner falsch an ein Datum erinnert oder wenn er grob fahrlässig die Wahrheit beugen sollte, um so seine Argumentation zu stützen.
Hat das Manuskript die Dokumentation passiert, so arbeiten die Redaktion und die Schlussredaktion Korrekturen in den Text ein. Doch die Arbeit der Dokumentation ist dann noch nicht zuende: In einem weiteren Arbeitsschritt kontrolliert sie, ob alle Korrekturen richtig übernommen wurden oder neue Passagen eingefügt wurden. Überschriften, Vorspänne, Randspalten und Bildunterschriften werden im Layout geprüft. Die Arbeitsbelastung der Dokumentation ist während der Produktionsphase hoch. Dann bleiben für die Verifikation oftmals nur wenige Stunden. Bei aller Kontrolle und Sorgfalt: Dokumentare sind auch nur Menschen und trotz aller Gründlichkeit rutscht, besonders unter Zeitdruck, manchmal ein Fehler durch. Doch wichtiger ist, dass die Dokumentation tatsächlich Fehler ausmerzt, bevor sie ein Leser im Blatt entdeckt. Harald Willenbrock, Autor bei brand eins, sagt über die Dokumentation: „Man verlässt sich auf sie. Und wenn man dann für Andere schreibt, die keine Dokumentation beschäftigen, ist das wie ein Absprung aus dem Flugzeug, bei dem man erst kurz vor dem Aufprall merkt, dass man dieses Mal gar keinen Fallschirm dabei hatte: Schmerzhaft." Damit die Arbeit ohne Dokumentation nicht allzu folgenreich ist, sollte man sich beim Schreiben und Korrigieren nach unserer Erfahrung stets folgende Fragen stellen – und auch beantworten:

Habe ich mindestens zwei unabhängige Quellen für einen Fakt vorliegen?
Sind die Quellen glaubwürdig?
Stammen die Informationen aus erster oder zweiter Hand?
Wer hat was erzählt und aus welchem Grund?
Was sagt die Konkurrenz oder Gegenseite dazu?
Sind die Informationen glaubhaft oder klingen sie nur gut?

Die Sicht der Kontrollierten:
Autoren von brand eins über ihre Erfahrungen mit der Dokumentation

„Es ist gut, dass es eine Instanz im Produktionsprozess gibt, die Fehler sucht und Schlimmeres verhindert, nicht nur für den Leser und den Autor, sondern auch für den inhaltlich Betroffenen. Wenn Verlage an der Sorgfalt im Umgang mit Fakten sparen, muss es einen nicht wundern, dass die Zukunft unseres Berufstandes öffentlich infrage gestellt wird. Der Wettbewerb wird weniger denn je auf dem Feld der Informationsbereitstellung entschieden werden, sondern bei Richtigkeit und Relevanz.
Eine „Garantie“ auf journalistische Qualität kann es jedenfalls nur mit einer Dokumentationsabteilung geben.“
(Bernhard Bartsch)

„Die Dokumentation macht die Texte besser, weil vom Autor aus falschen Fakten ebenso falsche Schlüsse gezogen werden können. Natürlich ist es unangenehm bei seinen Schwächen erwischt zu werden, doch bei brand eins fühle ich mich als Autor stets respektiert. Nur Profis können die Orientierung in diesem Ozean aus – nicht selten widersprüchlichen, voneinander abweichenden – Informationen behalten. Ich brauche die Dokumentation, weil sie meinen Texten hilft und weil sie dadurch meine Glaubwürdigkeit als Autor stärkt“
(Gerhard Waldherr)

„Ich brauche die Dokumentation, die selbst einfache, aber dafür doppelt so peinliche Fehler findet und behebt und weil ich erst einmal überhaupt wissen muss, dass ich einen Fehler gemacht habe. Diesen kann ich dann selber nachschlagen und beheben. Besser von der Dokumentation verbessert werden als von tausenden von Lesern und Kollegen. Man fühlt sich als Autor wunderbar.“
(Steffan Heuer)

„Warum schaffen es Autoren nicht, die absolute Sicherheit der Faktenlage zu garantieren? Neben einem Berg von Material, von dem nur ein Bruchteil Verwendung findet, stehen wir unter dem Eindruck des persönlich Erlebten, der bunten Broschüren und den fachlichen Gesprächen. Danach tritt der Entstehungsprozess des Textes in den Vordergrund. Da die Faktenlage nun nicht noch ein weiteres Mal geprüft wird, ist eine neutrale Sicht darauf hilfreich.“
(Dirk Böttcher)

RECHERCHE-JOURNALISMUS UND KRITISCHE MEDIENPOLITIK

Sven Preger
Mangelware Recherche
176 S., 9,90 €, br.,
ISBN 3-8258-8254-3

Ilona Wuschig
Anspruch ohne Wirklichkeit
15 Jahre Medien in Ostdeutschland
Die deutsch-deutsche Medienwelt ist im Jahr 15 Jahr nach der Einheit geteilt: Der Westen liest „Spiegel" und guckt „Tagesschau"; der Osten „Super-Illu" und „blitz". Die Chefredaktionen sitzen im Westen. Gesamtdeutschland nutzt die Erfahrungen von Ostdeutschen mit zwei Systemen, mit gesellschaftlichen Wandlungsprozessen nicht. Die Folge: Die Zufriedenheit mit der Staatsform Demokratie in Ostdeutschland nimmt ab!. Wie muss politische Kommunikation aussehen, damit beide Deutschlands die anstehenden Probleme diskutieren und angehen? Was ist falsch gelaufen im medialen Einigungsprozess? Und wie lässt sich eine funktionierende deutsch-deutsche Öffentlichkeit herstellen?
304 S., 29,90 €, br.,
ISBN 3-8258-9059-7

Julia Bönisch
Meinungsführer oder Populärmedium?
Das journalistische Profil von *Spiegel Online*
192 S., 12,90 €, br.,
ISBN 3-8258-9379-0

Matthias Armborst
Kopfjäger im Internet oder publizistische Avantgarde?
Was Journalisten über Weblogs und ihre Macher wissen sollten
264 S., 14,90 €, br.,
ISBN 3-8258-9633-1

Ingmar Cario
Die Deutschland-Ermittler
Investigativer Journalismus und die Methoden der Macher
Investigative Journalisten recherchierten in Deutschland bislang im Verborgenen. Dieses Buch gibt nun erstmals einen spannenden Einblick in die Methoden der Macher: Wie beschaffen sie sich interne Informationen und wie überprüfen sie diese? Wie schützen sie ihre Informanten und pflegen ihre Kontakte? Mit welcher Gegenwehr haben sie bei ihren Recherchen zu kämpfen? Befragt wurden investigative Journalisten unterschiedlicher Medien, die offen und ungeschminkt über ihre Arbeit berichten. Jeder kann nun von ihren Hinweisen und Erfahrungen lernen und diese auf die eigene Arbeit übertragen. Denn dieses Buch zeigt: Beim investigativen Journalismus kommt es weniger auf die berühmte Spürnase an als auf das richtige Handwerk, das erlernbar ist. Gleichzeitig macht es aber auch deutlich, wie schlecht die Bedingungen für investigative Recherchen in deutschen Redaktionen sind. Eine detaillierte Analyse auf der Grundlage der vorhandenen Literatur zeigt die Gründe für die Diskrepanz zwischen der großen Bedeutung des investigativen Journalismus und seinem geringen Stellenwert im deutschen Mediensystem. Dieses Buch ist mehr als nur eine wissenschaftliche Studie, es hat den Nutzwert eines Handbuchs: Ein Buch, das Einblicke in die Werkstatt von professionellen Recherche-Journalisten gibt. Ein Buch für alle, die wissen möchten, wie kritischer Journalismus funktioniert. Ein Buch, das zeigt, dass kritischer Journalismus die Voraussetzung für eine lebendige Demokratie ist.
248 S., 14,90 €, br.,
ISBN 3-8258-0080-6

Torsten Schäfer

Problemfeld Ausland: Fakten finden „am anderen Ende der Welt“

Torsten Schäfer studierte Journalistik und Politikwissenschaft sowie European Studies in Dortmund, Tours, Brüssel und Aachen. Seit Anfang 2009 arbeitet er als Redakteur bei GEO International. Zuvor war er freier Online-Redakteur bei der Deutschen Welle und Autor zu EU- und Umweltthemen für GEO, Süddeutsche Zeitung, taz, dpa. Als Dozent an Akademien und Hochschulen lehrt er Recherche und EU-Berichterstattung. Auf seinem Blog berichtet er regelmäßig zu diesen Themen: www.euroreporter.de

Auslandsberichterstattung steht in dem wenig rühmlichen Ruf, zumeist eine negative Perspektive zu vermitteln: Konflikt und Krise haben generell einen höheren Nachrichtenwert als positive Nachrichten. Mainzer Forscher haben mit Inhaltsanalysen zum Beispiel eine deutlich negative Perspektive in der Auslandsberichterstattung der großen Informationslieferanten, von dpa und AP, nachgewiesen (vgl. Wilke/Rosenberger 1991: 193). Und der frühere Leiter der dpa-Auslandsredaktion Gerd Rainer Neu erklärt den Negativmechanismus mit den Nachrichtenkriterien „Krieg", „Krisen", „Katastrophen", die für Agenturen und andere Medien besonders wichtig seien (vgl. Neu 2001: 18).

Auslandsberichterstattung ist darüber hinaus durch ihre Zentrierung auf Politik und die Fixierung auf Entscheidungseliten gekennzeichnet. Die Folge der Konzentration auf politische Eliten ist eine starke Personalisierung. Soziale und kulturelle Gruppen, politische Parteien und die Bevölkerung werden vernachlässigt. Inhaltsanalysen bestätigen wiederum für die Agenturberichterstattung die besondere Betonung der politischen Exekutive (vgl. Harseim/Wilke 2000: 107; Wilke/Rosenberger 1991: 183).

Ein weiterer Kritikpunkt ist die Vernachlässigung von Zusammenhängen und Hintergründen, die Kai Hafez als „Dekontextualisierung" bezeichnet. Der Kommunikationswissenschaftler führt die Kontextdefizite auf Raum- und Zeitvorgaben, die inhaltliche Steuerung der Berichterstattung durch Öffentlichkeitsarbeit sowie mangelndes Sachwissen der Journalisten zurück (vgl. Hafez 2002: 67). Besonders deutlich tritt in der Auslandsberichterstattung die mediale Fixierung auf die eigene geographische Herkunft hervor. Der Kommunikationswissenschaftler Winfried Schulz fand etwa heraus, dass das wichtigste Kriterium in der Auslandsberichterstattung der Faktor „Nähe" in Gestalt des Deutschlandbezuges ist (vgl. Schulz 1990: 116). Die mediale Aufmerksamkeit richtet sich danach vor allem auf Westeuropa und Nordamerika. Finanzkräftige Länder wie die USA, Frankreich, Deutschland und Großbritannien finden die meiste Beachtung. Wirtschaftsmacht wird somit zum weiteren bedeutenden Selektionskriterium (vgl. Schulz 1983: 283 ff.).

Schulz' Analysen der Auslandsberichterstattung von zehn deutschen Fernseh- und Rundfunksendern sowie Tageszeitungen geben einen Überblick über die Eigenschaften der Berichterstattung: Demnach kommen besonders die Nachrichtenfaktoren Thematisierung (Etablierung eines Themas), persönlicher Einfluss (Präsenz bekannter Politiker), Struktur (Komplexität und Überschaubarkeit), Relevanz (im Sinne von Betroffenheit), Nähe zu Deutschland bzw. Ethnozentrismus (Bezug auf eigene Bevölkerung) sowie politischer Erfolg in der Auslandsberichterstattung zum Tragen (vgl. Schulz 1990: 83 ff.).

Auslandsrecherche in der Heimat

Die ökonomischen Bedingungen haben sich in der Auslandsberichterstattung seit den 1980er Jahren verschlechtert. Die hohe Kostenintensität hat bei gleichzeitig abnehmendem Publikumsinteresse medienübergreifend zur Verringerung von Sendezeiten und Artikellängen geführt. In dieser Zeit kam es zu einer Kostenexplosion in der Auslandsberichterstattung, die einen Konzentrations- und Schrumpfungsprozess nach sich zog (vgl. Fischer 1982: 45). Diese Entwicklung setzte sich fort: Der Journalist Lutz Mükke stellte in einer Befragung von deutschen Afrika-Korrespondenten fest, dass Sparzwänge in Form von Platz- und Sendezeitlimits sowie Unterbesetzungen der Redaktion die Arbeit der Journalisten bedeutend einschränken (vgl. Mükke 2003: 84). Kommerzielle Überlegungen haben besonders beim Privatfernsehen dazu geführt, die Auslandsberichterstattung im Programm zu vernachlässigen, wie Miriam Meckel nachwies. Aber auch beim öffentlich-rechtlichen Rundfunk gab es Einschnitte in diesem Bereich (vgl. Meckel 1998: 268).

Darüber hinaus hat das Publikumsinteresse an Auslandsnachrichten seit dem Ende der 1980er Jahre generell abgenommen (vgl. Zschunke 2000: 92; Hafez 2002: 92). Der Soziologe Jürgen Gerhards weist in seiner Langzeitanalyse der Berichterstattung dreier deutscher Qualitätszeitungen nach, dass sich das Interesse an internationalen Themen Mitte der 1990er Jahre nach einer Zunahme mit dem Ende des Kalten Krieges auf das Niveau der 1950er Jahre zurückentwickelte (vgl. Gerhards 2000: 295).

Das beschriebene Desinteresse der Leserschaft an Auslandsthemen und die hohen Kosten der Auslandsberichterstattung haben in den ökonomisch prekären Zeiten seit 2000 ferner dazu geführt, dass Reiseetats in vielen Redaktionen zusammengestrichen wurden. Nicht nur wird also öfter auf einen Korrespondenten verzichtet, auch Rechercheeisen von Fachredakteuren aus der Redaktion werden reduziert.

Insgesamt ergibt sich daraus ein Trend, Auslandsrecherchen immer öfter aus der eigenen Redaktion heraus zu betreiben. Dabei wird eine örtliche Nähe suggeriert, die es faktisch gar nicht gibt. Das Gros der Leser geht davon aus, dass die Kompetenz der Redaktionen ein spezielles Wissen um die Verhältnisse vor Ort mit einschließt, und dass Journalisten also über einen fremden Ort berichten, weil sie ihn aus eigener Anschauung kennen oder zumindest tiefergehend die Verhältnisse vor Ort recherchiert haben.

Doch ist dies immer der Fall? Ist die Auslandsrecherche nicht auch ein „falsches Spiel", da sie geografische Kompetenz und Nähe suggeriert, diese oft aber nicht einlösen kann, da für Korrespondenteneinsätze, Reisen oder lange Recherchen in

der Heimatredaktion die Ressourcen fehlen? Die Arbeitsprozesse in den Redaktionen haben sich vielerorts durch Personalkürzungen und Etateinsparungen so verdichtet, dass gründliches Recherchieren allgemein schon zum Luxus wird. Die Auslandsrecherche, die schon allein durch Sprachbarrieren und Zeitunterschiede kompliziert wird, leidet unter den verschärften Bedingungen besonders. Dies hat auch der Fall „Bluewater“ gezeigt, bei dem der Regisseur Jan Henrik Stahlberg im Jahr 2005 den deutschen Journalismus vorgeführt hat. Es war Auslandsrecherche unter Zeitdruck, die hier misslang! Bei der Berichterstattung über ein deutsches Thema wäre die Inszenierung wohl schnell aufgeflogen. Gerade die Auslandsrecherche unterliegt also der Gefahr, dass sie zu schnell vermeintlich glaubwürdigen Onlinequellen vertraut. Dabei kann deren Glaubwürdigkeit oft schlechter eingeschätzt werden als die inländischer Quellen.
Aufgrund der oben beschriebenen Tendenzen geraten immer mehr Redakteure in derlei Situationen: Sie müssen Texte schreiben, die früher ein Korrespondent lieferte, oder aber über Themen berichten, die zuvor der Auslandsredakteur bearbeitete. Sie verrichten eine Arbeit, die in Redaktionen von Auslandsmedien wie etwa der Deutschen Welle ständig geschieht: Recherchieren am anderen Ende der Welt von Deutschland aus. Zwar berichten auch oder gerade für Auslandssender oft Korrespondenten, doch aufgrund der speziellen Ausrichtung auf andere Länder gehört die Berichterstattung über das dortige Geschehen zum klassischen Tagesgeschäft in der Redaktion. Das ändert nichts am grundlegenden Problem: Die Auslandsrecherche wird durch die fehlende Vor-Ort-Präsenz immer ein Stück weit ein „falsches Spiel“ bleiben. Lösbar sind aber in der Praxis auftretende, konkrete Probleme: Wo finde ich schnell Ansprechpartner zur wirtschaftlichen Lage in Armenien? Wie kann ich aktuell eine Nichtregierungsorganisation in Mali kontaktieren? Wo kann ich mich über die Parteien in Moldawien informieren? Folgende Quellen können Zugang zu Experten, Daten und Zahlen ermöglichen. Die Liste ist keineswegs vollständig, weshalb sie auf dem Blog www.euroreporter.de ständig fortgeschrieben wird.

Einige Quellen zur Auslandsrecherche

Länderdaten und -beschreibungen
- Länderportraits des Bundesaußenministeriums (Beachtung der dort angegebenen Links!)
- CIA-Factbook (Freizugängliche Daten jeglicher Art)
- Index-Mundi (Quelle ist CIA-Book; Fokus u. a. auf Energie, Ernährung)
- Laenderdaten.de (Quelle ist auch das Factbook)
- Fachinformationsverbund Länderkunde (Literatur, Studien)

Experten / NGOs finden
- Laenderkontakte.de
- Kooperation International (Bundesforschungsministerium)
- Idealist.org (NGO-Suche)
- Expertennetzwerk der Deutschen Welle (Journalisten)
- Länder-Parlamentariergruppen im Bundestag

Think Tanks / Stiftungen
- Stiftung Wissenschaft und Politik
- Deutsche Gesellschaft für Auswärtige Politik
- Friedrich-Ebert-Stiftung (Auslandsbüros)
- Konrad-Adenauer-Stiftung International
- Friedrich-Naumann-Stiftung (Ausland)
- Heinrich-Böll-Stiftung (Ausland)
- Hanns-Seidel-Stiftung (Ausland)

Wirtschaft
- Länderberichte der Bundesagentur für Außenwirtschaft
- Gesellschaft für Technische Zusammenarbeit
- Deutsche Außenhandelskammern: Links mit aktuellen Wirtschaftsdaten
- Kreditanstalt für Wiederaufbau (Länderinformationen)
- Economist-Research
- National Bureau of Economic Research (USA)

Fokus Europa: Besondere Probleme bei der EU-Recherche

Obwohl die Europäische Union (EU) einen Großteil der deutschen Rechtsrealität beeinflusst und somit vor allem ein maßgeblicher innenpolitischer Faktor ist, wird sie in manchen Redaktionen noch wie klassische Außenpolitik behandelt. Für viele Redakteure ist die Thematik an sich so sperrig und fremd, dass ihnen bisweilen klassische Auslandsthemen wie der Nahe Osten oder die USA vertrauter sind. Der unübersichtliche Gesetzgebungsprozess, der lange Zeitverzug bis zur Umsetzung der EU-Vorgaben in deutsches Recht, eine teils schlechte Pressearbeit und eine bisweilen bizarre Fachsprache („Eurospeak“) erschweren die Berichterstattung. Auch das generell eher negative Image der EU verhindert, dass sich Journalisten für sie interessieren. Die Dissertation des Verfassers zur regionalen EU-Berichterstattung, die auf einer Befragung in 24 Redaktionen basiert, zeigt, wie schwierig die Europarecherche für deutsche Redakteure ist – und wo die Fallstricke in der Praxis liegen. Ein Problem betrifft direkt das Fact-Checking: Durch fehlendes Fachwissen über die EU-Gesetzgebung und das politische System der Union bleibt die Überprüfung europapolitischer Aussagen von – teils ebenfalls wenig sachkundigen – Landespolitikern oder Wirtschaftsvertretern aus. Wissensdefizite, Zeitmangel und ein zu großes Vertrauen gegenüber den regionalen Politikern führen dazu, dass Journalisten nicht bei EU-Stellen anrufen, um Aussagen zu kontrollieren. Ein fast unbegreifliches Hindernis hierfür ist die teilweise Sperrung der Telefone von Lokalredakteuren für Auslandsgespräche.

Ein hilfreiches Rechercheinstrument sind Online-Fachportale zur EU-Politik. Sie werden in den Redaktionen aber nur sehr selten für die Recherche oder Hintergrundinformation genutzt. Oft sind die Dienste gar nicht bekannt. Der nützlichste Dienst wird mit am seltensten genutzt: Das Portal „EU for journalists", das eigens als umfassende Hilfe für die EU-Berichterstattung von Redaktionen außerhalb Brüssels konzipiert ist, findet kaum Beachtung.

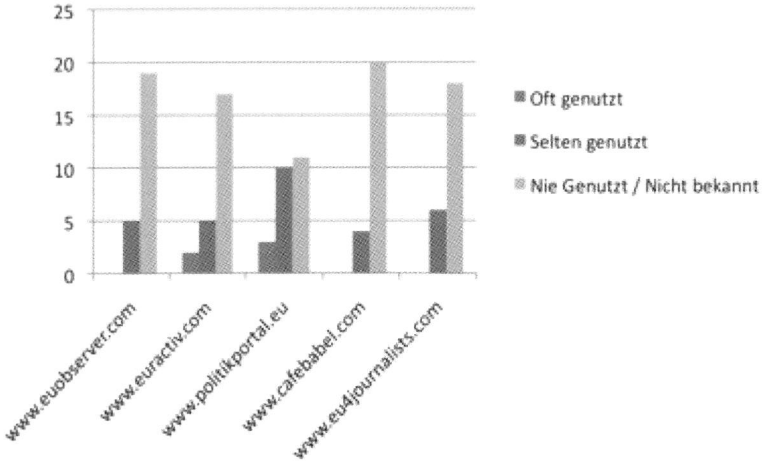

Abbildung 1: Nutzung ausgewählter Onlinequellen zur EU-Politik in 24 deutschen Redaktionen Quelle: Eigene Darstellung (Mehrfachnennung möglich).

Wichtiger im Redaktionsalltag sind persönliche Ansprechpartner, die telefonisch kontaktiert werden können. Die wichtigste Quelle in dieser Hinsicht, und damit das entscheidende mediale Scharnier zwischen der Region und Brüssel, sind die Europaabgeordneten. Schwächer ist die Zusammenarbeit der Redaktionen mit den nationalen Vertretungen der EU-Kommission ausgeprägt. Noch deutlich seltener wird bei der Recherche der Kontakt zur EU-Kommissionszentrale in Brüssel gesucht.

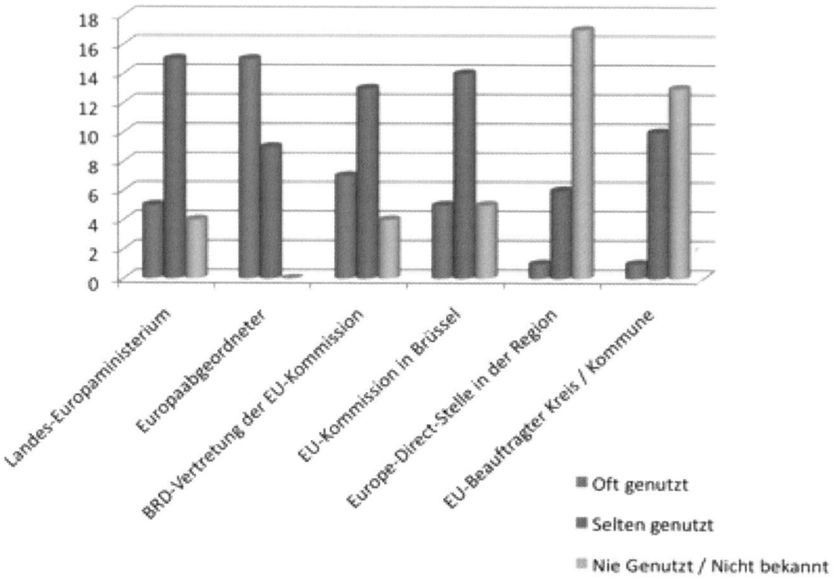

Abbildung 2: Nutzungshäufigkeiten von Recherchequellen in 24 deutschen Redaktionen
Quelle: Eigene Darstellung (Mehrfachnennung möglich).

Selten findet auch eine regelmäßige Kooperation mit Pressestellen der Landeseuropaministerien statt. Besonders gering für die Recherche ist der Stellenwert EU-spezifischer Quellen in der Region: Die EU-Beauftragten von Kreis und Kommunen werden kaum und die regionalen Europe Direct-Stellen fast nie befragt. Klar ist, dass die EU-Quellen vor Ort ein bislang noch meist ungenutztes Potenzial darstellen, um die EU-Berichterstattung regionaler und anschaulicher zu machen. Immer ist dabei daran zu denken, dass Regionalzeitungen das eigentliche Massenmedium sind, und dass damit die EU-Recherche vor allem hier ein Thema sein sollte.

Potenziale gibt es auch bei der Zusammenarbeit mit den EU-Abgeordneten. Das individuelle Engagement der Abgeordneten entscheidet also in starkem Maße darüber, ob eine Redaktion über sie berichtet. Dass die Berichterstattung über Abgeordnete mitunter ausbleibt – insbesondere auch in Form von lokaler Berichterstattung über Pressetermine – hat auch strukturelle Gründe wie die

Größe der Wahlkreise und das schmale Zeitbudget der Abgeordneten für die persönliche Präsenz vor Ort.

Reformen, die den Parlamentariern mehr Zeit und Aufmerksamkeit für ihre Region erlauben, könnten hier womöglich einiges bewirken. Insbesondere aber auch die Verbesserung der Pressearbeit der Abgeordneten, denen dafür selten geschultes Personal zur Verfügung steht. Würden Regionalbezüge in den Pressemeldungen öfter und besser eingebaut, stiege auch der Nutzwert dieser Texte für Redaktionen. Vor allem aber sollten Journalisten die bereits vorhandenen Quellen besser kennen und nutzen:

Einige Quellen zur EU-Recherche:

EU-Institutionen
- EU-Kommission (Ansprechpartner über Organigramme finden)
- EU-Pressroom (tägliche News)
- EU-Kommission in Deutschland
- Ständige Vertretung Deutschlands bei der EU
- Europäisches Parlament (Deutsche Abgeordnete)

EU-Datenbanken
- EUR-Lex (Gesetze)
- Eurostat (Statistik)
- IDEA (Personensuche)
- PRELEX (Gesetzgebungsstand)

Institute und Think Tanks
- Center for European Policy Studies
- Center for European Reform
- Centrum für europäische Politik
- Institut für europäische Politik
- Centum für angewandte Politikforschung (LMU München)
- Jean-Monnet-Lehrstuhl (Universität Köln)

EU-Fachdienste und Magazine
- Euractiv (mehrsprachige Übersetzung)
- EUobserver
- European Voice
- Politikportal EU (Presseschau auf Deutsch)
- The Parliament

- Europolitan
- Europa-digital.de (deutsch: Hintergründe, Eurospeak, EU-Lexika)
- Eurotopics (Übersetzte Presseschau)
- Café Babel (Junges, mehrsprachiges Europamagazin)
- Presseurop (Übersetzte Presseschau)

Recherche-Tools
- Brusselsreporter.org (Journalismus in Brüssel)
- EJC (Europäisches Journalistenzentrum, Maastricht)
- „EU 4 Journalists" (Lerntool zur EU-Berichterstattung)

Aus- und Weiterbildung zur Auslandsrecherche

Was zeigen diese Erkenntnisse? Und wie kann die Europarecherche verbessert werden? Zunächst ein grundlegender Gedanke: Es ist vermutlich sinnvoll, Journalisten im Rahmen der Aus- und Weiterbildung zu verdeutlichen, dass es zuerst nicht um die Berichterstattung über Themen aus Brüssel geht. Sondern vielmehr um die generelle Suche nach neuen, auch in Deutschland verorteten Themen, die sich aber nur aus einer (erlernten) europäischen Perspektive erkennen lassen. Diese Vorgehensweise könnte mitunter Hemmnisse abbauen und den Zugang zum fremden Gebiet der EU-Berichterstattung erleichtern.
Die Verwendung dieses Begriffs ist also bereits irreführend, da er suggeriert, dass es um Fragestellungen geht, die alleine in Brüssel angesiedelt sind. Tatsächlich ist die EU-Berichterstattung aber eine Hybridkategorie, die der Inlandsberichterstattung zuzuordnen ist. Vor diesen Hintergründen ist es für europajournalistische Aus- und Weiterbildung womöglich sinnvoller, in ihr „Angebot" die EU-Dimension der deutschen Politik und Berichterstattung stärker in den Blick zu nehmen, als nur nach Brüssel zu schauen.
Und da liegen die Probleme: In der deutschen journalistischen Ausbildung gibt es durchweg keine feste EU-Dimension. Es bleibt mehr oder weniger dem Zufall überlassen, ob sich ein angehender Journalist in seiner Ausbildungsinstitution mit der EU beschäftigen kann.
Letztlich muss vor dem Hintergrund und der absoluten Wichtigkeit der EU von jedem Politikredakteur verlangt werden können, dass er sich mit den EU-Strukturen auskennt. Es reicht nicht, wenn er einzelne Institutionen unterscheiden kann, etwa aber über das Mitentscheidungsverfahren als wichtigstes Gesetzgebungsverfahren keine Kenntnisse hat. Der Wissensstand „auf dem Niveau eines aufmerksamen Zeitungslesers", wie es ein Redakteur für seine Redaktion

beschreibt, ist ungenügend. Ziel muss der Aufbau einer strukturellen journalistischen Europakompetenz in der Redaktion sein, die von einem spezialisierten Fachredakteur mit einer hohen EU-Kompetenz sowie den europäisch geschulten Sachautoren getragen wird. Zu den verstärkten Kompetenzen treten dann gezielte Themenplanungen und Teamprojekte hinzu, die bislang fast vollständig ausbleiben.
Es wäre auch darüber nachzudenken, warum nicht das Volontariat, das immer noch die meisten Journalisten in Verlagen und Rundfunkhäusern in den Beruf führt, eine verpflichtende europäische Dimension erhalten sollte. Dies könnte durch entsprechende Vereinbarungen im Rahmen der Zentralverbände wie dem Bundesverband der Zeitungsverleger, dem Bundesverband der Zeitschriftenverleger sowie den öffentlich-rechtlichen Rundfunkhäusern geschehen. Solche Angebote, die strukturell eingeführt werden und deshalb nicht nur sporadisch wirken, könnten verhindern, dass das Ausland, insbesondere die EU, für viele Journalisten ein Buch mit sieben Siegeln bleibt.

Literatur

FISCHER, Heinz-Dietrich (1982): Akkreditierte Journalisten als Vermittler der Weltpolitik. In: FISCHER, Heinz-Dietrich (Hrsg.): Auslandskorrespondenten in der Bundesrepublik Deutschland: Status, Aufgaben, Arbeitsprobleme professioneller Berichterstatter aus Bonn. Düsseldorf.
GERHARDS, Jürgen (2000): Europäisierung von Ökonomie und Politik und die Trägheit der Entstehung einer europäischen Öffentlichkeit. In: Bach, Maurizio (Hrsg.): Die Europäisierung nationaler Gesellschaften. Sonderheft 40 der Kölner Zeitschrift für Soziologie und Sozialpsychologie. Wiesbaden.
HAFEZ, Kai (2002): Die politische Dimension der Auslandsberichterstattung. Baden-Baden.
HARSEIM, Christine; Jürgen Wilke (2000): Nachrichtenproduktion und Nachrichtenangebot der Deutschen Presseagentur. Mit einem Ausblick auf den Agenturvergleich. In: Wilke, Jürgen (Hrsg.): Von der Agentur zur Redaktion. Wie Nachrichten gemacht, bewertet und verwendet werden. Köln.
MECKEL, Miriam (1998): Internationales als Restgröße? Zur Auslandsberichterstattung in Fernsehnachrichten. In: Kamps, Klaus/Miriam Meckel (Hrsg.): Fernsehnachrichten - Strukturen, Funktionen, Prozesse. Opladen.
MÜKKE, Lutz (2003): Einzelkämpfende Allrounder. Eine Studie über Korrespondenten in Nairobi. In: Message, 2.
NEU, Gerd Rainer (2001): Hauptsache, es sind Deutsche betroffen. In: Journalistik-Journal, 1.
SCHULZ, Winfried (1990): Die Konstruktion von Realität in den Nachrichtenmedien. Freiburg.

Albrecht Ude

Problemfeld Internet: Fact-Checking im World Wide Web

Albrecht Ude arbeitet als freier Journalist, Rechercheur und Recherche-Trainer. Seine Arbeitsschwerpunkte sind Internet-Recherchen mit analytischen und forensischen Methoden, Computer Assisted Reporting (CAR) und Quellenprüfung. Er publiziert für Die Zeit, Zeit online, c't, journalist u.a. Über Recherchethemen bloggt er auf recherchenblog.ch und auf recherche-info.de. Unter eine-woche-ohne.de ruft er zu mehr Vielfalt in der Internet-Recherche auf.

Faktenkontrolle mit Informationsangeboten des Internet ist sehr gut möglich. Dies umso mehr, je mehr im Netz publiziert wird – in zunehmendem Maße ja auch exklusiv. Zudem bieten viele nachträglich digitalisierte Informationen einen schnelleren Zugriff als deren analoge Originale. Die Vertrauenswürdigkeit und Belastbarkeit der netz- und webbasierten Angebote ist jedoch im jeweils konkreten Fall zu prüfen.

Drei grundlegende Überlegungen helfen bei der Faktenkontrolle im World Wide Web:

1. Texte der Wikipedia taugen nicht als Quelle.

Die Wikipedia ist ein sehr nützliches Werkzeug in der Recherche, sie ist prall von Wissen, die Beschäftigung mit ihr bildet und macht Spaß – aber die Texte der Wikipedia-Artikel taugen nicht als Quelle. Ihre Stärken liegen in anderen Bereichen, etwa in der Erschließung von Wissen oder im Erkennen von Zusammenhängen – also eher in der „Navigation" durch Informationsbestände als in deren „Prüfung".
In Wikipedia kann jeder sofort schreiben. Jeder kann dort neue Artikel anlegen oder vorhandene modifizieren. Dieses Prinzip, das zur Mitarbeit einlädt, ist einer der Gründe für den Erfolg der Wikipedia. Es wird ergänzt durch das Prinzip der Protokollierung: Jede Änderung, und sei es nur die Korrektur eines Kommas, wird gespeichert und ist für alle Nutzer nachvollziehbar. Dadurch ist zum Beispiel so genannter Vandalismus (die nicht sachgemäße Änderung von Artikeln zu fremden Zwecken) nachvollziehbar und leicht reparabel. Darüber, was nicht sachgemäß ist, entscheiden die Bearbeiter des jeweiligen Textes - im Idealfall im Konsens. Dass Konsens der Bearbeiter aber keine Gewähr für Richtigkeit ist, liegt auf der Hand.
Die Grundidee der „freien Enzyklopädie" kann man in einem Satz so zusammenfassen: Viele Leute erzählen freiwillig, was sie wissen. Das ist – gerade für Journalisten! – eine traumhafte Situation. Allerdings: Wenn viele Leute erzählen, dann gibt es auch Fehlinformationen, Wissenslücken, falsche und nicht zuletzt bewusst verfälschte Informationen.
Ein Beispiel, wie leicht Wikipedia-Texte falsche Sachinformationen enthalten, ist der Fall des „Wilhelm zu Guttenberg". Der Artikel über Karl-Theodor zu Guttenberg wurde damals falsch, weil inkompetent, für die Faktenkontrolle genutzt. Darüber berichtete ein anonymer Gastautor am 12. Februar 2009 im Bildblog. In Kürze: Der Anonymus bei Wikipedia hatte dem Namen des fränkischen Adeligen, der ganze zehn Vornamen führt, einen elften angedichtet: Wilhelm. Als

Karl-Theodor zu Guttenberg zum Wirtschaftsminister ernannt wurde, brachten viele deutsche Medien seinen vollen Namen inklusive des falschen Wilhelms. Alle hatten entweder von anderen Medien – Medien sind keine vertrauenswürdigen Quellen! – abgeschrieben, oder aber Wikipedia zitiert, ohne die Versionsgeschichte des Artikels kritisch zu würdigen. Dabei ist diese mit nur einem Klick erreichbar unter dem Link „Versionen/Autoren", in der englischen Version unter „history".

So unbrauchbar der Text der Wikipedia ist, der Artikel ist insgesamt nützlich, genauer: Die Weblinks. Denn unter vielen Artikeln finden sich „Einzelnachweise" (engl. „References") und „Weblinks" (engl. „External links"). Sie verweisen auf Dokumente außerhalb der Wikipedia, die für die Faktenkontrolle nützlich sein können.

Im genannten Fall findet sich unter den Weblinks der Eintrag: „Literatur von und über Karl-Theodor zu Guttenberg im Katalog der Deutschen Nationalbibliothek", der „obersten" deutschen Bibliothek also, die etwa die Deutsche Nationalbibliografie erstellt. Ein Klick auf diesen Eintrag führt unmittelbar zum Eintrag in der so genannten „Personennormdatei" (PND). Diese Datenbank ist eine Quelle von hoher Verlässlichkeit. Gleichwohl bietet sie keine Informationen aus erster Hand: Bibliothekare sammeln darin Angaben über Autoren. Daher findet man dort etwa den Namen: „Guttenberg, Karl-Theodor Maria Nikolaus Johann Jacob Philipp Franz Joseph Sylvester /zu". Von einem „Wilhelm" fehlt dort jede Spur.

Ein anderes, weitaus bedenklicheres Beispiel für die falsche Nutzung der Wikipedia erwähnte der Spiegel am 11. März 2010. Unter dem Titel „Im Zweifel gegen die Opfer" schrieb Christoph Schult aus Jerusalem über die schleppende Entschädigung jüdischer Zwangsarbeiter, die im von Nazideutschland besetzten Polen in Ghettos hatten schuften müssen. Zuständig für Rentenanträge von Überlebenden aus Israel ist die Landesversicherungsanstalt (LVA) Rheinprovinz in Düsseldorf. Viele dieser Anträge wurden abgelehnt (in diesem Falle ist dann das Düsseldorfer Sozialgericht zuständig). Zitat aus dem Spiegel-Artikel: „Historiker wurden bei den Entscheidungen anfangs nicht zu Rate gezogen. Lieber verließen sich Versicherungssachbearbeiter und Richter auf oberflächliche Nachschlagewerke wie das Internetlexikon Wikipedia. In vielen Fällen behaupteten sie, es habe in der betreffenden Stadt gar kein Ghetto gegeben."

Zu behaupten, in einer Stadt habe es kein Ghetto gegeben, weil dies in Wikipedia nicht erwähnt ist, unterstellt der Wikipedia Vollständigkeit. Ein absurder Gedanke! Was mag ein jüdischer ehemaliger Zwangsarbeiter empfinden, wenn er von einem deutschen Sachbearbeiter oder gar Richter beschieden wird, das Ghetto, in dem er zwangsweise seine Lebenszeit verbracht hat, habe es doch gar nicht gegeben?

Ein letztes Beispiel zu den Klippen und Untiefen der Wikipedia-Texte: Echter Ostfriesentee. Ostfriesland, eine Halbinsel im Nordwesten Deutschlands an der Grenze zu den Niederlanden, ist eine Region der Teetrinker. Pro Kopf wird dort wesentlich mehr Tee getrunken als in Deutschland insgesamt. Typisch ist dort die „Ostfriesische Mischung", die als weltweit stärkste Schwarzteemischung gilt. Verschiedene Firmen bieten solche Mischungen an, die meisten ortsansässigen davon vermarkten ihre Tees nur in Ostfriesland, oder gar nur im eigenen Ort.

In der Wikipedia gibt es einen Artikel über Ostfriesentee: Er ist kurz und unverdächtig, hat keine Einzelbelege, keine Weblinks, es gibt keine Diskussion dazu und ein Klick in die Versionsgeschichte offenbart keine Betrugsversuche. Keine offensichtliche Gefahr also.

Abbildung 1: Ein völlig unverdächtiger Wikipedia-Artikel ohne offensichtliche Betrugsversuche – aus der Perspektive des Fact-Checking jedoch eine Ansammlung unbewiesener Behauptungen: http://de.wikipedia.org/wiki/Ostfriesentee

Gefährlich ist, was man nicht sieht: Der Artikel reiht Behauptungen aneinander, ohne auch nur einen einzigen Beleg zu liefern. Zum Beispiel der letzte Satz: „Nur in Ostfriesland gemischter Tee darf sich Echter Ostfriesentee nennen, die übrigen tragen die Bezeichnung ‚ostfriesische Mischung'. Diese Aussage legt nahe, die Bezeichnung „Echter Ostfriesentee" sei rechtlich geschützt.
Wenn dem so wäre, wer würde die Bezeichnung vermutlich schützen? Entweder die nationale Regierung oder die Europäische Union (EU). In der EU gibt es drei Gütezeichen für die Qualität hochwertiger landwirtschaftlicher Erzeugnisse und Lebensmittel und deren Schutz: g. U. (geschützte Ursprungsbezeichnung), g. g. A. (geschützte geografische Angabe), g. t. S. (garantiert traditionelle Spezialität). Darüber informiert die EU auf ihren Webseiten.

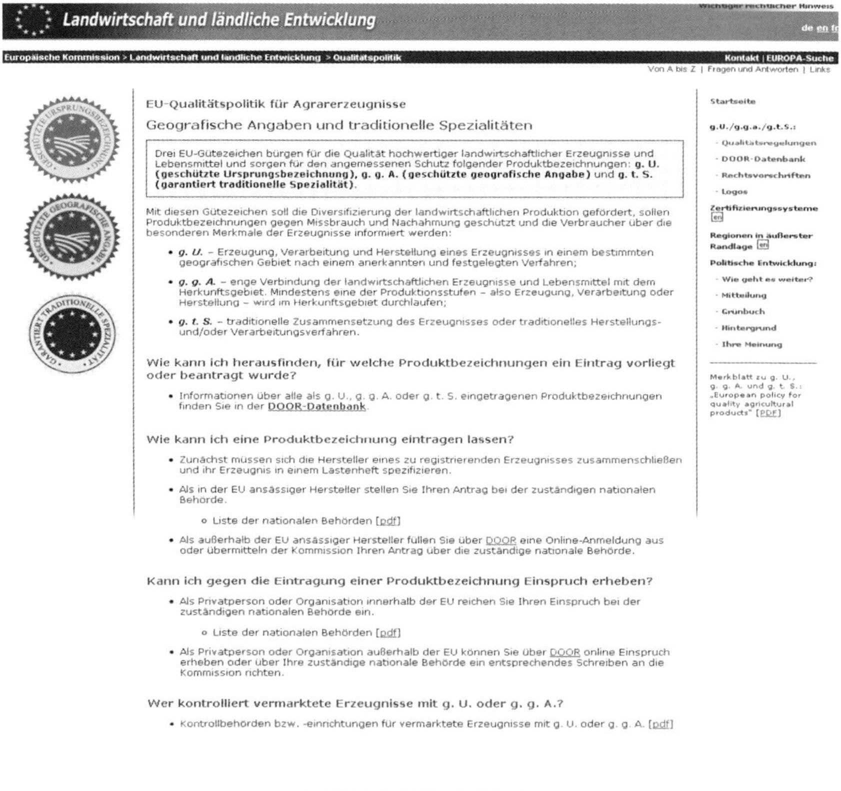
Wichtiger rechtlicher Hinweis

Landwirtschaft und ländliche Entwicklung

de en fr

Europäische Kommission > Landwirtschaft und ländliche Entwicklung > Qualitätspolitik

Kontakt | EUROPA-Suche

Von A bis Z | Fragen und Antworten | Links

EU-Qualitätspolitik für Agrarerzeugnisse

Geografische Angaben und traditionelle Spezialitäten

Drei EU-Gütezeichen bürgen für die Qualität hochwertiger landwirtschaftlicher Erzeugnisse und Lebensmittel und sorgen für den angemessenen Schutz folgender Produktbezeichnungen: **g. U. (geschützte Ursprungsbezeichnung), g. g. A. (geschützte geografische Angabe)** und **g. t. S. (garantiert traditionelle Spezialität)**.

Mit diesen Gütezeichen soll die Diversifizierung der landwirtschaftlichen Produktion gefördert, sollen Produktbezeichnungen gegen Missbrauch und Nachahmung geschützt und die Verbraucher über die besonderen Merkmale der Erzeugnisse informiert werden:

- ***g. U.*** – Erzeugung, Verarbeitung und Herstellung eines Erzeugnisses in einem bestimmten geografischen Gebiet nach einem anerkannten und festgelegten Verfahren;
- ***g. g. A.*** – enge Verbindung der landwirtschaftlichen Erzeugnisse und Lebensmittel mit dem Herkunftsgebiet. Mindestens eine der Produktionsstufen – also Erzeugung, Verarbeitung oder Herstellung – wird im Herkunftsgebiet durchlaufen;
- ***g. t. S.*** – traditionelle Zusammensetzung des Erzeugnisses oder traditionelles Herstellungs- und/oder Verarbeitungsverfahren.

Wie kann ich herausfinden, für welche Produktbezeichnungen ein Eintrag vorliegt oder beantragt wurde?

- Informationen über alle als g. U., g. g. A. oder g. t. S. eingetragenen Produktbezeichnungen finden Sie in der **DOOR-Datenbank**.

Wie kann ich eine Produktbezeichnung eintragen lassen?

- Zunächst müssen sich die Hersteller eines zu registrierenden Erzeugnisses zusammenschließen und ihr Erzeugnis in einem Lastenheft spezifizieren.
- Als in der EU ansässiger Hersteller stellen Sie Ihren Antrag bei der zuständigen nationalen Behörde.
  - Liste der nationalen Behörden [pdf]
- Als außerhalb der EU ansässiger Hersteller füllen Sie über DOOR eine Online-Anmeldung aus oder übermitteln der Kommission Ihren Antrag über die zuständige nationale Behörde.

Kann ich gegen die Eintragung einer Produktbezeichnung Einspruch erheben?

- Als Privatperson oder Organisation innerhalb der EU reichen Sie Ihren Einspruch bei der zuständigen nationalen Behörde ein.
  - Liste der nationalen Behörden [pdf]
- Als Privatperson oder Organisation außerhalb der EU können Sie über DOOR online Einspruch erheben oder über Ihre zuständige nationale Behörde ein entsprechendes Schreiben an die Kommission richten.

Wer kontrolliert vermarktete Erzeugnisse mit g. U. oder g. g. A.?

- Kontrollbehörden bzw. -einrichtungen für vermarktete Erzeugnisse mit g. U. oder g. g. A. [pdf]

Startseite

g.U./g.g.a./g.t.S.:
- Qualitätsregelungen
- DOOR-Datenbank
- Rechtsvorschriften
- Logos

Zertifizierungssysteme en

Regionen in äußerster Randlage en

Politische Entwicklung:
- Wie geht es weiter?
- Mitteilung
- Grünbuch
- Hintergrund
- Ihre Meinung

Merkblatt zu g. U., g. g. A. und g. t. S.: „European policy for quality agricultural products" [PDF]

Landwirtschaft und ländliche Entwicklung | Seitenanfang

Abbildung 2: Verlässliche Information aus erster Hand: Die EU schützt die Bezeichnungen landwirtschaftlicher Erzeugnisse und informiert darüber im Internet.

Es gibt sogar eine Datenbank (DOOR) für derartig geschützte Produktbezeichnungen, sortiert nach Land und Art des Erzeugnisses. Sie enthält neben eingetragenen Produktbezeichnungen auch solche, für die der Schutz erst beantragt ist. Eine Abfrage der Datenbank ergibt, dass weder „Tee“ noch „Ostfriesentee“ darin verzeichnet sind.
An diesem Punkt endet die Online-Recherche. Um zu klären, ob der Ostfriesentee vielleicht anderweitig geschützt ist, wie es die Wikipedia nahe legt, hilft ein Anruf beim Dachverband der Tee-Importeure und – Großhändler, dem Deutschen Teeverband e.V. Die weitere, via Telefon geführte Recherche zeigt: Es gibt ein Gerichtsurteil gegen eine in Deutschland ansässige Firma, die in ihrer Werbung den Anschein erweckte, eine „echt ostfriesische“ Teemischung zu liefern, wogegen eine der ostfriesischen Firmen klagte.
Mit allgemeinen Suchmaschinen wie Google wäre die abschließende Feststellung, dass Ostfriesentee nicht durch die EU geschützt ist, nicht möglich. Man hätte (nach vermutlich ermüdender Recherche) bestenfalls erkennen können, dass man nichts findet. Das aber ist eine andere Aussage als die, dass nichts zu finden ist.

2. Gute Hilfe bieten die Universalsuchmaschinen

Universalsuchmaschinen versuchen, das Internet ohne thematische, chronologische, nationale oder sprachliche Beschränkungen zugänglich zu machen. Sie versuchen, salopp gesagt, das „ganze“ Internet zu erfassen – was keiner Suchmaschine auch nur annähernd gelingt. Google ist die bekannteste Suchmaschine dieser Art, aber nicht die einzige.
Daneben sind Ask, Bing (von Microsoft), Exalead und Yahoo nützliche Suchwerkzeuge. Denn all diese Suchmaschinen erstellen ihre Datenbanken unabhängig voneinander. Was die eine nicht findet, kann im Index der anderen dennoch zu finden sein. Genau wie Google bieten sie die Möglichkeit zur „erweiterten“ Suche (engl. „advanced search“). Vor allem aber bieten die genannten Suchmaschinen fünf weitgehend unabhängige Möglichkeiten, Belege für eine Aussage zu finden.
Auch dies lässt sich anhand eines Beispiels illustrieren: Am Tag nach dem Amoklauf von Winnenden behauptete der Baden-Württembergische Innenminister Heribert Rech am 12. März 2009 bei einer Pressekonferenz, es gäbe ein Ankündigungsschreiben des Attentäters Tim K. in einem Internetforum namens krautchan.net.
Die Frage war einfach: stimmt das? Damals wurde ich telefonisch von einer Nachrichtenagentur um mein Urteil dazu gebeten; die Kollegen dort waren bereits

skeptisch und baten um einen zweiten Standpunkt. Das Problem: Schon während der Pressekonferenz war das webbasierte Forum krautchan.net nicht mehr erreichbar. Wegen des sofort einsetzenden Nutzerandrangs waren die Webserver überlastet. Später nahmen die Administratoren des Forums es für einige Zeit vom Netz. Am „originalen" Ort ließ sich also kein Fakt mehr prüfen.
Dennoch konnte ich diese Recherche binnen einer Viertelstunde erledigen. Hilfreich dabei waren die genannten Suchmaschinen: Für viele Suchergebnisse liefern sie nicht nur deren Beschreibung und den Link auf die gefundenen Webseiten, sondern sie haben auch Zwischenspeicher (engl. „Caches"), in denen man automatisch erzeugte Kopien der Webseiten findet. Sie zeigen die Pages zum Zeitpunkt, an dem die Suchmaschine sie das letzte Mal indiziert (engl. „gespidert") hat. Mit Hilfe der Caches in unterschiedlichen Suchmaschinen konnte ich krautchan.net fünf Mal untersuchen. Anhand von Kopien also, die unabhängig voneinander gemacht worden waren. Keine der zwischengespeicherten Seiten bot einen Beweis für die Richtigkeit der Behauptung des Innenministers. Diese wurde auch später nach einer Untersuchung des von der Polizei beschlagnahmten Computers von Tim K. widerrufen.
Besser dokumentiert ist ein anderes Beispiel der Faktenkontrolle: He Kexin, eine Chinesin aus der Volksrepublik China, nahm als Turnerin an den Olympischen Spielen 2008 teil. Die Regeln des Internationalen Olympischen Komitees (IOC) schreiben ein Mindestalter von 16 Jahren für Olympioniken vor. War He Kexin dafür alt genug? Diese simple Frage stellte Mike Walker, der das Blog „Strydehax" betreibt, wo er die nachfolgend skizzierte Recherche auch (mit vielen Screenshots) veröffentlichte.
Der Wikipedia-Artikel für He Kexin beginnt mit einer Merkwürdigkeit – er nennt zwei alternative Geburtsdaten: „He Kexin, 何可欣, Hé Kexin, (* 1. Januar 1992 oder 1994[1][2][3][4][5] in Peking) ist eine chinesische Sportlerin." Der einen Angabe zufolge wäre He Kexin zum Zeitpunkt der Olympischen Spiele 16 Jahre alt und dürfte teilnehmen, der anderen zufolge aber wäre sie erst 14 – also zu jung, um an den Start zu gehen.
Um das Problem zu lösen, hat Mike Walker nicht „gegoogelt", sondern mit Google recherchiert – ein wichtiger Unterschied. Er stellte sich die Frage: „Gibt es offizielle chinesische Dokumente, die für He Kexin das Geburtsjahr 1994 nennen?". Und übersetzte sie in eine Google-Abfrage: 何可欣, 1994 site:cn filetype:xls. Zur Erläuterung: Die drei chinesischen Zeichen, aus denen der Name der jungen Sportlerin besteht, kann man aus der Wikipedia kopieren und bei Google eingeben. Chinesisch muss man dafür nicht können (ein weiterer großer Nutzen der Wikipedia!). 1994 als gesuchtes Geburtsjahr muss nicht erklärt werden. „site:" ist einer der so genannten erweiterten Operatoren (engl. „advanced operators"),

die Google für die Suche in der eigenen Datenbank anbietet. Man kann auch von einem „Limitator“ sprechen, denn damit wird die Menge der Funde begrenzt. Der Site-Operator weist Google an, nur Ergebnisse einer bestimmten Domain auszugeben. Mit „site:spiegel.de“ findet man etwa nur Ergebnisse von den Webservern des Spiegels. „site:cn“ weist Google an, nur Dokumente aus der Domain „cn“ zu liefern, der Top-Level-Domain der Volksrepublik China.

„filetype:“ ist ebenfalls ein solcher Limitator. Damit weist man Google an, nur Ergebnisse eines bestimmten Dateiformates anzuzeigen. „filetype:pdf“ etwa führt dazu, dass Google nur PDF-Dateien liefert. „xls“ ist ein verbreitetes Dateiformat für Tabellen. Für jemanden, der nicht Chinesisch beherrscht, wäre ein Suchergebnis, das den Namen He Kexin irgendwo im Fließtext enthält, selbstverständlich nicht verwendbar. Mit tabellarischer Information lässt sich aber auch ohne Sprachkenntnis etwas anfangen.

In menschlicher Sprache lautet die Anfrage von Mike Walker also: Finde tabellarische Dokumente aus der Volksrepublik China, in denen 何可欣, und 1994 vorkommt.

Abbildung 3: Google liefert auf die Abfrage „site:cn 何可欣 filetype:xls 1994“ genau ein Suchergebnis (Foto: Strydehax).

Google lieferte daraufhin ein Suchergebnis – ein „Google Rack“, fast immer Zeichen einer kompetenten Abfrage.

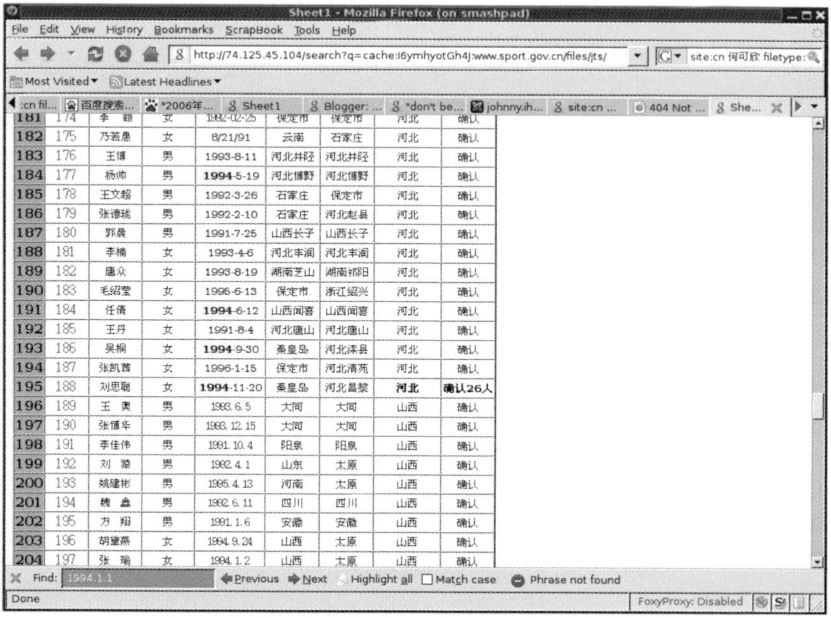

Abbildung 4: Leider ist das Suchergebnis auf dem Originalserver „www.sport.gov.cn“ nicht mehr vorhanden. Aber im Zwischenspeicher der Suchmaschine, dem Google-Cache, kann man es noch finden (Foto: Strydehax).

Das Dokument stammte vom Server „www.sport.gov.cn“. Solche Webadressen (engl. „**U**niform **R**esource **L**ocators“) kann man lesen, analysieren: „cn“ steht für die Volksrepublik China, „gov“ ist innerhalb dieser Top-Level-Domain die Second-Level-Domain für die Regierung der Volksrepublik. Wie einige andere Länder auch hat die Volksrepublik den eigenen Adressraum durch ein System von Second-Level-Domains vergrößert und geordnet). Aus dieser URL geht hervor, dass Google das Dokument auf dem Webserver der obersten Sportbehörde der Volksrepublik China („General Administration of Sport of China“) gefunden hat.

Mike Walker klickte auf den Link – und bekam eine Fehlermeldung mit dem Code 404, „File not found“. Das Dokument war vom Server gelöscht. Daraufhin klickte er auf die von Google zwischengespeicherte Version (Dokumente, die keine Webseiten sind, werden dabei automatisch in HTML-Dokumente konvertiert).

Mit einem sonderbaren Ergebnis: Die Version im Cache enthielt die Zeichen 何可欣 nicht – obwohl Google das Dokument als Ergebnis auf eine entsprechende Suchanfrage ausgegeben hatte! Kurzum: Ein höchst bemerkenswertes Resultat, aber kein Beleg.

An diesem Punkt angelangt, zeigte Walker eine der besten Eigenschaften von Rechercheuren: Hartnäckigkeit. Er informierte sich, ob es in der Volksrepublik China neben Google andere, relevante Suchmaschinen gibt. Das Ergebnis: Die Suchmaschine Baidu ist in den Funktionen Google ähnlich. Walker wiederholte seine Anfrage also bei Baidu und fand dort zwei Dokumente, beide vom bereits erwähnten Server „www.sport.gov.cn" (eines davon dasjenige, das auch Google schon genannt hatte). Auch das zweite Dokument war auf dem Server nicht mehr vorhanden, aber auch Baidu verfügt über einen Cache, einen Zwischenspeicher. Beide im Baidu-Cache enthaltenen Dokumente nannten für 何可欣 1994 als Geburtsjahr. Das ist ein Beweis: Es gab offizielle Veröffentlichungen der chinesischen Sportbehörden, die für He Kexin das Geburtsjahr 1994 angaben – folglich war sie für die Teilnahme an den Olympischen Spielen zu jung.

3. Es gibt viel mehr als Universalsuchmaschinen

Diese Beispiele zeigen deutlich den Nutzen digitaler Archive; in den genannten Fällen die Caches der großen Suchmaschinen. Aber es gibt noch viel bessere Archive als diese. Es entstehen immer mehr Projekte der digitalen Langzeit-Archivierung (einige von den Nationalbibliotheken initiiert). Sie verfolgen unterschiedliche Ziele, viele davon sind frei nutzbar. Diese Projekte zu kennen (und in die eigene, sorgsam gepflegte Bookmark-Sammlung aufzunehmen) lohnt sich sehr.

Das in der praktischen Arbeit wichtigste Web-Archiv ist die „WayBackMachine" (WBM), auch „Internet Archive" genannt. Es wurde bereits 1996 von Brewster Kahle gegründet. Diese digitale Bibliothek spidert und speichert in unregelmäßigen Abständen Webseiten und macht sie zugänglich. Auch andere Inhalte des Web wie Dokumente, Grafiken oder Videos werden gespeichert. Nach Aussage der Betreiber enthält die WBM derzeit 100 Milliarden Pages aus über 65 Millionen Webseiten in 37 Sprachen. Sie ist somit das größte öffentlich zugängliche Archiv.

Mit dem Internet Archive kann man also leicht einen Blick in die Vergangenheit werfen, die Entwicklung einer Webseite nachvollziehen, ja sogar vom Originalserver Gelöschtes noch finden. Leider ist die WBM weit davon entfernt, vollständig zu sein - wenn man dort etwas nicht findet, ist das also nicht unbedingt ein Beweis, dass nichts existierte oder existiert.

Abbildung 5: So sieht die Webseite des netzwerk recherche heute aus (Ausschnitt).

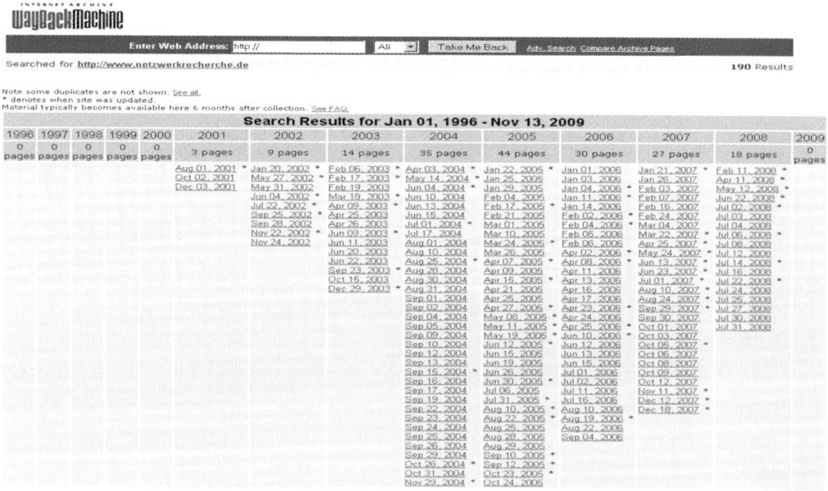

Abbildung 6: In der WayBackMachine (www.archive.org) kann man eine Vielzahl alter Versionen der Webseite des netzwerk recherche anklicken.

Gute Hilfen auf dem Weg zu Dokumenten für die Faktenkontrolle sind auch redaktionell bearbeitete Kataloge. Anders als Suchmaschinen, die nach programmierten Algorithmen arbeiten, werden diese Kataloge von Menschen mit semantischer Kompetenz erstellt. Sie erfassen zwar weniger Material als Suchmaschinen, doch ist dies mit menschlicher Intelligenz ausgewählt und eingeordnet. Eine Sonderstellung haben dabei die Kataloge, die von Bibliothekaren erstellt und gepflegt werden. Denn Bibliothekare sind Profis der Informationsverwaltung.

Auch Datenbanken sind gute Werkzeuge für die Faktenkontrolle. Allerdings sind sie Teil des „deep Web" (oder „hidden Web"): Suchmaschinen können zwar ihre Startseiten erfassen, aber nicht die Inhalte. Einige Datenbanken, die im „normalen" Internet kostenpflichtig sind, kann man durch das Projekt „Nationallizenzen" der Deutschen Forschungsgemeinschaft in wissenschaftlichen Bibliotheken kostenfrei abrufen. Eine weitere große Hilfe sind Datenbanken, die ihrerseits Datenbanken verzeichnen, und Listen von Datenbanken.

„CompletePlanete" etwa erfasst nach eigenen Angaben mehr als 70 000 Datenbanken und Spezialsuchmaschinen. Das „Datenbank-Infosystem" (DBIS) bietet Hinweise zu mehr als 8000 wissenschaftlichen Datenbanken.

Doch auch dort wird nur fündig, wer die richtigen Fragen stellt:

Fünf Fragen für das Fact-Checking im Internet

1.) Wer müsste die Antwort auf meine Frage haben?
(Wer hat die primäre Quelle?)
2.) Gibt es möglicherweise ein spezielles Suchwerkzeug genau für meine Frage?
3.) Wie finde ich dieses Werkzeug?
(etwa via Suchmaschinen, in Katalogen oder Datenbanken)
4.) Kann/muss ich die Quelle prüfen?
5.) Wann muss ich erkennen, dass ich online nicht weiterkomme?

Der Text ist auch im Internet mit zahlreichen Links zu finden: www.factchecking.de

Hanna Klenk-Schubert

Problemfeld Archivierung: Wie man Rechercheergebnisse verwaltet

Hanna Klenk-Schubert leitet das Archiv der Stuttgarter Zeitung und der Stuttgarter Nachrichten. Nach einem Diplom-Studium der Chemie in Tübingen absolvierte sie ein Bibliotheksreferendariat in Stuttgart und arbeitete als Dokumentarin in der pharmazeutischen Industrie. Als Lehrbeauftragte der Hochschule der Medien in Stuttgart unterrichtet sie Bibliotheks- und Informationsmanagement.

Nach meiner Erfahrung ist auch im digitalen Zeitalter das Handarchiv die beste Methode für den einzelnen Journalisten. Es ist schlichtweg übersichtlicher als ein Digitalarchiv. Man bekommt eher ein Gefühl für Redundanzen; Wachstum und Veränderungen sind haptisch erfahrbar. Das Wachstum einer Datei dagegen lässt sich noch nicht einmal am Umfang zuverlässig erkennen. Und was beim Archivieren immer unterschätzt wird: Ein Handarchiv ist leichter zu pflegen.
In der Medizin werden Handarchive „Patientenakten" genannt: Zu Lebzeiten des Patienten werden jegliche Veränderungen seiner medizinischen Daten in die Akte eingetragen – später wandern die Akten ins Krankenhausarchiv. Im Journalismus wird das Handarchiv entsprechend so lange gepflegt, bis die Recherche beendet ist und veröffentlicht wird: Nicht umsonst ist der englische Ausdruck für Textarchiv „morgue", also „Leichenhalle".
Grundsätzlich gilt: Handarchive sind Sammlungen von Dokumenten zu einem oder mehreren LAUFENDEN Vorgängen. Daraus folgt: Die zu ordnenden Informationen sind überschaubar hinsichtlich ihres Umfangs und ihrer Anzahl. Im Gegensatz zu Pressearchiven hat ein Handarchiv daher auch keinen Anspruch auf Vollständigkeit hinsichtlich der Quellen. Wohl aber sollte ein Handarchiv Vollständigkeit hinsichtlich der Fakten zu den bearbeitenden Vorgängen anstreben. Das erfordert eine regelmäßige und aufmerksame Pflege. Aber: Ein Handarchiv ist ein Arbeitsinstrument und darf deshalb nicht mehr Pflege erfordern als die Recherche.
Die Herausforderungen des Handarchivs sind: Es muss Lücken darstellen können. Es muss multimedial sein – weil man für eine Recherche nicht nur einen Sinn verwendet, sondern hört, sieht und denkt. Und es muss die Vernetzung der Medien perfekt organisieren. Was macht aber aus einer bloßen Sammlung ein gutes Handarchiv? Zunächst einmal muss es „unmittelbaren Zugriff" auf die Informationen bieten. Das bedeutet, alle Elemente des Handarchivs sollten möglichst vom Schreibtischstuhl aus greifbar sein. (Manchmal müssen Ausnahmen gemacht werden, etwa bei Karten, die auf einer Weichfaserplatte aufgepint sind). Dafür sind vor allem vier Dinge erforderlich:

1. Die Nutzung der geeigneten Ordnungs-Systeme: Die benutzten Systeme (Datenbank, Schreibprogramm, Kalender, Mailprogramm etc.) sollten einer Produktfamilie angehören oder zumindest aufeinander abgestimmt sein.
2. Eine zum System „passende Erschließungsform": Die Ordnungsmerkmale der Verzeichnishierarchie, etwa die obersten „Klassen", müssen immer gleich sein, durchgängig benutzt werden und dürfen keine redundanten Elemente enthalten.
3. Ein Überblick über den Umfang: Sobald eine Systemstelle unverhältnismäßig wächst, muss nach den Gründen geforscht werden. Muss das System

erweitert werden? Sind die gespeicherten Dokumente redundant? Muss dazu etwas publiziert werden, weil zu viel geschehen ist? Oder: Wenn eine Systemstelle „vertrocknet" muss sie eliminiert oder einer anderen zugeordnet werden?

4. Ein Überblick über den Pflegeaufwand: Steigt der wöchentliche Pflegeaufwand, ist Ursachenforschung notwendig. Muss das Arbeitsgebiet angepasst werden (nicht in die Breite, sondern in die Tiefe)? Wie lässt sich die Archivpflege effizienter gestalten?

Da ein unmittelbarer Zugriff unerlässlich ist, müssen die Eigenschaften der Speichermedien beachtet werden. Die klassischen Speichermedien, die eine unmittelbare Aufnahme der gespeicherten Informationen erlauben (Papier, Pergament, klassische Fotoabzüge), haben eine Lebensdauer, von der angenommen werden kann, dass sie länger ist als die Lebenszeit des Handarchivs. Für Fotoabzüge gilt etwa die Faustregel: Schwarzweißabzüge = 100 Jahre, Farbabzüge = 75 Jahre bei nachlassender Farbintensität. Bei elektronischen Speichermedien umfassen die Lebenszeiten viel geringere Zeiträume: Magnetische Speichermedien wie Floppys und Bänder haben nur eine Lebenszeit von 10 bis 15 Jahren, DVDs und CDs kaum mehr (es sei denn, sie werden optimal gelagert). Bei Festplatten steigt die Gefährdung für die Daten durch thermische Einflüsse schon nach drei Jahren dramatisch an.

Bereits diese kleine Aufzählung zeigt, dass nicht nur die Speichermedien, sondern auch die Nutzungssysteme sehr schnelllebig sind. Wer nutzt heute noch Bänder oder Floppys? Deswegen ist es nicht nur ein Gebot der Ökonomie, sondern auch der Sicherheit, die Anzahl der benutzten Medien und Systeme zu minimieren. Schreibsystem, Datenbanksystem und Kalender aus einer Produktfamilie sind meist vollkommen ausreichend.

Die geordnete Erschließung

Viele Anfänger setzen sich zunächst hohe Ziele und erarbeiten ein elaboriertes Erschließungssystem – schließlich dienen die Annotationen auch der Information über Herkunft, Quelle, und Inhalt. Bei Fotos sind besonders auch Belichtungszeiten beliebt. Meist vergessen sie dabei, die Annotationen auch unter dem Gesichtspunkt der Sparsamkeit und Effizienz zu betrachten: Als formale Kriterien bei Zeitungsausschnitten genügen meist Quelle und Datum. Weitere Notationen wie Ressort, Auflagen, Ausgaben etc. machen, wenn sie stringent durchgehalten werden, sehr viel Arbeit und haben einen geringen Nutzwert – denn schneller machen sie die Suche im Archiv nicht. Bei Fotos helfen schon Aufnahmeort, Zeitpunkt und das dargestellte Thema weiter. Technische Notati-

onen wie Blende oder Verschlußzeit sind allenfalls für künstlerisch Interessierte von Belang, haben aber in einem Handarchiv nichts zu suchen. Gesprächsnotizen lassen sich am besten mit Angaben über den Ort, die Zeit und das Medium ablegen – aber Telefonnummern nicht vergessen!
Inhaltliche Kriterien richten sich nach den Arbeitsgebieten: Man sollte ein paar Grundüberlegungen beachten: Wer sich ein Erschließungssystem überlegt, steht vor der Wahl: Sollen Sachverhalte oder geografische Begriffe den Vorrang haben? Ich würde den Sachverhalten als strukturgebendes Element den Vorzug geben: Denn Sachverhalte, die das Arbeitsgebiet repräsentieren, können sich ändern. Das ist bei geographischen Begriffen nur selten der Fall. Statt alle möglichen Themen unter einem geografischen Ort zu subsumieren, sollten lieber geografische Orte unter immer neuen Arbeitsgebieten auftauchen.
Ein Beispiel: Nehmen wir einmal an, Sie recherchieren zum Sachverhalt „Stadthallen“, etwa in einem bestimmten Landkreis. Ein Landkreis hat rund 50 Orte. Dann legen Sie eine Karteikarte an, in der alle Orte des Landkreises aufgezählt werden. Jeder Ort mit einer Stadthalle, erhält ein Kreuzchen.
Das bedeutet: Wenn sich jetzt das Arbeitgebiet ändert, so können Sie den abgeschlossenen Teil mit der Karteikarte in einem Ordner abheften. Sie wissen auch noch nach 15 Jahren, dass diese oder jene Gemeinde zu einem bestimmten Zeitpunkt keine Stadthalle und kein Schwimmbad hatte. Und sollten sie einmal wieder zum Thema recherchieren, so finden sie alles gebündelt an einem Ort.

Was gehört ins Handarchiv?

Die Klassen, die in einem Handarchiv verwendet werden, richten sich nach dem Arbeitsgebiet des Archivnutzers. Ein Beispiel: Ein Journalist arbeitet für eine Medizinseite. Daher spielen für ihn Krankheiten, Gesundheitspolitik und Gesundheitsratschläge die Hauptrolle. Entsprechend sind die Klassen, die der Medizinjournalist anlegt, etwa: Aids, Gesundheitspolitik, Grippe, Herz-Kreislauf-Erkrankungen, Krankheiten a-z, Krankenhäuser, Krankenkassen, Krebs, Medizintechnik, Rettungswesen.
Natürlich wird es noch mehr Klassen geben. Aber das Handarchiv darf, ja muss Lücken haben. An manchen Stellen muss die Klassifikation ausgefeilt sein, an anderen darf sie oberflächlich bleiben. Augenfällig sind die Klassen Aids, Grippe, Herz-Kreislauf-Erkrankungen und Krebs. Denn es sind die einzigen Krankheiten, die einer eigenen Klasse zugeordnet werden. Alle anderen Krankheiten werden in diesem Beispiel unter „Krankheiten a-z“ zusammengefasst. Herz-Kreislauf-Erkrankungen und Krebs sind die häufigsten Todesursachen und spielen auch bei den Krankheitskosten eine große Rolle. Entsprechend häufig wird

über diese Krankheiten auch berichtet. Diesen Sachverhalt bildet das Archiv ab – und kann dazu dienen, auch hin und wieder alte, aber längst vergessene Tatsachen zu diesen Krankheiten in Erinnerung zu rufen. Fragestellungen im Zuge der Berichterstattung über Grippeepidemien, die sich mittels eines guten Handarchivs schnell beantworten lassen, könnten etwa lauten: Warum tauchen die schweren Grippeepidemien nur alle fünf bis zehn Jahre auf? Was unterscheidet eine virale Grippe von einer bakteriellen Erkältung? Warum wirken Hausmittel wie Sauna und Abhärtung so gut? Manche Schlagworte der Medizinberichterstattung fehlen im Klassensystem des Beispieljournalisten: Ärzte und Marburger Bund, Pharmaindustrie oder Stammzellen etwa. Die Erklärung ist einfach: Der Journalist schreibt vorwiegend für die Medizinseite. Die Pharmaindustrie wird auf den Wirtschaftsseiten abgehandelt, die Ärzte-Modelle und Ärzte-Körperschaften sind der Innenpolitik zugeordnet und die Gesundheitspolitik ist auf der Medizinseite ein Randgebiet. Anders als ein Archiv, das von Dauer sein soll, darf ein Handarchiv Lücken aufweisen, die den Anforderungen des Nutzers entsprechen! Auch das vergessen ambitionierte Archivanfänger allzu oft.

Ein Muss: Das Personenarchiv

Unabdingbar ist ein Personenarchiv. In Pressearchiven enthalten die einzelnen Personenarchivalien meist ein Formblatt, das eine Kurzvita und den vollen Namen enthält. Dahinter werden Dokumente gesammelt, die für die jeweilige Person erheblich sind. Unabhängig davon werden die Bilder zur Person gesammelt und an einer dritten Stelle die Daten, die für ein Jubiläum genutzt werden. Ein Handarchiv dagegen sollte wie bereits beschrieben alle Medien an einer Stelle zusammenführen. Die Reihenfolge der Personenakten ist dabei am besten alphabetisch. Als zweckmäßig erweist sich eine Dreiteilung der Personenakten:

1. Die Karteileichen: Eine Kartei, in der die nicht mehr aktiv am gesellschaftlichen Leben teilnehmenden Personen enthalten sind. Die Karteileichen werden zweimonatlich umgewälzt. Dabei lassen sich etwa anstehende Geburtstagsdaten in den Terminkalender eintragen. Stirbt eine Karteileiche, so wird die Karte entweder eliminiert oder einem Langzeitarchiv zugeführt.
2. „Dünne" Personen: Als „dünne" Personen werden solche Personenakten bezeichnet, in denen wenig Material ist oder jene Personenakten, die nur aus einer Karte bestehen. Sie werden im gleichen Karteikasten wie die Karteileichen geführt, aber mit Karteikarten einer anderen Farbe. Neben der Kurzvita sind auf der Karte nur Kontaktdaten, Lebens- und Karrieredaten sowie Netzwerke notiert. Sollten Dokumente zu dieser Person anfallen, so werden sie an die Karteikarte angeheftet.

3. „Dicke“ Personen: Namen, unter denen viel Material gesammelt wird, sollten in Mappen abgelegt werden. Diese enthält eine Formkarte mit den oben geschilderten Daten und die wichtigen Dokumente zur Person.

Das Verhältnis der „Dicken” zu den „Dünnen” beträgt im Allgemeinen 1:10. Selbst bei Gesellschaftsreportern sollten sie insgesamt kaum die Zahl 500 überschreiten. Denn 500 Karteikarten brauchen ungefähr einen Kasten, der kürzer als 50 Zentimeter ist und somit leicht auf jedem Schreibtisch Platz hat.

Intensive Pflege

Um ein Handarchiv überschaubar zu halten, bedarf es der Pflege. Je weniger intensiv ein Archiv gepflegt werden muss, umso effizienter wird es. Die Pflege des Archivs ist eine Arbeit, die nicht besonders beliebt ist. Ich kann diese Haltung nicht verstehen, denn die Pflege kann auch eine weitere nützliche Funktion haben: Man lässt alle Sachverhalte noch einmal Revue passieren, ordnet ein, relativiert und bewertet die eigene Arbeit. Diese Arbeit ist keine langweilige Routine, sondern eine Möglichkeit zur Reflexion über das eigene Tun – und somit eine wichtige Hilfe, um Fehler zu vermeiden.

Das digitale Handarchiv

Von Ulf Grüner

Wer seine Informationen elektronisch speichern möchte, muss vor allem immer an eines denken: Je sensibler die archivierten Informationen sind, umso sicherer müssen diese verstaut werden. Die Lagerung auf Webservern kommt schon mal gar nicht in Frage. Im Zweifel: Runter auch vom Computer (bzw. erst gar nicht dort sichern) und rein in verschlüsselte Tresore. Das kann schon ein mit Truecrypt (truecrypt.org) gesicherter normaler USB-Stick sein. Darauf passt dann auch gleich ein mobiles Büro für heikle Recherchen (portableapps.org). Wer es noch sicherer braucht, wählt einen speziell via Hardware verschlüsselten USB-Stick. Einer der derzeit kleinsten, AES-gesicherten USB-Speicher ist der Pico-C von SuperTalent mit 32 GB Platz drauf (leider nur für Windows). Vergleichbare Produkte etwa von SanDisk (Cruzer Enterprise) sind ein wenig größer, bieten teils aber noch eine hochwertigere AES-Verschlüsselung mit FIPS-Zertifizierung.
Für die Archivierung von Inhalten aus dem Web bieten zwei Firefox-Addons schon ausreichende Möglichkeiten: Die kostenlose Software „Scrapbook“ sichert nicht nur die Webadresse, sondern zugleich die gewünschten Texte, Bilder und Dateien und protokolliert Datum sowie Uhrzeit der Archivierung. Sie eignet sich perfekt für kleine Alltagsrecherchen. Eine simple Volltextsuche und ein flexibles Ordnersystem erleichtern das Wiederfinden. Informationen und Installation via https://addons.mozilla.org/firefox/427/. Komplexere Materialsammlungen lassen sich besser mit dem Firefox-Addon „Zotero“ sichern und verwalten. Diese Software wurde für wissenschaftliches Arbeiten entwickelt und bietet entsprechend filigrane Sortier- und Verwaltungsfunktionen wie Verknüpfungen mit lokalen Dateien, Verschlagwortung und einer erweiterten Suchfunktion. Dafür gibt es derzeit kein besseres Add-on als Zotero. Es beherrscht das korrekte Zitieren und Bibliografieren genauso wie die Sicherung von Webseiten, Verschlagwortung (“tags“), lokale Suche in PDFs und Notizen sowie eine präzise erweiterte Suche. Die neue Version 2.0 ermöglicht darüber hinaus die Zusammenarbeit mit Kollegen. Das Zotero-Fenster hat drei Spalten: links „Meine Bibliothek“ mit der Übersicht aller Ordner (hier Sammlungen genannt). In der Mitte jeweils der Inhalt des links markierten Ordners. Rechts die Details zum in der Mitte markierten Eintrag, das können Notizen zu einer gespeicherten Webseite sein, Schlagworte oder Verknüpfungen zu einer Videodatei. Zugegeben: die Vielfalt erfordert Einarbeitung. So einfach wie „Scrapbook“ ist „Zotero“ nicht. Aber es lohnt sich. Ausführliche Hilfen für die umfangreichen Funktionen bietet die Website www.zotero.org/support/quick_start_guide (Installation via https://addons.mozilla.org/de/firefox/addon/3504/).
Wer aber große Mengen an Informationen und unterschiedliche Informationstypen auf seinem Rechner archivieren möchte, braucht ein noch leistungsfähigeres Programm:

„LitLink" zählt zu den bewährten Helfern des Rechercheurs (www.litlink.ch). Ebenfalls für wissenschaftliche Arbeit entwickelt, basiert es technisch auf der Profi-Datenbank Filemaker, ist aber kostenlos für Windows und Mac-Computer auch ohne Filemaker-Software benutzbar. Besonders hilfreich ist die assoziative Verknüpfung aller gespeicherten Informationen, etwa Web-Inhalte, Gesprächsnotizen oder Exzerpte. Selbst einfache Social-Network-Analysen lassen sich damit realisieren: Die integrierte Personen-Datenbank ist ursprünglich für die Erfassung von Autorinnen und Autoren gedacht, taugt aber natürlich für die systematische Dokumentation aller Personen einer Recherche – und die Auswertung in Form von „Netzwerken".

Manche Journalisten schwören bei der lokalen Archivierung auf „Wikis". Diesen fehlt aber die elegante automatische Sicherung von Webinhalten inklusive automatischer Quellenangabe und Datumsstempel, wie bei „Scrapbook", „Zotero" und „LitLink". Wer es dennoch versuchen will: www.wikimatrix.org hilft bei der Auswahl geeigneter Software. Deutlich vertrauter ist vielen Excel, für das der Kollege Luuk Sengers mit „DigitalFile" eine kostenlose Erweiterung geschaffen hat – speziell für Journalisten: www.luuksengers.nl/?page_id=3

Neben diesen kostenlosen Programmen gibt es eine ganze Reihe von weiteren digitalen Helfern, die zwar Geld kosten, aber bei intensiver Nutzung lohnen. Dazu zählen beispielsweise:

- flexible Datenbanken wie „DevonThink" (www.devon-technologies.com, nur für Mac) und „askSam" (www.asksam.com, nur für Windows)
- der Scanner-im-Kugelschreiber „Smartpen", der gleichzeitig ein Gespräch als Ton aufzeichnet, die schriftlichen Notizen automatisch der passenden Stelle im Mitschnitt zuordnet und die Handschrift auf Wunsch in digitalen Text umwandelt (sofern das Programm die Handschrift erkennen kann): www.livescribe.com/smartpen/

Je nach persönlichem Bedarf reicht manchmal eine Software zur Sicherung von Informationen, wie „Scrapbook". Wer zudem die Daten auch aufbereiten will, braucht mindestens sehr gute interne Suchfunktionen wie bei „Zotero", „LitLink", „DevonThink" und „askSam". Nur so findet man Verknüpfungen, die einem nicht sofort auffallen. Etwa mit einem Firmennamen, der schon einmal bei einer Recherche eine Rolle gespielt hat. Oder Verknüpfungen rund um eine Person. Dafür lohnt sich auch der Einsatz zusätzlicher Analyse-Software, etwa das für Social Network Analysis bewährte UCINET: www.analytictech.com/ucinet/

Aber bei aller Begeisterung für die Chancen digitaler Archive: Es klappt natürlich nur, wenn man kontinuierlich und systematisch die Daten erfasst, verschlagwortet oder zumindest vorsortiert und regelmäßig mit einem Backup sichert.

Ulf Grüner ist Journalist und Recherchetrainer. Weitere Informationen stehen auf seiner Webseite bereit: www.ulfgruener.de

Holger Wormer

Problemfeld Interview: Zitatcheck und Autorisierung

Holger Wormer ist Professor für Wissenschaftsjournalismus und war bis April 2010 Geschäftsführender Direktor des Instituts für Journalistik an der Technischen Universität Dortmund. Von 1996 bis 2004 war er als Wissenschaftsredakteur bei der Süddeutschen Zeitung spezialisiert auf rechercheintensive Themen. Seit mehr als zehn Jahren ist er in der Aus- und Weiterbildung von Journalisten engagiert, u.a. als Dozent für die Henri Nannen-Schule, die Akademie der Bayerischen Presse und den WDR. Interview- und Gesprächsführungstechniken bis hin zu Fragen der Autorisierung spielen dabei immer wieder eine wichtige Rolle – und wurden zum Teil auch bereits in kleineren Forschungsprojekten untersucht. Homepage: www.wissenschaftsjournalismus.org

„Du hörst mir ja gar nicht zu, Schatz!“ Kaum ein Satz dürfte in deutschen Wohnzimmern und Küchen häufiger ausgesprochen werden als dieser. Und oft wird er sogar stimmen. Mindestens ebenso oft aber ist er wohl nur ein Indiz für die Schwierigkeiten, die immer auftreten, wenn man das aufnehmen will, was ein anderer mitteilen möchte. Oder nach Konrad Lorenz: Gesagt ist eben nicht gehört und gehört ist noch nicht verstanden. Und was für Menschen gilt, die sich so gut kennen, dass sie Wohnzimmer und Küche miteinander teilen, gilt für weniger gute Bekannte – wie Journalisten und ihre Interviewpartner – umso mehr.

Sprachwissenschaftler haben sich Experimente ausgedacht, um deutlich zu machen, wie sehr Menschen aneinander vorbeireden können, weil sie unterschiedliche Welten im Kopf haben. Beispielsweise sollen sich zwei Menschen darüber unterhalten, dass sie „einen Tisch bestellt“ haben. Mensch Nr. 1 bekommt als Vorgabe, dass es sich um die Bestellung eines Tisches im Restaurant handelt; Mensch Nr. 2 hingegen glaubt, es ginge um den beim Möbelhaus bestellten Tisch. Im Experiment werden beide eine Weile brauchen, um zu bemerken, dass sie völlig aneinander vorbeireden – gleiche Worte, gleiches Wohnzimmer, unterschiedliche Welten.

Derlei Beispiele lassen sich viele finden; man spiele das Experiment etwa durch mit dem „schlechten Empfang“ (beim Bürgermeister) und dem „schlechten Empfang“ (des eigenen Handys). Sie machen deutlich, dass in Gespräch und Interview mitgeteilte „Fakten“ für beide Gesprächspartner eben noch lange nicht das Gleiche bedeuten müssen. In der Folge wäre es dann nicht verwunderlich, wenn der Satz „Das habe ich nie so gesagt“ in deutschen Redaktionen ungefähr den gleichen Stellenwert hätte wie die eingangs zitierte Klage über mangelndes Zuhören. Ein Grund dafür sind die verschiedenen Welten, in denen Journalisten und die meisten ihrer Gesprächspartner leben.

Welche Dimension der Streit um Fakten und Zitate bereits ein in einem – für den Laien völlig harmlos erscheinenden – Artikel annehmen kann, illustriert ein Beispiel über die „Kommunikation von (über) Bienen“ (siehe am Ende dieses Textes). Am Schluss rät der betroffene Wissenschaftler, auf eine Autorisierung von Artikeln zu bestehen; der Journalist wirft dem Wissenschaftler indes Unredlichkeit vor, habe er doch vorher mehrfach den Inhalt des Beitrags für gut befunden. Über die Gründe kann man im Detail nur spekulieren: Gab es hier tatsächlich einige Missverständnisse zwischen Journalist und Wissenschaftler? Oder war die Ächtung des Forschers durch (einflussreiche!) wissenschaftliche Fachkollegen so groß, dass er den Rückzug antreten musste, um nicht von den Geldmitteln der Scientific Community abgeschnitten zu werden?

Das echte Missverständnis ist jedoch ohnehin nur eine Variante von jenen Fällen, bei denen Gesagtes und/oder Notiertes nicht mit den realen Fakten übereinstimmt. Es lassen sich mindestens sechs Fehlerquellen für Fakten aus Zitaten unterscheiden:

Fehlerquellen in Interviews

Fall 1: Echtes Missverständnis durch verschiedene Welten („mindmap", „setting") von Interviewpartner und Journalist.
Fall 2: Interviewpartner glaubt den von ihm geschilderten Sachverhalt xy wirklich, xy ist aber in Wirklichkeit falsch (echter Irrtum).
Fall 3: Interviewpartner deutet im Gespräch bereits Zweifel an seiner eigenen Aussage an (Signalwörter: „offenbar", „vielleicht", „wahrscheinlich", „schätzungsweise").
Fall 4: Interviewpartner hat xy zwar gesagt, überlegt es sich aber später, z.B. bei der Autorisierung anders (Achtung: Rückzug kann verschiedene Gründe haben!).
Fall 5: Interviewpartner versucht bewusste Irreführung (Gegenmittel: Hintergrund und Interessen des Partners klären; W-Fragen der zweiten Generation).
Fall 6: Interviewpartner ist völlig ungeeignet, um nachgefragte Fakten zu liefern (Beispiel: Elsbeth M. aus Castrop-Rauxel macht im Regionalfernsehen allgemeingültige Gesundheitsaussagen zum Infektionsrisiko durch Grippeviren).

Seitens der Journalisten stellt sich die Frage, warum sie sich angesichts der vielfältigen Risiken und Unwägbarkeiten, die mit der Nutzung von Zitaten und Fakten aus Recherchegesprächen verbunden sind, überhaupt auf Zitatgeber auch als Faktengeber verlassen. Zum einen handelt es sich dabei natürlich um eine schnelle und bequeme Informationsquelle; bei einem guten Experten können viel gezielter und differenzierter Fragen gestellt, Meinungen, Fakten (samt deren Einordnung durch den Gesprächspartner) abgefragt werden, als das etwa bei einer Online-Recherche der Fall sein mag (die zudem oft ein größeres Vorwissen voraussetzt, um den gewünschten Erfolg zu erzielen). Und während das Internet prinzipiell für jedermann zugänglich ist, sprechen Politiker, Sportler, Künstler oder Experten noch lange nicht mit jedermann, wohl aber – meistens – mit Journalisten. Insofern gilt: Das Interview ist der Mehrwert des Journalismus gegenüber dem Internet! Gleichwohl sollten Fakten aus Zitaten eben nicht einfach übernommen, sondern – wie sonst auch – durch weitere Quellen geprüft werden. Idealerweise beginnt die Überprüfung von Fakten bereits im Gespräch. Für die verschiedenen Fälle können dabei folgende Strategien hilfreich sein (in Anlehnung an die zuvor identifizierten Fehlerquellen):

Gegenstrategie Fall 1: Das Problem der „verschiedenen Welten" wurde eingangs bereits beispielhaft erläutert. Man sollte immer damit rechnen, dass die gleichen Worte für beide Gesprächspartner nicht das Gleiche bedeuten – zum einen wegen unterschiedlicher Lebenswirklichkeiten, zum anderen auf Grund von Fachsprachen (etwa Juristendeutsch versus Allgemeinsprache). Und wenn die Bedeutung vielleicht manchmal nicht komplett verschieden ist, so mag es doch graduelle Unterschiede geben: So wird ein Journalist, der vor Ort von einem Unfall berichtet, das Gesehene vielleicht ganz furchtbar finden (weil er ohnehin kein Blut sehen kann), während der Notarzt, der täglich mit Verletzten konfrontiert ist, das Unfallgeschehen noch als recht harmlos empfindet. Auch die berüchtigten „Peanuts" für Banker gehören – jedenfalls ein Stück weit – in diese Kategorie. Die „journalistische Zuspitzung" eines Sachverhaltes tut hier ein Übriges. Eine banale Empfehlung gegen echte Missverständnisse lautet daher: So gut es geht in die Lebenswelten und die akute Situation des Gesprächspartners hinein versetzen! Es haben eben nicht alle Leute in jenem Moment, in dem der Journalist anruft, gerade darauf gewartet, ein Interview mit präzisen Statements und genauen Fakten zu geben. In der Regel haben sie sich vorher mit etwas ganz anderem beschäftigt als der Journalist. Im Gespräch sollte man sich daher regelmäßig fragen, wie der Interviewte das gerade Gesagte noch gemeint haben könnte.

Gegenstrategie Fall 2: „Ich hätte schwören können" lautet ein weiterer alltäglicher Satz, der sich auf Gesprächssituationen im Journalismus übertragen lässt: Da hat man mit viel Mühe den richtigen und vertrauenswürdigen Experten gefunden, der zudem auch noch drei gerade Sätze nacheinander sprechen kann, und dann stimmt es gar nicht, was er sagt! Das Gegenmittel ist in diesem Falle: Wann immer möglich sollte der Journalist Faktenaussagen von Gesprächspartnern gegenchecken oder zumindest auf Plausibilität prüfen. In der redaktionellen Realität sind hingegen andere Tendenzen zu beobachten. Wenn man sich schon selber nicht auskennt, soll es wenigstens der Experte tun: „Zitieren statt recherchieren" scheint oft das journalistische Motto zu sein. Für viele Zahlen und andere Fakten aber sind Online-Recherchen und Nachschlagewerke zuverlässiger und vielschichtiger als das, was ein noch so guter Fachmann gerade im Kopf hat. Auch Experten können irren!

Gegenstrategie Fall 3: Weniger gefährlich (da leichter erkennbar) sind Fälle, in denen Gesprächspartner bereits Zweifel an den eigenen Aussagen andeuten – sofern die Zweifel gehört werden! Fängt der Gesprächspartner an zu „vermuten", zu „glauben" oder zu „schätzen" ist kritisches Nachfragen geboten: „Sind sie sicher?", „Weiß man das genau?", „Wo könnte man das nochmals prüfen?". Bei Zahlen hilft mitunter schon die Frage weiter, wie genau man die Angabe eigentlich wissen und zählen kann. Wer die Aussage des Stadionsprechers zitiert, im Stadion hätten sich zur Halbzeit genau 61.738 Menschen auf den Rängen befunden, macht sicherlich einen Faktenfehler – denn so genau kann man das gar nicht wissen: Einige Zuschauer sind womöglich gerade auf der Toilette, andere wegen des schlechten Spiels früher gegangen; „rund 60.000" ist in diesem Falle die unpräzisere und doch richtigere Angabe. Auch in anderen Fällen empfiehlt es sich, die Zweifel an Zahlen und Fakten – sofern sie sich nicht durch andere Quellen ausräumen lassen – im Beitrag zumindest aufzugreifen. Dabei reicht es allerdings kaum, den Zweifel nur durch ein eingestreutes „vermutlich" deutlich zu machen, das sich schnell versendet. Vielmehr sollte man die Unsicherheit wirklich zum Thema machen („Sicher ist sich Professor Müller nicht, aber er wagt dennoch eine Schätzung").

Gegenstrategie Fall 4: Nicht immer ist das Zurückziehen eines Zitats gleichzusetzen mit der Identifikation eines Lügners – und schon gar nicht ein Indiz für die Richtigkeit des ursprünglich Gesagten. So mag gerade der besonders geschickte Frager im Interview ein Risiko produzieren, das ihm vielleicht gar nicht bewusst ist: Womöglich hat er sein Gegenüber durch besonders geschickte Befragungstechnik tatsächlich zu einer Aussage gebracht, die dieser sonst gar nicht gemacht hätte. Und erst beim ruhigen Nachdenken fällt dem Gesprächspartner auf, dass er an einer Stelle im Gespräch vielleicht zu unpräzise war oder sich eben zu einer falschen Aussage hat nötigen lassen. Interviews mit Journalisten sind für viele Menschen per se Stress-Situationen, in denen sie tatsächlich Dinge sagen, die sie so eigentlich nicht meinen. In diesen Fällen ist die Autorisierung (siehe unten) ein hilfreiches Korrektiv.
Kaum weniger häufig dürften jene Fälle sein, in denen den Interviewten erst später klar wird, welche Konsequenzen das Gesagte für sie haben könnte – und manches deshalb plötzlich nie so gesagt haben wollen. Das kann der Kronzeuge sein, der plötzlich mit Schadensersatzforderungen konfrontiert ist, weil er Kollegen, seine Firma oder seinen Verein kritisiert hat. Es kann aber auch der erwähnte Wissenschaftler sein, der befürchten muss, keine Forschungsgelder mehr zu bekommen, weil er sich gegen die Meinung der Mächtigen seines Fachs gestellt hat (siehe Beispiel am Ende des Textes). Und noch viel öfter sind es – vermutlich – die puren Eitelkeiten der Selbstdarsteller zwischen Promis und Politikern, die an ihrem Image in der Öffentlichkeit (und damit auch an ihren Zitaten) feilen.
Vor allem im letzten Fall sollte der Journalist so hart wie möglich bleiben; durch genaue Dokumentation belegen, dass etwas an einem bestimmten Tag zu einer

bestimmten Uhrzeit (notieren!) tatsächlich so gesagt und in den Schreibblock gekritzelt wurde. Im anderen Falle aber trägt er – gerade bei Medien-Unerfahrenen – auch ein Stück weit die Verantwortung für die „Zitatfolgenabschätzung“: Dem zufälligen Passanten oder dem Lottogewinner sollte er deutlich machen, was es bedeuten könnte, wenn ein bestimmtes Zitat mit vollem Namen vor einem Millionenpublikum über den Sender geht.

Gegenstrategie Fall 5: Die W-Fragen sind das A und O des Journalistenanfängers, der Profi und Zitatchecker bringt sie jedoch gleich in eine neue Reihenfolge; man könnte sie die „W-Fragen der zweiten Generation“ nennen: „Warum sagt wer was wann wo und wie?“ Warum etwa wird die Ankündigung des Lokalpolitikers, dass die neue Schule nun doch gebaut wird, auf dem Sommerfest der örtlichen IHK am Samstag vor der Kommunalwahl gemacht? Warum rechnet ein industrienahes Institut medienwirksam aus, dass es Beamten im Unterschied zu leitenden Angestellten finanziell besonders gut geht? Und warum sagt der Vertreter des Einzelhandelsverbands kurz vor dem letzten Adventssamstag, dass in diesem Jahr bereits besonders viele hochwertige Geschenke gekauft wurden? Auch Wissenschaftler, die im Ruf stehen, unabhängige Experten zu sein, neigen schon einmal dazu, just dann einen „Durchbruch“ in ihren Labors zu vermelden, wenn gerade die Finanzierung eines Forschungsprojekts zur Verlängerung ansteht.
Nun muss man weder diesseits noch jenseits des Labors überall weiße Mäuse sehen und „das Wort ‚Zufall‘ ist“ eben doch nicht immer, wie es Lessing gesagt haben soll (Zitat ungeprüft!), gleich „Gotteslästerung“. Dennoch: Keine Aussage findet ohne Kontext statt. Und ein Zitat ist eben nur so gut und zuverlässig wie sein Zitatgeber.
Wer nicht hinterfragt, welche Interessen sein Gesprächspartner mit seinen Aussagen verfolgen könnte, lässt sich leicht in die Irre führen. Und er macht sich zum Vertreter der Interessen des Interviewten. Selbst in offensichtlichen Fällen sind manche Journalisten geradezu fahrlässig: Wenn Wissenschaftler im Auftrag eines Schokoladenherstellers berichten, wie gesund Schokolade sei, und der Journalist berichtet dies brav und unkommentiert weiter, erinnert das schon an den Kalauer des Blödelbarden Otto. Der witzelte einst: „Wissenschaftler haben herausgefunden, dass Rauchen doch nicht gesundheitsschädlich ist. Gezeichnet, Dr. Marlboro.“ Auch in weniger offenkundigen Fällen sollte man den Gesprächspartner gleich selbst nach seinen Interessen und seiner eventuellen Befangenheit fragen. Das geht manchmal sogar harmlos und elegant: „Mit dieser Idee können Sie doch jetzt bestimmt viel Geld verdienen, oder?“. Die Hürde zu lügen ist bei direkter Nachfrage jedenfalls naturgemäß höher - wer erst gar nicht gefragt wird, kann bequem lügen durch Verschweigen.

Gegenstrategien Fall 6: Die Wahl der richtigen Gesprächspartner ist mindestens ebenso wichtig wie die Gesprächsführung selbst. Was für alle geschilderten Fälle gilt, scheint in der Realität häufig unterzugehen. Wem die Suche nach dem Experten zu mühsam und das Gespräch mit demselben zu kompliziert ist, der greift gerne mal auf den „Surrogat-Experten" zurück: Kann der Bauer mit seinen volkstümlichen Regeln nicht auch Fundiertes über das Wetter von morgen oder vielleicht sogar die Verbreitung von Aschewolken in der oberen Atmosphäre sagen? Und wenn man gar nicht weiter weiß, fragt BILD Promis von Beckenbauer bis Vicky Leandros, ob man sich gegen Schweinegrippe impfen sollte. Denn die müssen es ja wissen! Dabei spricht natürlich nichts dagegen, den Beitrag durch den Promi oder den berühmten „Betroffenen" lebensnäher zu gestalten; oder eben mal zu hören, was bei einer Straßenumfrage rauskommt. Wer dann aber zu den eigentlichen Fakten kommen will, sollte schon jemanden fragen, der sich mit so etwas auskennt.

Weitere Gegenstrategien: Auch viele der allgemeinen Empfehlungen zur Interviewführung, wie sie in der Praxisliteratur beschrieben sind (z.B. Haller 2001; Linden & Bleher 2005; Thiele 2008; Wormer 2008) können helfen, die Zuverlässigkeit von Faktenaussagen aus Interviews zu erhöhen. So senkt etwa das oft empfohlene „aktive Zuhören" (oder Paraphrasieren: „Ich habe Sie also richtig verstanden, dass") nicht nur die Zahl der echten Missverständnisse, sondern gibt dem Gesprächspartner auch Gelegenheit darüber nachzudenken, ob das von ihm Gesagte tatsächlich korrekt war. Und es ist auch eine vorbeugende Maßnahme gegen ein verbreitetes Ärgernis: die ausufernde Autorisierung.

Das Problem der Autorisierung

Wenn sich acht deutsche Tageszeitungen von der taz über die Süddeutsche und Die Welt bis zur Frankfurter Allgemeinen in ihrer Berichterstattung absprechen, muss etwas Wichtiges passiert sein: Am 28. November 2003 starteten sie eine gemeinsame Aktion, um gleichzeitig mit unterschiedlichen Artikeln in allen Blättern gegen einen um sich greifenden Missbrauch der Autorisierung zu protestieren. „In Berlin ist es üblich geworden, dass Abgeordnete selbst kleinste Zitate vorgelegt bekommen wollen", konstatierte Hans Leyendecker in der Süddeutschen Zeitung. Das Interview werde im Zuge der Autorisierung zum PR-Vehikel umfunktioniert. Konkreter Anlass für die Aktion war ein Wortlautinterview des SPD-Generalsekretärs Olaf Scholz mit der taz, bei dessen Autorisierung dann gleich auch die Fragen umgeschrieben wurden, die dem Politiker offenbar bereits zu forsch waren. Doch auch jenseits der Extreme ist das Thema „Autorisierung"

ein Dauerbrenner in der Journalistenweiterbildung. All das ist Grund genug, um sich bereits vor dem Gespräch darüber Gedanken zu machen. So muss dem Gesprächspartner zunächst klar sein, dass sein Gegenüber Journalist ist und mit ihm gerade ein Interview und nicht nur ein bloßes Hintergrundgespräch führt. Alles weitere ist vor allem eine Frage der Vereinbarung: Gibt der Gesprächspartner seine Auskünfte nur unter der Bedingung, dass er seine Zitate (und ggf. ihren engsten Zusammenhang im Text) vor der Veröffentlichung noch einmal sehen darf, so ist der Journalist verpflichtet, sich an diese Absprache zu halten – nicht anders, als man verpflichtet ist, sich an einen geschlossenen Vertrag zu halten. Nicht verpflichtet ist der Journalist dagegen, den ganzen Text zur Autorisierung vorzulegen. Wer aber geschlampt und Zitate nicht gleich im Gespräch geprüft und sauber aufgeschrieben hat, wird wohl nicht um das Gegenlesen herumkommen. Denn wie der Medienrechtswissenschaftler Udo Branahl immer wieder betont: Zitate müssen nun mal stimmen! Und das gilt auch für die sinngemäße (also nicht wörtliche) Wiedergabe eines Zitats. Formuliert der Journalist Antworten um (über grammatikalische Berichtigungen oder die Beseitigung von „ähs" hinaus), darf er sie nur dann als wörtliches Zitat verwenden, wenn der Gesprächspartner dem zugestimmt hat. Gerade mit Blick auf das Fact-Checking kann es aber in Einzelfällen sinnvoll sein, den Gesprächspartner über die Zitate hinaus einen kompletten Beitrag prüfen zu lassen – jedenfalls sofern dieser keine heiklen Passagen enthält. Wenn Fact-Checker gelegentlich sogar die im Artikel genannten Personen kontaktieren, um Fakten zu prüfen, wieso sollte das der Autor bei einem reinen Sach- oder lexikalischen Hintergrundtext nicht gleich selber tun, wenn sich so objektive Fehler in der Berichterstattung vermeiden lassen?
Neben dem organisatorischen und zeitlichen Aufwand spricht jedoch auch bei harmlosen Sachtexten etwas gegen einen allzu vorauseilenden Autorisierungsgehorsam: Je mehr die Journalisten ihre Gesprächspartner daran gewöhnen, dass sie jeden Beitrag autorisieren dürfen, umso leichter resultiert daraus ein Gewohnheitsrecht oder unnötiges Misstrauen („Also Ihre Kollegen haben mir die Texte immer noch einmal vorgelegt"). In der Konsequenz kann das dazu führen, dass sich auch die Rechtssprechung daran orientiert, wenn das Autorisieren bereits als „allgemein üblich" angesehen wird. Wie eine Untersuchung am Lehrstuhl Wissenschaftsjournalismus der Technischen Universität Dortmund bestätigt hat, gehört es bereits heute bei den meisten deutschen Printmedien zum redaktionellen Automatismus, Wortlautinterviews autorisieren zu lassen (vgl. Seifert 2008). In der Studie wurde die Autorisierungspraxis (bzw. das Copy Approval) in Deutschland und England ebenso verglichen wie deren rechtliche Grundlagen. Befragt wurden dazu deutsche und englische Tageszeitungsjournalisten aus den Ressorts Politik, Wirtschaft und Wissenschaft. Folgt man

den Angaben der deutschen Journalisten, so lassen diese etwa neun von zehn Wortlautinterviews autorisieren; Zitate in Artikeln werden immerhin in mehr als zwei von zehn Fällen zur Autorisierung gegeben. Für englische Journalisten ist es der Studie zufolge zwar keineswegs „undenkbar" (wie dies in der deutschsprachigen Literatur oft behauptet wird), einen Text gegenlesen zu lassen. Die Grundtendenz, dass englische Journalisten deutlich weniger zur Autorisierung (insbesondere von Wortlautinterviews) neigen, wurde dennoch klar bestätigt (Tabelle 2):

Deutschland (n=94)	Immer	Nach Vereinbarung	Nie
Interviews	53 (56%)	41 (44%)	- (0%)
Zitate	8 (9%)	66 (70%)	20 (21%)
Ganze Artikel	- (0%)	15 (16%)	79 (84%)
England (n=24)	Always	By Agreement	Never
Interviews	- (0%)	5 (21%)	19 (79%)
Quotes	- (0%)	13 (54%)	11 (46%)
Articles	- (0%)	6 (25%)	18 (75%)

Tabelle 2: Antworten von englischen und deutschen Tageszeitungsjournalisten auf die Frage „In welchen Fällen lassen Sie eine Autorisierung (Copy Approval) bei Wortlautinterviews, Zitaten und ganzen Artikeln zu?" (vgl. Seifert 2008).

Trotz der vergleichsweise schlechten Rücklaufquote bei englischen Journalisten wird deutlich, dass eine generelle Autorisierung auch bei Wortlautinterviews als absolut unüblich gelten kann. In Deutschland lässt sich das Recht auf eine Autorisierung vor allem aus den allgemeinen Persönlichkeitsrechten (Schutz des eigenen Wortes, informationelle Selbstbestimmung und Imageschutz) ableiten. Zwar gibt es auch in England Rechtsfiguren, die Zitierungen gewisse Grenzen setzen, im Endeffekt sind englische Journalisten nach Seifert (2008) jedoch „weder rechtlich noch standesrechtlich zum Copy Approval verpflichtet". Inwieweit das unterschiedliche Autorisierungsverhalten nun vor allem Ausdruck unterschiedlicher Journalismuskulturen ist oder darauf beruht, dass es in Deutschland – anders als in England – ein ausgeprägtes Recht gibt zu bestimmen, was von einem selbst in einer Zeitung steht, ist für die Praxis müßig zu entscheiden. Wie aber kann man einem ausufernden Autorisierungswahn vorbeugen? Dazu sieben Vorschläge:

1. Lassen Sie zentrale Zitate möglichst schon im Gespräch durch aktives Zuhören mündlich „autorisieren“, etwa indem Sie komplexe Aussagen mit eigenen Worten paraphrasieren. Der Gesprächspartner wird dann womöglich leicht zu überzeugen sein, dass eine erneute Autorisierung auf schriftlichem Weg nicht mehr notwendig ist.
2. Machen Sie Ihren Gesprächspartner darauf aufmerksam, dass eine Autorisierung im – bei vielen ja hoch angesehenen – angloamerikanischen Raum eher unüblich ist und von englischen Journalisten (und auch von Ablegern englischer Zeitungen in Deutschland) nicht akzeptiert würde.
3. Weisen Sie ggf. darauf hin, dass der Text noch Zitate anderer Gesprächspartner enthält, die ihrerseits noch nicht autorisiert sind.
4. Weisen Sie auf die knappe Zeit bis zum Redaktionsschluss hin, die eine Zusendung von Zitaten schwierig bis unmöglich macht.
5. Lassen Sie allenfalls Textpassagen autorisieren, die die wörtliche oder in indirekte Rede gefasste Aussage des Gesprächspartners (inklusive des unmittelbaren Kontextes) enthalten, nicht aber den gesamten Beitrag (Ausnahmen siehe oben) und schon gar keine Überschriften!
6. Wenn Sie einen Text oder einzelne Zitate autorisieren lassen müssen, dann vereinbaren Sie bereits im Vorfeld eine angemessene, aber doch möglichst knappe Frist (von beispielsweise x Stunden) für die Antwort: Da Sie dem Gesprächspartner entgegen kommen und ihm die Autorisierung ermöglichen, ist es recht und billig, wenn er sich ein Stück weit Ihrem Arbeitsrhythmus anpasst.
7. Kommt ein Text doch verunstaltet zurück, lohnt es sich, erneut zu verhandeln: Machen Sie Ihrem Gesprächspartner klar, dass viele seiner Änderungen übertrieben, unüblich oder unnötig sind. Argumentieren Sie, dass manches in der ursprünglichen Fassung sicherlich besser beim Leser ankommt. (Hier kann bei manchen Partnern auch der dezente Hinweis hilfreich sein, dass Sie der Textprofi sind, der das vielleicht am besten beurteilen kann). Auch der Hinweis, man werde bei zu starken Eingriffen in der Zeitung darauf hinweisen, dass es sich um ein stark vom Gesprächspartner überarbeitetes Interview handelt, kann ein probates Mittel sein.

Wenn es trotz allem einmal gar nicht klappen will mit einem Zitat und seiner Autorisierung, hilft am Schluss vielleicht ein kleiner Trost: Es spricht viel dafür, dass Zitate im Text bei weitem überschätzt werden – da mag der Volontär noch so oft gehört haben: „Zitate lockern auf“. Denn erstens gilt: Höchstens lockere

Zitate lockern wirklich auf. Und zweitens, dem Readerscan-Forscher Carlo Imboden folgend: Schlecht eingeführte Zitate lassen Leser oft aussteigen.

Literatur

BRANAHL, U. (2006): Medienrecht. Eine Einführung. Wiesbaden.

HALLER, M. (2001): Das Interview – ein Handbuch für Journalisten. Reihe Praktischer Journalismus, Konstanz.

LEYENDECKER, H. (2003): Nicht fummeln, Liebling! – Politik gegen Presse: Die Sache mit der „Autorisierung", Süddeutsche Zeitung, 28.11.2003.

LINDEN, P.; Bleher, C. (2005): Journalisten-Werkstatt „Das Interview". Beilage zum MediumMagazin, Freilassing.

SEIFERT, J. (2008): Autorisierung und Copy Approval – Gegenlesen in Deutschland und England. Ein Vergleich aus rechtlicher und praktischer Sicht mit besonderer Berücksichtigung der Politik-, Wirtschafts- und Wissenschaftsressorts in Tageszeitungen. Diplomarbeit am Lehrstuhl Wissenschaftsjournalismus, Dortmund.

THIELE, C. (2008): Journalisten-Werkstatt „Gute Gespräche. Die Kunst des Interviews II", Beilage zum MediumMagazin, Freilassing.

WORMER, H. (2008): Google ist Silber, reden ist Gold. Wer es versteht, seinen Gesprächsstil an verschiedene Typen von Wissenschaftlern anzupassen, erfährt (und versteht) mehr als andere In: Hettwer, H.; Lehmkuhl, M.; Wormer, H.; Zotta, F. (Hg.): Wissenswelten. Wissenschaftsjournalismus in Theorie und Praxis. Gütersloh.

Hinweis: Mehr Informationen zum Thema `Interviewtechnik´ in der nr-Werkstatt Nr. 13 „Interview-Kulturen"

Kommunikation von (über) Bienen: Ein folgenreicher Streit um harmlose Zitate

Schwänzeltanz entzaubert (Süddeutsche Zeitung, 2. Dezember 2009)

Jedes Schulkind lernt, dass Bienen sich durch Tanzen verständigen. Doch die Insekten verstehen den Hüftschwung vermutlich gar nicht – oder er lässt sie schlicht kalt.

Anfangs lachte der junge Zoologe Karl von Frisch nur über die merkwürdigen Wackelbewegungen seiner Bienen. Er lud befreundete Imker ein, und zusammen vergnügten sie sich ganze Sommertage lang damit, diesen „Scherz der Bienen" zu beobachten. 1923 notierte Frisch in den Zoologischen Jahrbüchern: „Ich behaupte, dass auch die Bienen, wenn der Stock in gutem Zustand ist, gewisse Lustbarkeiten und Freuden unter sich haben, dass sie sogar zuweilen einen gewissen Tanz anstellen." Ein halbes Jahrhundert später erhielt Frisch den Nobelpreis unter anderem für die Erforschung des Schwänzeltanzes. (...) Mit Hilfe des Schwänzeltanzes informiert eine Biene ihre Artgenossen im Stock über die exakte Position der Futterquelle und die Entfernung dorthin, war Frisch schließlich überzeugt. Die anderen Bienen beobachten die Choreographie, entschlüsseln die darin codierten Informationen und steuern dann zielsicher den Futterplatz an. Jedes Schulkind lernt seitdem etwas über diese Kommunikationsleistung der Bienen. Nun gerät das Dogma vom unmissverständlichen Schwänzeltanz in die Kritik. Immer selbstbewusster greifen Wissenschaftler die These an. „Wir haben untersucht, ob Bienen allein anhand der Informationen aus dem Schwänzeltanz eine einzelne, nicht duftende Futterquelle finden können. Unsere Ergebnisse weisen darauf hin, dass dies nicht der Fall ist", schreibt der Würzburger Bienenforscher Jürgen Tautz. (...)

Reaktionen bei der Fachgesellschaft der deutschen Biologen

Kontroverse um den Schwänzeltanz (www.vbio.de/informationen/alle_news -› kontroverse um den schwaenzeltanz (Stand: 19. April 2010))

Der Artikel „Schwänzeltanz entzaubert" (...), veröffentlicht in der Süddeutschen Zeitung vom 02. Dezember 2009, hat bei Bienenforschern für einigen Wirbel und Unmut gesorgt. Am 09. Dezember 2009 erschien daraufhin in der Süddeutschen Zeitung ein Interview mit Prof. Randolf Menzel, der die wesentlichen Fehler korrigiert hat: „Und sie tanzen doch". Wir dokumentieren hier stellvertretend die Positionen des Karl-von-Frisch-Schülers Prof. Dr. Karl Daumer und diejenige

von Prof. Dr. Jürgen Tautz von der Universität Würzburg, den die Autorin in ihrem Artikel zitiert hatte. Bilden Sie Sich selbst ihre Meinung.
(...)

Prof. Dr. Jürgen Tautz, BEEgroup, Biozentrum, Universität Würzburg: Von den Risiken, ein Wissenschaftskommunikator zu sein

Ein erst kürzlich erschienener Beitrag der Süddeutschen Zeitung zum Schwänzeltanz der Honigbienen hat leider zu heftigen Reaktionen aus Biologenkreisen geführt. An dieser Stelle möchte ich mich lediglich über MEINE Rolle in diesem Kontext äußern.
Eine Mitarbeiterin der SZ hatte mich angerufen und um ein Gespräch gebeten, da ihr eine Fach-Publikation zu neuen Aspekten der Futterplatzrekrutierung bei Honigbienen untergekommen war. (...)
Ich habe in diesem Zusammenhang einen GROSSEN FEHLER begangen, hier selbstkritisch hervorgehoben, zur Warnung, insbesondere an junge Kollegen/Innen, die sich um Vermittlung von Fachwissen, auch an Nichtfachleute, bemühen wollen. Ich habe NICHT darauf bestanden, das Konzept des SZ-Beitrags, Teile des Textes und/oder den Endtext vor dessen Veröffentlichung zu sehen. Der Beitrag gibt so wenig den Geist, den Tenor und die Details meiner etwa einstündigen Ausführungen wieder, dass ich dessen Veröffentlichung so NIE autorisiert hätte. Ich hätte den Verdacht schöpfen können, dass eine derart komplexe Geschichte das hohe Risiko von input ungleich output beinhaltet. Diese Gefahr habe ich unterschätzt. (...)
Publikationen der BEEgroup zur Tanzsprache sind zu finden unter http://www.beegroup.de. Sie geben wieder, welche Haltung von mir und meinen Mitarbeitern in diesem Zusammenhang gegenüber den überragenden Lebensleistungen Karl von Frischs und Martin Lindauers in Fachorganen aber auch in Sonderheften für Schulen und anderen Medien AUTORISIERT öffentlich gemacht worden sind.

Dazu der Ressortleiter Wissen der Süddeutschen Zeitung (Dr. Patrick Illinger)

Als für Wissenschaft verantwortlicher Redakteur der Süddeutschen Zeitung habe ich in den vergangenen drei Wochen versucht, den ausufernden Wirbel um einen am 2.Dezember in der SZ erschienenen Text über den Schwänzeltanz der Bienen, in dem Aussagen von Prof. Jurgen Tautz aus Würzburg eine wichtige Rolle spielen, möglichst zu dämpfen. Nun muss ich (...) feststellen, dass Prof. J. Tautz die Entstehung des umstrittenen Beitrags auf eine Weise darstellt, die meine Mitarbeiterin und das Ansehen der Süddeutschen Zeitung in Misskredit bringen.

Prof. J. Tautz versucht nun, sich quasi als Opfer eines journalistischen Überfalls darzustellen und rät sogar Fachkollegen, zurückhaltender gegenüber Journalisten zu sein. Abgesehen davon, dass dies nachteilig für den deutschen Wissenschaftsjournalismus wäre, stellt Tautz die Abläufe unkorrekt dar. J. Tautz erklärt, er hätte den in der SZ am 2. Dezember erschienenen Text „so NIE autorisiert". Ich halte es daher für nötig, die tatsächliche Rolle von Prof. Tautz in dieser Angelegenheit zu erläutern.
Auch mehrere Tage nach dem Erscheinen des SZ-Beitrags vom 2. Dezember kommunizierte Prof. J. Tautz in Sachen Bienentanz mit der Süddeutschen Zeitung, wobei er keinerlei Kritik an dem erschienenen Beitrag äußerte, sondern im Gegenteil mündlich wie schriftlich seine Aussagen sowie den Beitrag selbst bestärkte (...) , so zum Beispiel am 7. Dezember in einer E-Mail an meine Mitarbeiterin (...): „Ihr Beitrag hat aufgerührt, was sich nun als Folge bestimmt zu einem klaren Bild setzen wird."
In zustimmendem Tenor äußerte sich Prof. J. Tautz der Süddeutschen Zeitung gegenüber auch in einem weiteren Telefongespräch (...) Tautz erklärte meiner Mitarbeiterin, dass er zwar erschrocken sei über die heftigen Reaktionen, aber dennoch froh sei, dass der ursprüngliche Artikel so erschienen sei, weil es ja manchmal gut sei, wenn ein Konflikt, den es schon lange unterschwellig gebe, einmal heftig losbreche. (...)
Da Prof. Jürgen Tautz nun versucht, sich auf Kosten meiner Mitarbeiterin zu rechtfertigen, sehe ich mich gezwungen, dieser unwahren Darstellung der Abläufe zu begegnen: Was Prof. J. Tautz seit dem 18. Dezember in seiner Stellungnahme auf der website des vbio äußert, hinterlässt in unserer Redaktion völliges Unverständnis (...). Prof. J. Tautz war bis vor wenigen Tagen nachweisbar einverstanden mit dem SZ-Beitrag über den Schwänzeltanz der Bienen vom 2. Dezember 2009.

Dokumentationen

Die Dokumentation

nr-Werkstatt:
Werte und Orientierungen

kann kostenfrei gegen einen adressierten und ausreichend frankierten Rückumschlag (DIN C5, 1.50 Euro) beim netzwerk recherche bezogen werden.

Bezugsadresse:
netzwerk recherche e.V.
Geschäftsstelle
Stubbenhuk 10, 5. OG
20459 Hamburg

www.netzwerkrecherche.de
info@netzwerkrecherche.de

nr
netzwerk
recherche

message - Werkstatt: Fact-Checking

Sei skeptisch und glaube nichts

Von Michael Haller

Überprüfen gehört zum kleinen Einmaleins der Recherche – und doch schleichen sich immer wieder Fehler ein. Hier einige Grundregeln des Fact-Checking.

Wenn man Leser, Fernsehzuschauer oder Radiohörer fragt, was für sie das wichtigste Qualitätsmerkmal der Medien sei, lautet die Antwort übereinstimmend: Zuverlässigkeit. Diese in verschiedenen Repräsentativbefragungen gewonnene Auskunft bezieht sich auf die aktuellen Informationsmedien, allen voran die Tageszeitung (weniger auf Illustrierte und Boulevardblätter). Von der Zuverlässigkeit der Berichte hängt es ab, ob die Leser ihrer Zeitung »Glaubwürdigkeit« zusprechen. Und diese wiederum – so belegen die Erhebungen – ist maßgeblich, ob die Leser ihrem Blatt treu bleiben oder sich bei passender Gelegenheit verabschieden.

Das Image der Zuverlässigkeit gewinnen Zeitungen oder Rundfunksendungen dann, wenn stimmt, was berichtet wird. Also muss der Journalist nur überprüfen, ob stimmt, was er berichten will – und schon ist alles in Ordnung. Das klingt simpel und selbstverständlich, schließlich heißt es in den Landesmediengesetzen, dass die Medien die Informationen auf »Wahrheit, Inhalt und Herkunft« zu prüfen hätten. Dasselbe steht auch im Pressekodex. Und doch ist es so schwer – aus drei Gründen.

Erstens: Fakten sind nicht immer Fakten

Am Anfang jedes Berichts stehen Ausgangsinformationen: Die Erzähle eines Zeugen oder eines Betroffenen; die Darstellungen in älteren Texten, die man im Archiv, der Datenbank oder über Google findet. Dieses Material ist meist ein Gemisch aus Sachaussagen, Eindrücken, Empfindungen, Meinungsäußerungen und Urteilen. Manches kann man überprüfen, vieles jedoch nicht.

Angenommen, Sie sollten wegen des Notverkaufs der Hypo Alpe Adria einen Recherchenbericht schreiben über das Missmanagement des Chefs der Bayerischen Landesbank (BayernLB), Michael Kemmer. Angenommen, Sie stoßen bei der Materialauswertung auf dieses Zitat: »Kemmer hat im Umgang mit dem Problem Hypo Alpe Adria versagt« (ich zitiere im Folgenden aus der Süddeutschen Zeitung vom 15.12.2009). Was ist daran faktisch? Erstens die Frage, ob der Satz wirklich gesagt wurde. Doch leider heißt es in Bezug auf die Quelle nur: »aus der Belegschaft«. Die Quelle ist also anonym, der Reporter kolportiert nur oder fabuliert. Und die Aussage des Zitats ist eine subjektive Einschätzung, Juristen nennen dies eine Meinungsäußerung. Also nichts Faktisches und insofern auch nicht überprüfbar.

Überprüfen kann man nur Aussagen, die Sachverhalte betreffen. Das sind überwiegend Angaben

- über Personen (Name, derzeitige Funktion, Alter, Zivilstand, Wohnort)
- über Örtlichkeiten (Stadtname, Straßenname, Hausnummer, Lage des Zimmers)
- über die Ortszeit (wann genau, seit wann, bis wann, Zeitzone, Datum)
- über den Gegenstand (eine Tat, ein Beschluss, eine Rede oder Aussage, ein Naturereignis usw.)
- über Merkmale eines Gegenstands (Abmessungen, Dauer, Farbe, Temperatur, Lautstärke, Beschaffenheit).

Tipp: Die klarste Checkliste sind die vier W-Fragen Wer, Was, Wann, Wo. Alle Aussagen, die auf diese Fragen eine Antwort geben können, sind im Prinzip überprüfbar.

Problematisch sind Aussagen über die Art und Weise, über das »Wie«, weil es Einschätzungen nennt und meist in Sinnbildern oder Metaphern zur Sprache kommt. »Dieser Umgang mit der Vergangenheit treibt offenbar einen Keil in den Vorstand der CSU« – Klar, was gemeint ist. Aber was ist daran faktisch? Es ist nicht diese Aussage selbst (diese ist eine Interpretation), es sind die Belege, die diese Aussage stützen (hier: die Meinungen des Alt-Vorstands der CSU, Stoiber, Beckstein, Huber).

Tipp: Antworten auf Wie- und Warum-Fragen sind meist keine Fakten, sondern Interpretationen von Fakten. Also müssen zuerst diese Belege und dann die Angemessenheit ihrer Interpretation überprüft werden.

Zweitens: Die Sachen sind kompliziert

Fakten allein ergeben keinen Sinn. Sie sind wie Mosaiksteine, die zusammen ein ganzes Puzzle – den Zusammenhang – geben sollen. Das Puzzle selbst kann man nicht überprüfen, es muss aber als Ganzes plausibel sein. Die Aussage »Michael Kemmer hatte es sich am Ende mit allen verdorben« ist so ein Puzzle – und wenn die Belege fehlen, ist es eine (oftmals überzogene oder verallgemeinerte) Behauptung, die wie eine These funktioniert.

Manchmal sind Vorgänge und Abläufe auch viel zu unübersichtlich (»komplex«), um sie wie ein Puzzle beschreiben zu können. Und manchmal ist nur ein Teil des Ganzen erkennbar; über den unbekannten Teil existieren nur Spekulationen. Das Hypo-Alpe-Adria-Desaster habe den Freistaat Bayern »mindestens 3,75 Milliarden Euro gekostet« heißt es. Dass der Staat diesen Betrag aus Steuergeldern hat aufbringen müssen, kann überprüft werden, indem beim Pressesprecher nachgefragt wird. Aber sagt der alles, was für die Einordnung des Vorgangs wichtig ist? Was verbirgt sich hinter dem »mindestens«?

Tipp: Aussagen über Zusammenhänge, Abläufe und Folgen kann man nicht überprüfen. Man sollte sie wie Thesen behandeln – also nur zitieren (aber mit präziser Quellenangabe).

Drittens: Das unsichere Wissen

Wer überprüft, sucht vielleicht die Wahrheit – doch was er findet, ist etwas anderes, nämlich »Unstrittigkeit«. Das geht so: Indem ich eine Sachaussage überprüfe, vergleiche ich sie mit Aussagen anderer Quellen; wenn die anderen dasselbe sagen, gilt die Aussage als gesichert, d.h. sie ist eine unstrittige (verifizierte) Tatsache. Doch wie zuverlässig sind diese anderen Quellen? Bewege ich mich vielleicht im Zirkel, weil alle Quellen aus derselben Ursprungsquelle geschöpft haben? Oder fallen alle demselben Irrtum, demselben Vorurteil anheim? Man kann es nicht ganz ausschließen, doch die Gefahr lässt sich durch eine kritische Quellenüberprüfung wenigstens reduzieren.

Tipp: Jede Faktenüberprüfung beginnt mit dem Quellen-Check: Auf welche Primärquelle gehen sie zurück? Welche ist authentisch?

Die meisten Fehler sind die Folge von Gutgläubigkeit und Schlafmützigkeit: Man liest etwas und glaubt es nur schon deshalb, weil es andere auch schon geglaubt haben. Auch Message kennt das Problem dieser Betriebsblindheit: Da untersuchte ein Autor aktuelle Trends bei den Bloggern und nennt in seinem Manuskript den bekannten Blog »Spreeblick« plötzlich »Spreewald« (vielleicht hatte er im Laufe jener Nachtschicht Hunger bekommen). Das Skript wird gegengelesen, redigiert, Korrektur gelesen, nochmals gecheckt – und dann steht im Heft »Spreewald« (Message 4/2008: 17). Ähnliche Fehler finden sich tagtäglich in fast allen gedruckten Medien; in den Onlinemedien nur deshalb so selten, weil rasch korrigiert werden kann.
Motto: Glaube deinem eigenen Wissen nicht und markiere jeden Namen, jede Sachaussage, auch wenn du sie schon X-mal gelesen oder sogar irgendwann einmal selbst geschrieben hast.
Ob ein journalistischer Text am Ende zutreffend informiert, darüber entscheidet nicht nur die Sachrichtigkeit der Fakten, sondern die Darstellung des ganzen Vorgangs. Und ob diese trifft, hängt letztlich von der Einstellung des Autors, des Gegenlesers, Fact-Checkers, Korrektors ab. Und diese Einstellung sollte lauten: Sei skeptisch! Glaube nichts, auch nicht dir selbst!

Michael Haller ist Professor für Allgemeine und Spezielle Journalistik an der Universität Leipzig und Herausgeber von „Message - Internationale Zeitschrift für Journalismus“.

Im Dickicht der Details

Von Erwin Koch

Fehler vermeiden im Schreibprozess! Das Recherchematerial gehört gut strukturiert, um beim Schreiben in den gesammelten Fakten nicht die Orientierung zu verlieren.

Vor einem Jahr, ausgestattet mit dem Segen der Zeit, fuhr ich auf die Osterinsel, ein kleiner Lebenstraum. Ich wollte dort, in Form einer Reportage, der Theorie nachforschen, dieser einsame Punkt im südlichen Pazifik habe vor dreihundert Jahren vorweggenommen, was der Erde noch bevorstehe, der ökologische und soziale Kollaps.
In der Tat hatten die Holländer, die die Osterinsel im Jahr 1722 entdeckten, eine Gesellschaft vorgefunden, die in Auflösung begriffen war. Es gab keinen einzigen Baum mehr auf der Insel, aus dem man hätte ein Boot bauen können, um dem Elend zu entkommen, Rapa Nui war leergeholzt, es herrschten Hunger, Krieg, Kannibalismus.
Ich bin Reporter. Nach Möglichkeit mache ich mich kundig, bevor ich irgendwohin aufbreche. Ich will vorbereitet sein, auf dass ich gewisse Fragen oder Themen vor Ort nicht unangesprochen lasse. Andere Reporter machen es anders, ich pflege zuerst zu lesen, zu lesen, zu lesen.

Erster Schritt
Aus dem Internet kitzelte ich, was mir nützlich erschien, Stichworte Osterinsel und Rapa Nui. Ich druckte es aus, insgesamt 71 Seiten. Die ordnete ich in chronologischer Reihenfolge, beginnend mit dem ältesten Dokument, einem Zeitungsartikel aus dem Jahr 1998, und nummerierte den Stapel, 1 bis 71, oben rechts.
Dann las ich die Papiere, unterstrich die Informationen, von denen ich glaubte, sie könnten vielleicht Teil meines Textes werden.

Zweiter Schritt
Ich setzte mich an meinen Computer, öffnete den Ordner Stichwortverzeichnisse und schuf mir eine neue Datei: Osterinsel. Ich bückte mich über meine 71 Seiten, fasste die erste Information auf Seite eins, die ich unterstrichen hatte, in wenigen Worten – doch immerhin in so vielen, dass ich auch Wochen später noch verstünde, was damit gemeint war – zusammen und vermerkte dazu die Zahl der Seite, auf der eben diese Information zu finden war. Seite nach

Seite behandelte ich auf diese Weise: Stichwort plus Seitenzahlen. Das sah dann, einige Beispiele, so aus:

- O. entstand vor 2,5 Mio Jahren, vulkanisch 1
- Geogr. Koordinaten 1
- Distanzen zu anderen Inseln 3
- Fläche 2
- 41 % davon ist National-park 3
- ›30 000 archäolog Punkte = bestuntersuchter Ort 4

Dritter Schritt

Nachdem ich alle Informationen auf den 71 Seiten in Stichworten zusammengefasst und jedes Stichwort mit einer oder mehreren Herkunftsnummern versehen hatte, erfand ich mir, der thematischen Übersicht zuliebe, einige Kapitel.
Jene Stichworte zur Pflanzen- und Tierwelt auf der Osterinsel, damals und heute, zog ich zum Kapitel Flora/Fauna zusammen, jene, die sich auf Kunst und Götter bezogen, zum Kapitel Kunst/Kultur/Religion. Andere Kapitel hießen Geographisches, Historisches, Administratives, Soziales, Zukunftsszenarien.

Vierter Schritt

Ich ging in die Bibliothek. Unter dem Begriff Osterinsel waren dort 33 Schriften vermerkt, sechs nahm ich mit nach Hause, alle neueren Datums. Ich blätterte und las und unterstrich mit zartem Bleistift, was mir nützlich werden könnte. Schließlich zeichnete ich jedes Buch mit einem Buchstaben aus und ergänzte mein Verzeichnis mit den Informationen, die ich aus diesen sechs Büchern gewonnen hatte. Dabei übernahm ich die Seitenzahl des jeweiligen Buches und setzte ihr den entsprechenden Buchstaben, den ich für das jeweilige Buch vergeben hatte, voran:

A = Iwanowski's, Chile mit Osterinsel
B = Reise Know-How, Chile und die Osterinsel
C = Osterinsel, Ein Reiseführer, M. Kasparek Verlag
D = Josef W. Schmid, Osterinsel
E = Jared Diamond, Kollaps

- Vor der polyn. Besiedlung gab es auf O. 24 Arten von See- und 6 Arten von Landvögeln, heute nur noch 4, keine davon indigen C26
- Verschiedene Besiedlungstheorien 5,55 A607 B577
- Heyerdahl vertrat eine Besiedlung durch südamerik. Indianer A607 B577 E107

Fünfter Schritt

Ich reiste auf die Osterinsel und war eine Woche lang dort, suchte Menschen, deren Biografie oder Aussagen mir geeignet schienen, dem Thema gerecht zu werden, ihm Gestalt zu geben – mein Personal.

Insgesamt unterhielt ich mich mit dreizehn Personen, acht davon nahm ich in meine engere Wahl, eine alte Sippenhauptfrau, die Inselpsychologin, einen Reiseleiter schweizerischer Herkunft, einen Unabhängigkeitsfanatiker, der sich König nannte, ein Mädchen, die Kandidatin bei einem Schönheitswettbewerb, den Inselkaplan und die Gouverneurin. Was ich hörte, was ich sah, was ich roch und fühlte, notierte ich in ein kleines Buch. Wieder zu Hause, las ich meine Notizen, versah jede Seite des Notizbuchs mit einer Zahl und unterstrich, was mir wichtig vorkam – und komplettierte schließlich mein Verzeichnis mit den Informationen aus dem Notizbuch, N für Notizbuch.

Wieder schuf ich mir einige Kapitel, eines für jede der acht Personen, für die ich mich entschieden hatte, ein weiteres Kapitel hieß einfach Szenisches.

Sechster Schritt

Damit war mein Stoff organisiert, chronologisch und thematisch geordnet. Endlich begann die Schreiberei, der erste Satz, dann der zweite, der dritte. Mein Verzeichnis, 40.000 Zeichen lang, lag ausgedruckt neben mir, ich saß und wusste nicht weiter, blätterte durch den Wald der Stichworte und überlegte, welches vernachlässigbar sei und welches nicht. Entschied ich mich für eines, las ich noch einmal die Quelle, die sich darüber ausbreitete: D154, also Seite 154, im Buch D für Osterinsel von Josef W. Schmid.

Wahrscheinlich kamen nicht mehr als zehn Prozent meiner Erinnerungsstützen zum Zug und wurden, in vernünftige Sätze gegossen, Teil des Textes. Aber die zehn besten Prozent, hoffentlich.

Siebenter Schritt

Ich überließ den Aufsatz meinem Gegenleser, einem Freund, der seit Jahrzehnten fast alles liest, was ich schreibe, und es tüchtig ausmistet.

Der Kisch-Preisträger Erwin Koch lebt als freier Journalist in der Zentralschweiz und schreibt u.a. für Die Zeit und Geo.

Sich selbst auf die Schliche kommen

Von Betram Weiß

Nach der Recherche ist vor der Recherche! Wenn kein Fact-Checker Ihr Manuskript überprüfen kann, müssen Sie selber ran. Dabei kann man sich einige Arbeitsschritte von den professionellen Fehlersuchern abschauen.

Artikel ohne Fehler gibt es wohl nur selten. Auch dieser wird sicherlich nicht fehlerfrei sein. Aber es gibt Mittel und Wege, die Zahl der Irrtümer so gering wie möglich zu halten – und so die höchsten Werte des Journalismus zu wahren: Korrektheit und Glaubwürdigkeit. Fehler kann vermeiden, wer sorgfältig recherchiert. Fehler kann vermeiden, wer im Schreibprozess aufmerksam und akkurat seine Quellen im Blick behält. Und Fehler kann vermeiden, wer nach dem Schreiben systematisch nach Unstimmigkeiten in seinem Manuskript fahndet.

Die sorgfältige Überprüfung des eigenen Textes wird aber allzu oft vergessen oder fällt schlichtweg dem Zeitdruck oder niedrigen Honoraren zum Opfer. Manche Magazine wie Spiegel, Geo, The New Yorker oder Focus haben deshalb eigene »Fact-Checker« angestellt, die zumindest alle Sachverhalte im Werk eines Journalisten vor dem Druck noch einmal kontrollieren. Es ist eine Besonderheit, der Journalisten bei Zeitungen und Nachrichtenagenturen, beim Radio und Fernsehen oder im Internet nur selten begegnen.

Die meisten Journalisten müssen selbst für die Richtigkeit ihrer Arbeit Sorge tragen. Doch dafür können sie sich von den professionellen Fehler-Suchern der Zeitschriften manches abschauen. Wer wie sie die Suche nach Fehlern in seinem Manuskript zu einem eigenständigen Arbeitsschritt macht, wird zweifellos Fehler entdecken. Und sich so vielleicht manchen Ärger ersparen können.

Schritt eins: Lesen!

Die Arbeit der Faktenprüfer ist vielleicht eine der letzten Bastionen des Papiers: Ein Fact-Checker mag das Manuskript elektronisch erhalten und im Arbeitsprozess elektronisch weitergeben, doch für seine eigentliche Tätigkeit, das Überprüfen, vertraut er auf einen Papierausdruck. Dieser bietet Übersichtlichkeit und Raum für Anmerkungen, Notizen und Korrekturzeichen. Ganz am Anfang steht aufmerksames Lesen. Lesen mit den Augen eines skeptischen, immerzu kritischen Zweiflers. Das ist keine revolutionäre Neuigkeit. Doch ebenso wie alles Folgende kann es nützlich sein, sich den Wert dieses Blicks von Zeit zu Zeit ins Gedächtnis zu rufen, um ihn zu üben und zu stärken. Bei diesem ersten Lesedurchgang lässt sich schon mancher »Stolperstein« entdecken. Zumindest diesen Schritt sollte jeder Journalist in jeder Situation leisten können.

Schritt zwei: Auswählen!

Beim zweiten Lesedurchgang gilt es zu entscheiden, was geprüft werden muss: Unterstreichen Sie mit einem farbigen Stift alles, was einer Überprüfung anhand von Quellen standhalten muss – also alle »Fakten«. Was genau gehört also unterstrichen und was nicht? Muss ich diese Kleinigkeit wirklich überprüfen? Sobald sich diese Ungewissheiten beim Lesen einschleichen, sollte man sich folgende Fragen stellen, empfiehlt die kanadische Fact-Checkerin und Journalisten-Ausbilderin Cynthia Brouse. Lassen sie sich mit „Ja“ beantworten so ist eine Überprüfung geboten:

- Gibt es eine andere Möglichkeit, dies auszudrücken?
- Könnte ich die Quelle missverstanden haben?
- Würde es jemanden stören, wenn dies falsch wäre? (Eine Frage, die nach Brouse vor allem dann wichtig wird, wenn eine Aussage allzu gut in die Drama turgie eines Textes passt.)

Gerade Fehler in Basisfakten wie Namensangaben sorgen schnell für Aufruhr und werden ungern verziehen, wie etwa die Posse um den »falschen Wilhelm« im Namen des CSU-Politikers zu Guttenberg im Februar 2009 zeigte. Auf Wikipedia wurde dem Politiker ein weiterer Vorname hinzugedichtet, welchen viele Medien ungeprüft übernahmen.
Hilfreich beim Unterstreichen der zu prüfenden Sachverhalte ist es, nicht Wort für Wort zu markieren, sondern nur Fakten, die eine Einheit bilden. Der Name »Karl-Theodor zu Guttenberg« wird also als ein Faktum unterstrichen. Handelt es sich um ein umfangreiches Manuskript, kann es überdies nützlich sein, für verschiedene Faktentypen unterschiedliche Farben zu verwenden. So lässt sich etwa auch die Wichtigkeit der zu prüfenden Details hierarchisieren.
Während des ersten Lesens müssen noch keine einzelnen Details in den Blick geraten. Im Fokus stehen vielmehr die Gesamtheit des Textes, seine Struktur und logische Entwicklung. Folgende Fragen könnten dabei eine Antwort finden:

- Wirkt der Beitrag glaubwürdig und sind seine Argumente überzeugend?
- Wie wirkt der Artikel im Vergleich zu anderen, die dieses Thema behandeln?
- An welchen Stellen könnte Übertreibung oder unbegründete Mutmaßung vermutet werden?
- Enthält der Text Vorwürfe? Wenn ja, lassen sich diese wirklich rechtfertigen?

Schritt drei: Überprüfen!
Im dritten Schritt machen Sie sich daran, alle unterstrichenen Sachverhalte anhand von Quellen zu überprüfen. Dabei können Sie den Text systematisch von Anfang bis Ende durchkämmen. Mitunter lässt sich die Arbeit aber auch beschleunigen, wenn Sie sich jeweils auf einen Informationstypus beschränken, etwa zunächst nach allen Namen schauen, dann nach allen historischen Zusammenhängen, dann nach allen Zitaten usw.
Suchen Sie das gesamte Quellenmaterial zusammen, das Sie beim Schreiben des Textes verwendet haben: Notizbücher, Tonbänder, Bücher, Artikel und Studien. Alles gehört dazu. Es ist hilfreich, wenn Sie das Material bereits während der Recherche systematisch aufbereitet haben. Jedes Faktum, dessen Richtigkeit Sie guten Gewissens belegen können, streichen Sie durch einen Haken ab. Überprüfen Sie die korrekte Schreibweise eines Wortes, so empfiehlt es sich, jeden einzelnen Buchstaben mit einem diagonalen Strich abzustreichen. So gewinnt man im Arbeitsprozess Klarheit darüber, welche Informationen bereits auf welche Weise überprüft wurden. Ist eine Änderung im Manuskript erforderlich, so sollte diese nicht nur im Text, sondern auch an dessen Rand kenntlich gemacht werden – damit die Korrektur bei der Übertragung in eine elektronische Fassung nicht übersehen wird. Als Markierung eignen sich etwa ein senkrechter Strich am Anfang der betreffenden Zeile oder kleine Kreuze, die man auf eine durchgezogene senkrechte Linie am Seitenrand setzt.

Die »richtige« Quelle wählen!
Idealerweise versieht man jeden überprüften Sachverhalt in seinem Dokument mit einem Quellenhinweis, so dass die Herkunft der Angabe auch später nachvollziehbar ist. Erst dann ist die Information im eigentlichen Sinne »dokumentiert«. Im besten Falle belegt ein gewissenhafter Fact-Checker eine Aussage durch mehrere, voneinander unabhängige Quellen. Nur so kann er einigermaßen sichergehen, sich nicht zu irren und der so genannten »Wahrheit« nahezukommen. Steht nur eine Quelle zur Verfügung, ist sie mit folgenden Fragen abzuklopfen:

- Bin ich an der Originalquelle?
- Gibt es eine abweichende Quelle?
- Warum halte ich die Quelle für belastbar?
- Kann die Quelle überhaupt recht haben (z. B. fachliche Qualifikation)?
- Macht die Quelle selbst womöglich eine falsche Angabe?
- Wurde die Quelle sinngemäß wiedergegeben?
- Wenn nicht, trifft dann die Umformulierung noch den inhaltlichen Kern?

Vorsicht, Fehlerquelle!
Wer ein Manuskript sorgfältig und systematisch überprüft, wendet dafür mitunter Stunden auf. Unter realistischen Bedingungen ist oftmals nur ein Minimum möglich. Zumindest die wichtigsten Fehlerquellen sollte man kritisch beäugen, bevor man den Text für fertig erklärt:

- Superlative
- Zahlen und statistische Angaben
- Namens- und Altersangabe
- Zeitangaben und zeitgeschichtliche Bezüge
- Ortsangaben und geografische Bezüge
- Fachbegriffe, insbesondere aus Medizin, Technik und Naturwissenschaft

Fehler entstehen vor allem, wenn man Vermutungen anstellt oder etwas aus dem Gedächtnis beschreibt; wenn man glaubt, auf sein eigenes Wissen vertrauen zu können. Dies lässt sich nur durch hartnäckige Suche nach belastbaren Quellen vermeiden. Doch eben diese steht der nötigen Freiheit im kreativen Prozess des Formulierens oft im Wege.
In Redaktionen, die eine eigenständige Faktenprüfung in ihren Arbeitsprozess integriert haben, tragen Autoren daher an Stelle eines Fakts mitunter einen Platzhalter ein, den der Faktenprüfer dann durch den entsprechenden Sachverhalt ersetzt. Platzhalter sind beispielsweise »XX«, »oo«, »TK« für »to kome«. Die falsche Orthografie (statt »TC« für »to come«) ist beabsichtigt, damit der Platzhalter nicht übersehen wird. Es lohnt sich, dieses Vorgehen auch einmal in der eigenen Arbeit zu erproben. Denn so lässt sich die mühsame Suche nach einem einzelnen Detail vom Schreibprozess lösen, in dem man sich womöglich lieber auf Textstruktur und Dramaturgie konzentriert.

Richtig mit Fehlern umgehen!
Fehler sind unangenehm und manchmal schwer zu verzeihen. Besonders, wenn sie einfach zu vermeiden gewesen wären. Die Fehlerquote aber kann ein Autor senken, so der US-Journalismusforscher Scott Maier: Zum einen, wenn er sich die Zeit nimmt, seine Arbeit Satz für Satz zu überprüfen; und zum anderen, wenn er offen für seine Verantwortung einsteht, wenn Fehler auftauchen – und sich so für das Aufspüren von Fehlern sensibilisiert. Ebenso wichtig wie die Vermeidung von Fehlern ist also der Umgang mit ihnen. Daher gilt das Credo der Washington Post: »Richtigkeit ist unser Ziel und Aufrichtigkeit unsere Verteidigung«.

Freigabe zum Start?: Checklisten

Bevor ein Pilot zum Abflug ansetzt, überprüft er mit einer Checkliste, ob das Flugzeug wirklich funktionstüchtig ist. Auch jeder Journalist sollte routiniert einige Prüffragen beantworten, bevor er seine Arbeit der Öffentlichkeit präsentiert. Um zu lernen, wie Checklisten oder allgemein verbindliche Handwerksregeln zum Umgang mit Informationen und Quellen aussehen können, lohnt ein Blick in die USA. Dort weist etwa die Tageszeitung Detroit Free Press jedem Arbeitsprofil in der Redaktion eine eigene Checkliste zu, um Fehler in der Berichterstattung zu vermeiden. Bevor etwa Reporter ihr Manuskript abgeben, sollen sie sich fragen:

- Habe ich alle genannten Namen, Titel und Orte doppelt überprüft?
- Habe ich alle genannten Telefonnummern und Webadressen getestet?
- Ist der Artikel ausgewogen?
- Wer oder was könnte in dem Artikel fehlen?
- Habe ich allen Betroffenen eine Chance gegeben, mit mir zu sprechen?
- Habe ich Rechtschreibung und Zahlenangaben überprüft?
- Habe ich alle Informationen zu Fotos und Grafiken überprüft?

Allen Redakteuren gibt die Detroit Free Press dagegen folgende Fragen an die Hand:

- Hat der Autor alle genannten Namen, Titel und Orte überprüft?
- Hat der Autor alle genannten Telefonnummern und Webadressen getestet?
- Sind alle Zitate korrekt und angemessen verwendet?
- Erfasst jedes Zitat, was der jeweils Befragte gemeint hat?
- Ist der Artikel ausgewogen?
- Wer oder was könnte in dem Artikel fehlen?
- Werden Hintergrund und Kontext ausreichend erläutert, um die Relevanz des Themas plausibel zu machen?
- Erfassen Titel und Vorspann den Inhalt korrekt?
- Erfassen Bildunterschriften und Grafiktexte den Inhalt korrekt?
- Wurden Änderungen im Text mit dem Autor abgesprochen?

Die Society of Professional Journalists fordert in Ihrer »Accuracy Checklist«, dass Journalisten noch härter mit sich selbst zu Gericht gehen:

- Haben Sie Vertrauen in die Tatsachenbehauptungen in Ihrem Artikel und zu den Quellen, die sie geliefert haben?
- Können Sie alle Tatsachen belegen?

- Haben Sie für alle Schlüsselinhalte die Gegenprobe gemacht?
- Können Sie die korrekt geschriebenen Namen und die richtigen Telefonnum mern aller zitierten Quellen angeben?
- Sind Sie sich ganz sicher, dass alle im Artikel genannten Tatsachen der Wahr heit entsprechen?
- Sind Sie darauf vorbereitet, Ihre Inhaltskontrolle öffentlich zu verteidigen oder auf sonstige Maßnahmen zur Überprüfung Ihres Textes zu antworten?
- Sind die Zitate in Ihrem Text korrekt, in ihrem richtigen Zusammenhang präsentiert?
- Zitieren Sie anonyme Quellen? Wenn ja, warum? Sind Sie darauf vorbereitet, sich öffentlich für die Verwendung solcher Quellen zu rechtfertigen?
- Verwenden Sie Material, Dokumente oder Bilder von anonymen Quellen? Warum? Wie groß ist Ihr Vertrauen in die Gültigkeit dieses Materials? Sind Sie darauf vorbereitet, die Verwendung dieses Materials öffentlich zu rechtfertigen?
- Haben Sie Personen, Minderheiten, Kulturen, Nationen oder Gesellschafts-gruppen beschrieben und dabei stereotype Adjektive verwendet? Sind diese Beschreibungen genau und in dem dargestellten Kontext bedeutungsvoll?
- Haben Sie anstößige Formulierungen oder Bilder in Ihrem Artikel verwendet?
- Gibt es einen triftigen Grund für die Verwendung solcher Informationen? Wäre der Artikel weniger korrekt, wenn man die Formulierung oder das Bild weg lassen würde?
- Geben Ihre Überschriften (oder Programmankündigungen oder Titel) genau die Tatsachen und den Kontext des Artikels wieder, auf die sie sich beziehen?

Bertram Weiß ist Kommunikationswissenschaftler und lebt in Hamburg. Als Fachberater stand ihm Dr. Martin Seidl zur Seite, Leiter der Dokumentationsabteilung des Focus.

Vorsicht! Unsichere Infos

Von Gerd Roth

Nicht immer legt ein Journalist für seine Quelle die Hand ins Feuer. Denn manchmal war es ihm nicht möglich, die Information zu überprüfen. Was tun?

Die Information ist stets nur so sicher wie ihre Quelle. Aus diesem Grund verwenden seriöse Medien zu Recht viel Energie auf Quellen und ihre Nennung in den Texten. »In jeder Meldung müssen Informationen oder Ansichten durch Angabe der Quellen nachvollziehbar sein«, heißt es etwa in den Standards der Deutschen Presse-Agentur (dpa). Nur Quellen eröffnen den Lesern die Möglichkeit, Genauigkeit und Zuverlässigkeit eines Textes beurteilen zu können. Doch nicht immer können Quellen klar benannt werden. Oder die Quelle kann vom Autor nicht richtig eingeschätzt werden, gilt gar als unsicher. Und schon fangen die Schwierigkeiten an. Was mache ich jetzt mit meiner schönen Information?

Umschreibungen nur wenn notwendig

Ich kann meine Quelle verschleiern. Doch eine Verschleierung deckt nicht nur den Informationsgeber, sondern macht den Inhalt auch weniger nachprüfbar. Deshalb: Wenn Verschleierungen und Umschreibungen der Quelle notwendig sind, sollten sie so zuverlässig wie möglich sein. Eine Information »von zuständiger Stelle« oder »von offizieller Seite« sollte aus einer Quelle stammen, die für das Beschriebene tatsächlich inhaltlich oder formal zuständig ist. Auch Funktionen sollten einen direkten Bezug zur Information haben. Berichte aus der Sitzung eines Gremiums können etwa »Teilnehmer« oder »Mitglieder« sicher wiedergeben. Die sprachlich wenig schönen und inhaltlich allgemeinen »Kreise« sollten nur ausnahmsweise verwendet werden. Wer seine Informationen im Text aber nur auf Quellen wie »von zuständiger Seite«, »informierte Kreise« oder gar das völlig nichts sagende »Beobachter« stützt, gefährdet die notwendige Glaubwürdigkeit. Leser müssen sich in solchen Fällen allein auf die Seriosität des Mediums verlassen. Niemals sollten Umschreibungen einer Quelle eine mangelnde Recherche verdecken.

In wirtschaftlich schwierigen Zeiten verschwimmen bei vielen Medien journalistische Arbeit und Eigendarstellung. Auf Exklusivität der eigenen Darstellung wird zu Gunsten des schnellen PR Effekts und damit mittelfristig verbundener Werbeeinnahmen verzichtet. Informationen werden nicht mehr nur wegen ihrer Brisanz, sondern auch zur Nennung des eigenen Mediums noch vor der Veröffentlichung vor allem an Multiplikatoren wie etwa Nachrichtenagenturen übermittelt.

Mit dieser Entwicklung einher geht die Häufung von umschriebenen oder verschleierten Quellen, aber auch von Informationen, die sich bei Nachrecherche als unzusammenhängend, überzogen interpretiert oder gar falsch erweisen. Da regt sich dann der Verdacht, dass die häufige Verwendung umschriebener Quellen mit dem Mangel sicherer Informationen zusammenhängt. Ein journalistisch höchst unbefriedigender Zustand.

„Nach Fernsehbildern"

Auch Medien müssen als Ursprung einer Information genannt werden. Das ist nicht nur fair gegenüber den Kollegen und notwendig gegenüber den Rezipienten, sondern in einigen Fällen auch technisch erforderlich. So können TV-Bilder etwa wegen optischer Verzerrungen schnell eine eigene Realität oder nur einen unzuverlässigen Eindruck des gesamten Geschehens vermitteln. In solchen Fällen macht ein Quellenhinweis wie »nach Fernsehbildern« die mögliche Unsicherheit deutlich.

Unsichere Informationen

Vorsicht ist bei elektronischen Quellen und Übermittlungswegen geboten. E-Mails und Faxabsender können problemlos gefälscht werden. Doch selbst wenn der Absender stimmt, heißt das noch nicht, dass die Information auch daher stammt oder richtig ist. Jenes folgenschwere Fax, mit dem Helmut Kohl vermeintlich die Enttarnung seiner angeblichen Spender ankündigte, kam tatsächlich aus einer CDU-Fraktion. Dennoch war es eine Fälschung. Deswegen müssen Absender und Authentizität der Information stets überprüft werden.
Auch das Internet ist unabhängig von seinen guten und schier unbegrenzten Recherchemöglichkeiten eine sehr unsichere Quelle. Eine web-Information muss daher mit weiteren Quellen gecheckt werden.

Unbekannte Quellen

Informationen aus unbekannten Quellen müssen nicht automatisch schlecht oder unzutreffend sein. Allerdings sollte die Seriosität der Quelle zunächst überprüft und so gesichert werden. Dazu können Referenzen eingeholt werden. Wer kennt die Quelle? Womit hat sie normalerweise zu tun? Ist sie kompetent für ihre Angaben? Je nach Art der Quelle können geeignete Ansprechpartner im Umfeld, bei Kontaktpersonen, selbst bei offiziellen Stellen sitzen. Auch eine Rückfrage bei Journalistenkollegen kann hilfreich sein. Eine unbekannte Quelle lässt sich zudem gegenchecken mit gezielten Fragen zu Aspekten, die durch anderweitige Recherche bereits bekannt sind.

In einigen Fällen wird versucht, zur Deckung des oder der Informanten die Aufmerksamkeit in eine ganz andere Richtung zu lenken. Dazu die dpa-Standards: »Es darf in keinem Fall aus Gründen der Tarnung eine Information einer anderen Quelle ‚untergeschoben' werden.»

Lieber auf eine Information verzichten
Es werden sich trotz aller Vorsichtsmaßnahmen im Redaktionsalltag immer wieder Zweifel ergeben, weil sich eine Quelle nicht »hart» machen lässt. So schwer es engagierten Mitarbeitern auch fallen mag: In solchen Fällen sollte mit Blick auf die journalistische Verantwortung auf eine Verwendung der Informationen verzichtet werden.

Gerd Roth leitet die Abteilung „Coaching und Weiterbildung" bei der Deutschen Presse-Agentur in Berlin.

Quellen prüfen, Spuren löschen

Von Albrecht Ude

Recherchieren Journalisten im Internet fahrlässig, können Falschmeldungen entstehen. Viel gefährlicher aber sind die Spuren, die manche im Netz hinterlassen. Durch sie droht sogar der Quellenverrat.

Nicht alle Journalisten wissen richtig mit dem Internet umzugehen, wie zahlreiche Presseenten zeigen, die durch kompetente, strukturierte Online-Recherche hätten vermieden werden können.
Eine der bekanntesten Enten, die durch das Netz in Umlauf gebracht wurden, sind die Forderungen des »Bund Deutscher Juristen«. Am 1. Januar 2006 verbreitete Associated Press dessen Pressemitteilung. Der Verein unterstütze die »Folterforderung von Bundesinnenminister Schäuble«. Der Vorsitzende des Richtervereins, Claus Grötz: »Die Gewinnung von Aussagen mittels leichter Foltermaßnahmen und die Verwertung solcher Aussagen sind zukünftig möglich zu machen.« Die per E-Mail verbreitete Pressemeldung verwies auf die Webseite bunddeutscherjuristen.org des angeblich 1952 gegründeten Vereins. Zahlreiche Medien, darunter MDR, N-TV, WDR und Spiegel Online brachten die Meldung.
Vielleicht hatten die zuständigen Redakteure sogar im Netz recherchiert und waren auf die Wikipedia-Artikel zum »Bund Deutscher Juristen« und zu »Dr. Claus Grötz« gestoßen. Doch beide gibt es nicht.
Zum Beispiel hätte bereits stutzig machen können, dass die Webseite des Bundes Deutscher Juristen kein Impressum hat, wie es deutsches Recht vorschreibt. Was auch bei solchen Seiten nicht gefälscht sein kann: die URL-Adresse. Mit der simplen Frage »Wem gehört diese Webseite und wer betreibt sie?« hätte man den Fake entlarvt.

Rechercheaufwand: Zwei Minuten

Für Webseiten mit unterschiedlichen Endungen sind in der Regel auch unterschiedliche Organisationen zuständig. Beispielsweise ist das Deutsche Network Information Center (Denic) für alle Domains zuständig, die auf .de enden. Über die Root Zone Database (www.iana.org/domains/root/db), eine Art Nachschlagewerk für Webadressen, die von der US-amerikanischen Internet Assigned Numbers Authority (IANA) betrieben wird, lässt sich die zuständige Organisation nachrecherchieren und über einen Direkt-Link erreichen. Die Webseite des Bundes Deutscher Juristen endete auf .org. Somit ist die Organisation Public Interest Registry (PIR) zuständig. Dort nachge-

schaut erfährt man über die »Who-is«-Suchfunktion, dass bunddeutscherjuristen.org am 28. Dezember 2005 eingerichtet wurde – nur drei Tage vor der Pressemeldung (http://pir.org/node). Die Domain gehört einer US-Firma, die mit der Dienstleistung Geld verdient, die Namen ihrer Auftraggeber zu verschweigen.
Die Root Zone Database aufzurufen, dem Link zur Who-is-Datenbank zu folgen und dort den Domain-Eintrag nachzuschlagen, dauert etwa zwei Minuten.

Wikipedia-Eintrag, um PM zu decken
Am Tag, an dem die Ente über den Bund Deutscher Juristen die Runde machte, gab es auch Wikipedia-Einträge über den Verein und seinen angeblichen Vorsitzenden Claus Grötz. Beide Einträge wurden von Mitgliedern der Wikipedia-Community an diesem Tag als »Fakes« enttarnt und gelöscht. Schon vorher hätte ein Klick auf den Link »Versionen/Autoren« gereicht, um zu erkennen, dass die Einträge ‚just in time' für die Pressemeldung eingerichtet wurden. Dieser Link ist in jedem Wikipedia-Artikel vorhanden.

Die richtige Site für die Recherche-Frage
Bei kompetenten Online-Recherchen müssen die eingesetzten Suchwerkzeuge und die angewendeten Methoden zu den gestellten Fragen passen. Ein Beispiel: Wer nach einem Buch sucht, kann danach googeln. Wer nach der korrekten Titelaufnahme für das Buch sucht, ist mit dem Katalog der zuständigen Nationalbibliothek (in Deutschland die Deutsche National Bibliothek, d-nb.de) besser bedient. Wer das Buch aus einer Bibliothek (möglichst in der Nähe) entleihen möchte, sollte einen Verbundkatalog (etwa den Virtuellen Katalog der Universität Karlsruhe, KVK) konsultieren, und wer das Buch kaufen möchte, sucht am besten bei einem kommerziellen Anbieter wie Libri oder für alte Bücher beim Zentralen Verzeichnis Antiquarischer Bücher (ZVAB). Diese Entscheidung und das Vorwissen kann kein Suchwerkzeug dem Suchenden abnehmen.

Gottesgeschenke für den Rechercheur
Gefährliche Wissenslücken gibt es bei den Metadaten digitaler Dokumente und der sicheren elektronischen Kommunikation. Beides berührt den Informantenschutz. So kam es im Oktober 2007 beim Spiegel durch ein unachtsam zusammengestelltes Dossier im PDF-Format zum Quellenverrat.
Metadaten sind Angaben über Inhalt und Entstehung des Datei-Inhaltes. Es gibt sie in fast allen Datei-Formaten. Wer beispielsweise eine neue Word-Datei im Verzeichnis »Eigene Dateien« speichert, hat bereits drei solcher Spuren darin hinterlassen. Standardmäßig trägt Word Autor und Firma in die »Datei-Informationen« ein. Lässt der Nutzer diese Felder frei, übernimmt Word stattdessen die Angaben, die bei der

Registrierung des Programmes eingetragen wurden. Auch der Speicherort wird im Dokument vermerkt (als »C:\Dokumente und Einstellungen\[Nutzerverzeichnis]\Eigene Dateien«). Das »Nutzerverzeichnis« ist dabei oft der Name oder das Kürzel des Dateiautors – ein relevanter Hinweis auf die Quelle. Das Wissen um solche Metadateien, die man auf dem Bildschirm oder ausgedruckt nicht sehen kann, benötigt jeder Journalist: Zwar können sie bei der digitalen Veröffentlichung von Dateien Fallstricke sein – für einen Rechercheur sind sie aber Gottesgeschenke.

Durch Mausklick eigene Daten hinterlassen

Auch beim ganz normalen Surfen verrät jeder User vieles über sich im Netz. Wie viel, lässt sich testen: Wer den »Privacy Test« auf tools-on.net klickt, dem zeigt die Webseite an, welche Daten allein durch diesen Mausklick an den Webserver geflossen sind: IP-Adresse, Browserversion, Betriebssystem, Referer (das ist die Webseite, über die man per Link gekommen ist) und vieles mehr. Besonders heikel: Wer unter »Client's hostname« oder »Preferable Mail Server« den Namen des eigenen Mediums liest, hinterlässt bei jedem Surfen im Internet quasi die eigene Visitenkarte.

Standards der Online-Recherche

1. Webbrowser als Basis-Werkzeuge der Online-Recherche beherrschen
2. Universalsuchmaschinen und deren erweiterte Suchfunktionen einsetzen
3. Wikipedia nicht als Quelle verwenden
4. Kollaborative Projekte (»Social Media«) wie Newsgroups, Social Networks, Weblogs, Social Bookmarks, Twitter etc. laufend nutzen
5. Spezialisierte Suchdienste verwenden
6. Quellen und Informanten so effektiv schützen wie bei anderen Recherchen
7. Digitale Quellen prüfen
8. Recherchen anonymisieren und verschleiern
9. Recherchen planen und protokollieren
10. Recherche-Ergebnisse gerichtsfest archivieren

Quelle: recherche-standards.wikispaces.com

Weiterführende Links:

»Handbook of Journalism« von Reuters mit einem Abschnitt »Reporting from the Internet and using social media http://handbook.reuters.com/index.php/Main_Page

Diskussion über Recherchestandards: recherche-standards.wikispaces.com

Albrecht Ude arbeitet als freier Journalist und Trainer. Seine Schwerpunkte sind Online-Recherche und Kommunikationssicherheit.

Fakten, Fiktionen, Fälschungen

Von Jakob Vicari / Arno Nehlsen

Vertrauen ist gut – Kontrolle ist besser! Das zeigen wir zum einen anhand des folgenden Beitrags über den Reporter Stephen Glass. Zum anderen haben wir einen erfahrenen Fact-Checker gebeten, den Beitrag des Autors zu überprüfen.

Ian Restil, 15 Jahre alter Computer-Hacker, der aussieht wie eine jugendliche Ausgabe von Bill Gates, bekommt einen Wutanfall.« So beginnt die Geschichte »Hack Heaven«, erschienen am 18. Mai 1998 im Politmagazin The New Republic. Geschrieben hat ihn ein 25 Jahre alter Reporter: Stephen Glass.
Sein Artikel entfaltet den Kosmos der Hacker-Welt farbig und lebendig. Restil ist es gelungen, in die Systeme der Softwarefirma »Jukt Micronics» einzudringen, von einem Bibliothekscomputer aus. Der junge Hacker fordert von der Firma unter anderem ein lebenslanges Playboy-Abonnement. Der Hacker-Newsletter Computer Insider schätzt, dass Firmen in den letzten Jahren 900 Hobby-Hacker wie Restil engagiert haben.

Hacker, Firma, Newsletter – alles erfunden
Reporter Glass nimmt den Leser mit in diese Welt. Er scheint mittendrin zu stehen, in der Verhandlung dieses Hackers im ausgefransten Baseball-T-Shirt. Der Artikel ist brillant geschrieben, und er ist vor der Veröffentlichung durch eines der besten Fact-Checking-Verfahren gegangen, die es in amerikanischen Medien gibt. Und doch: Er ist gefälscht.
Der Hacker Ian Restil, die Firma, der Newsletter – sie alle entsprangen dem Kopf des jungen Autors Glass. Denn er selbst ist eine Art Hacker: ein Hacker des Qualitätsjournalismus. Er ist in eine Bastion eingedrungen und hat alle Sicherungsmechanismen ausgehebelt. The New Republic, gegründet im Jahr 1914, ist ein Magazin mit Tradition, bei dem Prestige mehr gilt als Auflage.

Überprüfungsrecherche: Drei-Tage-Foltertest
Zum Qualitätsverständnis des Blattes gehört auch die Dokumentation, ein Drei-Tage-Foltertest. Chefredakteur Michael Kelly installierte, als er vom New Yorker kam, dafür eine der ausgefeiltesten Redaktionsroutinen. Doch Glass fabrizierte fast drei Jahre lang, zwischen 1995 und 1998, als aufstrebender Star 41 Artikel; in 27 davon fanden sich später Fälschungen. In einer Nachricht an die Leser schreibt die Redaktion: »Wir haben keine Ausrede für all das. Unser Mitgefühl gilt allen Betroffenen.«

Penenberg entlarvt Glass

»Mein Leben war eine Kette aus Lügen«, sagt Glass später in einem CBS-Interview. Glass, schwarze Brille, Locken, der naive Blick aus den graugrünen Augen – er beherrscht seine Rolle immer noch. Die Rolle des arglosen Journalisten, dem man die Arbeit zu leicht machte. Ausgedachte Figuren haben einen Vorteil, sagt er: »Solche Leute schreiben keine Leserbriefe«.

Entlarvt wird Glass kurz nach der Veröffentlichung seiner Geschichte »Hack Heaven« durch den Journalisten Adam Penenberg. Eigentlich soll Penenberg für Forbes.com die Geschichte über den Hacker Ian Restil neu schreiben. Doch der ausgewiesene Hacker-Experte hat Schwierigkeiten, Restil zu finden. Er meldet sich bei Glass' Vorgesetztem, Charles Lane. Als sich Penenbergs wachsende Zweifel nicht ausräumen lassen, fährt Lane mit Glass an den Ort der vermeintlichen Hacker-Konferenz, von der Glass in seinem Artikel berichtet hat. Das ist das Ende der Lügengeschichte.

»Es ist tough, das Gegenteil zu beweisen. Es ist sehr viel tougher zu beweisen, dass jemand oder etwas nicht existiert.« So beginnt Penenbergs Artikel über den Fall, erschienen auf Forbes.com. Später wird auch ein Hollywoodfilm namens »Shattered Glass« über den Fall Stephen Glass gedreht. In dem Spielfilm sieht man die Szenen, die Glass für seinen Hacker-Report erfunden hatte. Und plötzlich sind Glass' Hirngespinste nicht mehr ganz so überzeugend. Ian Restil ist pickelig und trägt eine Mütze, blau mit nach hinten gedrehtem Schirm. Er ist das Klischee eines rotzigen Computer-Nerds. Überraschend genug, dass das staubtrockene Fact-Checking ein Thema für Hollywood wurde.

Kein Fälscher im Journalismus ging so weit

Zeitzeugen, die die Redaktion kannten, wie Glass' Kollegin Hanna Rosin und Slate-Redakteur David Plotz, halten den Film für nahe an der Realität. Tatsächlich kommt er ohne den obligatorischen Kerzenschein in der Fälscherwerkstatt aus, ohne Bettszene und Verfolgungsjagd. Die Internet Movie Database listet dennoch Fehler wie diesen auf: Als der Schwindel auffliegt, treffen Glass und sein Vorgesetzter Lane aufeinander. Glass soll gestehen. Tatsächlich duellierten sich dabei allein die Anwälte.

Kein Fälscher im Journalismus ging je so weit wie Glass. Als sein Schwindel aufzufliegen droht, installiert er sogar Anrufbeantworter und Webseite für die fiktive Firma »Jukt Micronics« – auch für alle seine fiktiven Figuren. Als vermeintlicher Hacker Restil schreibt er seinem Vorgesetzten eine E-Mail: »i hope you rot in hell«.

So heißt es zumindest im Film. Ob es diese Mail wirklich gab?

Jakob Vicari arbeitet als freier Wissenschaftsjournalist in Hamburg.

Faktencheck des Beitrags über Stephan Glass:

Der Dokumentar Dr. Arno Nehlsen überprüfte das Manuskript und zeigt, welche Fakten es zu hinterfragen gilt: Die Verifikation beginnt mit dem genauen Lesen des Textes. Erste Unstimmigkeiten oder Rechtschreibfehler werden am Rand vermerkt. Danach wird der Text »gestrichen«, das bedeutet, alles, was verifiziert werden soll, wird unterstrichen. Und das betrifft alles, was objektivierbar, also nicht bloß Meinung des Autors ist. Jedes Faktum, unabhängig davon, ob es überhaupt verifizierbar ist oder ob der Dokumentar glaubt es zu kennen, wird in Frage gestellt. Diese Dokumentation erfolgte allein mit Hilfe des Internets und dem Film »Shattered Glass«. Ein weiterer Schritt der Verifikation wäre die Recherche nach anderen Quellen (z. B. Archive) mit denen sich die Sachverhalte auf die Gegenprobe stellen ließen. Doch erweiterte Möglichkeiten sind in diesem Mini-Experiment – für den Autoren des Manuskripts, ebenso für den Dokumentar – nicht vorgesehen.
Geänderte Textpassagen sind ~~durchgestrichen~~, alternative Formulierungen unterstrichen. An einigen Passagen steht eine Frage. Hier wurde in einer vertretbaren Zeit keine Quelle gefunden. In diesen Fällen ist es ökonomischer, den Autor nach den entsprechenden Quellen zu fragen. Im Folgenden sind jene Passagen aufgeführt, in denen Korrekturen angebracht wären:

»Ian Restil, 15 Jahre alter Computer-Hacker, der aussieht wie eine jugendliche Ausgabe von Bill Gates, bekommt einen Wutanfall.« So beginnt die Geschichte »Hack Heaven«, erschienen im Mai 1998 im Politmagazins The New Republic.
Anmerkung: Der Artikel kann nicht am 18. Mai erschienen sein, weil die New York Times bereits am 12. Mai über den Rauswurf von Glass berichtet, der Text von Penenberg auf Forbes.com ist datiert auf den 11. Mai 1998.

Geschrieben hat ihn ein ~~25 Jahre alter~~ junger Reporter: Stephen Glass.
Anmerkung: 25 Jahre alt macht ihn zwar die New York Times 1998. Aber andere Quellen liefern widersprüchliche Aussagen: Die deutsche Wikipedia gibt das Geburtsjahr 1974 an, die englischsprachige 1972. Deshalb muss das Alter hier gestrichen werden.

Der Hacker-Newsletter Computer Insider schätzt, dass Firmen in den letzten vier Jahren 900 Hobby-Hacker wie Restil engagiert haben. (...) Zum Qualitätsverständnis des Blattes gehört auch die Dokumentation, ein journalistischer ~~Drei-Tage-~~Foltertest.
Anmerkung: Wieso drei Tage? Dauern lange und kurze Geschichten gleich lang?

Angeblich installierte der ehemalige Chefredakteur Michael Kelly ~~installierte~~, als er vom New Yorker kam, dafür eine der ausgefeiltesten Redaktionsroutinen.
Anmerkung: Kelly wurde schon 1997 entlassen, war also zum Zeitpunkt von »Hack Heaven« nicht mehr im Amt, deshalb ist er der ehemalige Chefredakteur. Dass Kelly vom New Yorker kam ist ok, aber dass er die Routine mitbrachte stammt aus dem Film, deshalb »angeblich«.

Doch Glass fabrizierte fast drei Jahre lang, zwischen 1995 und 1998, als aufstrebender Star 41 Artikel für The New Republic; in 27 davon fanden sich später Fälschungen.
Anmerkung: Er hat in dieser Zeit auch für andere Magazine geschrieben.

In einer Nachricht an die Leser schreibt die Redaktion: »Wir haben keine Ausrede für all das. Unser Mitgefühl gilt allen Betroffenen.«
Frage: Gibt es überhaupt eine Quelle für dieses Zitat?

»Mein Leben war eine Kette aus Lügen«, sagt Glass später in einem CBS-Interview. Glass, schwarze Brille, kurze Haare, der naive Blick aus den graugrünen Augen.
Anmerkung: Das Aussehen ist fraglich, denn ich kann auf dem Bild auf cbsnews.com keine Locken erkennen; auch der Blick ist eher wach als naiv. Da Letzteres eine subjektive Bewertung ist und wichtig für den Duktus der Geschichte, bleibt der Fakt drin.

(...) Doch der ~~ausgewiesene Hacker-Experte~~ investigative Reporter hat Schwierigkeiten, Restil zu finden. Er meldet sich bei Glass‘ ~~Vorgesetztem~~ Chefredakteur, Charles Lane.
(...) »Es ist tough, das Gegenteil von etwas zu beweisen. Es ist ~~sehr viel~~ noch tougher zu beweisen, dass jemand oder etwas nicht existiert«. So beginnt ~~Penebergs~~ Penenbergs Artikel über den Fall, erschienen auf Forbes.com.
(...) Tatsächlich kommt er ohne den obligatorischen Kerzenschein in der Fälscherwerkstatt aus und ohne ~~Bettszene und~~ Verfolgungsjagd. Die Internet Movie Database listet dennoch Fehler wie diesen auf: ~~Als der Schwindel auffliegt,~~ Am Ende des Films treffen Glass, ~~und~~ sein Vorgesetzter Lane und ihre Anwälte aufeinander. Glass soll gestehen, welche seiner Storys gefälscht sind. (...) ~~Kein~~ Ich kenne keinen Fälscher, der im Journalismus ging je so weit ging wie Glass.
Anmerkung: Der Superlativ ist nicht zu verifizieren; Es gab in der amerikanischen Mediengeschichte sehr viele Fälscher.

Als sein Schwindel aufzufliegen droht, installiert er sogar Anrufbeantworter und Webseite für die fiktive Firma »Jukt Micronics« – auch für alle seine fiktiven ~~Figuren~~ Informanten. Als vermeintlicher Hacker Restil schreibt er ~~seinem Vorgesetzten~~ an Glass, also an sich selbst eine E-Mail: »i hope you rot in hell«. So heißt es zumindest im ~~Film~~ CBS-Interview.

Quellen im Internet:

- www.google.de/#hl=de&source=hp&q=cal+ripken+jr.&btnG=Google-Suche& meta=&aq=f&oq=cal+ripken+jr.&fp=72afe6b104a77c1d
- www.docstoc.com/docs/17288188/Hack-Heaven
- de.wikipedia.org/wiki/Stephen_Glass
- en.wikipedia.org/wiki/Stephen_Glass_(reporter)
- www.cbsnews.com/stories/2003/05/07/60minutes/main552819.shtml brunofranchini.files.wordpress.com/2009/05/stephen-glass.jpg
- www.imdb.com/title/tt0323944/goofs
- www.slate.com/id/2088948/
- www.kellyaward.com/mk_about_mk.html
- www.nytimes.com/1998/05/12/us/magazine-dismisses-writer-accused-of-hoax.html?scp=20&sq=%22stephen+glass%22&st=nyt
- www.forbes.com/1998/05/11/otw3_print.html#
- www.penenberg.com/biography.html

Dr. Arno Nehlsen leitete von 1985 bis 2009 die Abteilung »Dokumentation» und Verifikation der Geo-Gruppe.

Medien-Echo zur nr-Fachkonferenz „Fact-Checking": Einige Beispiele

Die Fact-Checker. In: B5 aktuell – Das Medienmagazin. Sendung vom 9.5.2010. Online zugänglich unter: http://www.br-online.de/podcast/mp3-download/b5aktuell/mp3-download-podcast-medienmagazin.shtml

Faktenchecker auf Fehlersuche. In: NDR Zapp. Sendung vom 31.3.2010. Online zugänglich unter: http://www3.ndr.de/sendungen/zapp/archiv/ethik_journalismus/faktchecker100.html

1153 Fehler in einer Ausgabe. In: Wiener Zeitung, 26.04.2010

Factchecker beim „New Yorker": Wie wahr sind Fakten? In: Süddeutsche Zeitung, 19.04.2010

Inside the World's Largest Fact-Checking Operation: A conversation with two staffers at Der Spiegel In: Columbia Journalism Review, 09.04.2010

Das Zwei-Quellen-Missverständnis. In: recherche-info.de, 29.3.2010

Fact-Checking. Journalisten-Werkstatt. In: Medium Magazin, Mai 2010. (Sonderbeilage).

„Korrigieren Sie das bitte". Wie Pinguine in der Arktis die Glaubwürdigkeit eines Mediums untergraben. In: info7, 1/2010.

Fact-Checking. Message-Medienwerkstatt. In: Message, 1/2010 (Sonderbeilage).

Fact-Checking. Werkstatt Journalismus. In: Edito, 1/2010 (Sonderbeilage).

Leseempfehlungen zum Thema „Fact-Checking“

Cynthia Brouse: After the fact. A guide to fact-checking magazines and other media. Lulu, 2007.

Sandra Hermes: Qualitätsmanagement in Nachrichtenredaktionen. Herbert von Halem, 2006.

Susan Shapiro: Caution! This article has not been fact checked. Read at your own risk. American Bar Foundation, 1995, Working Paper 9511.

Craig Silverman: Regret the error. How media mistakes pollute the press. And imperil freen speech. Union Square Press, 2007.

Sarah Harrison Smith: The fact checker's bible. A guide to getting it right. Anchor Books, 2007.

Bertram Weiß: Fact-Checking in deutschen Printredaktionen. In: Info7, 1/2010.

Bertram Weiß: Die im Dunkeln sieht man nicht. In: Message, 4/2009.

Vinzenz Wyss: Redaktionelles Qualitätsmanagement. Ziele, Normen, Ressourcen. UVK Verlagsgesellschaft, 2002.

Informationen zum Thema Fact-Checking bietet die Webseite www.fact-checking.de

Eine Webseite des netzwerk recherche e. V.

Fact-Checking:
Fakten finden, Fehler vermeiden

Herausgeber: netzwerk recherche e. V.
Geschäftsstelle, Stubbenhuk 10, 20459 Hamburg
Verantwortlich: Prof. Dr. Thomas Leif, Wiesbaden
Konzept/Redaktion: Bertram Weiß, Hamburg
Gestaltungskonzept & Titel: Nina Faber de.sign, Wiesbaden
Umschlagfoto: Photomish Dan / flickr
Artwork/Fotos: Simon Kremer, Dresden
ISBN: 978-3-9812408-4-9
Druck: ColorDruck Leimen

info@netzwerkrecherche.de
www.netzwerkrecherche.de
www.facktchecking.de

Wir danken allen Referenten und Förderern für die Unterstützung bei der nr-Fachkonferenz „Fact-Checking: Fakten finden, Fehler vermeiden“, die am 27. und 28. März 2010 im Spiegel-Redaktionsgebäude in Hamburg stattfand, sowie den Autoren dieses Dokumentationsbandes zur Tagung.

Sie können die Arbeit von netzwerk recherche e. V. unterstützen:
Spendenkonto: Sparkasse Köln, Konto-Nr. 69863, BLZ 37050299
netzwerk recherche e. V. ist vom Finanzamt Wiesbaden als gemeinnützig anerkannt.